CW00594771

A GUIDE TC

SPCK International Study Guides

This SPCK series was originally sponsored and subsidized by the Theological Education Fund of the World Council of Churches in response to requests from many different countries. The books are inter-cultural, ecumenical and contextual in approach. They are prepared by and in consultation with theological tutors from all over the world, but have from the outset been as widely used by students and parish groups in the West as by those for whom English may be a second language. The text and pictures are regularly amended to ensure that both scholarship and relevance to contemporary issues are kept up to date. Fully revised editions are marked (R). Titles at a slightly more advanced level are marked (A).

General Editors: Daphne Terry and Nicholas Beddow

ALREADY PUBLISHED

IN PREPARATION

SPCK International Study Guide 27

A GUIDE TO ACTS

John Hargreaves

First published in Great Britain 1990
SPCK
Holy Trinity Church
Marylebone Road
London NW1 4DU

Third impression, 1995

Copyright © John Hargreaves 1990

All rights reserved. No part of this book may be reproduced
or transmitted in any form or by any means, electronic or
mechanical, including photocopying, recording, or by any
information storage and retrieval system, without permission
in writing from the publisher.

Unless otherwise stated, the Scripture quotations in this publication are
from the Revised Standard Version of the Bible, Ecumenical Edition
Copyrighted 1973 by the Division of Christian Education
of the National Council of the Churches of Christ in the USA.

The photographs are reproduced by courtesy of Camera Press Ltd (pp. 8, 38, 124,
156); Photos-Service Vivant Univers (pp. 24, 49, 84, 218); The Observer (p. 69);
Popperfoto (p. 94); Oxfam (p. 112); The Church Missionary Society (p. 142); The
Mansell Collection (pp. 165, 226); Inter-Church Travel Ltd (p. 181); and the Basel
Mission (p. 203).

British Library Cataloguing in Publication Data

Hargeaves, John, *1911–*
A guide to Acts.
1. Bible. N.T. Acts — Critical studies
I. Title   II. Series
226'.606

ISBN 0–281–04367–1
ISBN 0–281–04366–3 (special edition for Africa,
Asia, S. Pacific and Caribbean)

Printed in Great Britain by
Latimer Trend & Company Ltd, Plymouth

Contents

Preface

I want to thank warmly all those who have helped me in the preparation of this book, especially:

The congregation of St Luke's Church, Sevenoaks, Kent, whose generous present enabled me to travel extensively in Greece and Turkey. As a result I have been able to see most of the places mentioned in Acts (having already worked for some years in Jerusalem);

The staff of Inter-Church Travel, particularly Canon Ron Brownrigg, for expert advice and carefully arranged journeys;

Dr Athanasius Delikostopoulos of Athens, who shared his knowledge of Paul's journeys, and also the many other Christians who are living in the countries where Paul did his work;

Students of Selly Oak Colleges and Readers of Rochester Diocese who joined me in the study of Acts;

Those who commented on the book out of their experience in many different parts of the world: my brother, the Rev. Cecil Hargreaves, formerly of Bishops College, Calcutta; the Rev. Monrelle Williams of Codrington College, Barbados; and the Rev. Pandang Yamsat of Bukuru, Northern Nigeria;

Miss Elizabeth Spence, who typed the first draft with her usual accuracy, and Mr Stephen Ridout, who helpfully suggested many amendments and corrections;

The Rev. Nick Beddow, whose careful comments were always welcome;

Daphne Terry, who for over thirty years has given me the great benefit of her professional skill and stimulating and kindly comment (and indeed has been a sort of expert midwife to the whole series), and who has enlivened the present book in countless ways.

JOHN HARGREAVES

Using this Guide

The plan of this book follows much the same pattern as that of other biblical Guides in the series.

In the Introduction we consider the reasons why Luke wrote the 'second volume' of his two-part book, Gospel and Acts, and why it is of special interest and importance for the Church in the modern world.

Each section of the Guide consists of:

1. An *Outline* in which the Bible passage is briefly summarized so as to make quite clear the sequence of events Luke was describing and the chief subjects he was dealing with;
2. An *Interpretation* in which we discuss Luke's main purpose in writing, the message he wanted to pass on and what it meant to readers of his own time, and how we should understand and apply it to our own lives today;
3. *Notes* on particular words and verses which seem to need further explanation or discussion; and
4. *Suggestions* for revision and further study.

Special Notes

These three background notes, on Luke's accuracy as a historian, Paul's background, and the manuscripts of Acts, are separate from the sections dealing with the Bible passages because each relates to some extent to the book as a whole. Some readers may prefer to read them immediately after the Introduction, before going on to detailed work on the text of Acts.

Additional Notes and Word Studies

Extended notes on nine key subjects, which were of particular concern to Luke on account of their significance in the life of the early Church—and are equally significant today—follow the regular notes at appropriate points in the text. The regular notes themselves include detailed studies of many important Bible words which Luke used in Acts. The Index references to these studies and to the subjects of the Additional Notes are given in bold type.

Study Suggestions

These suggestions for further study appear at the end of each section and each Special Note. As well as helping readers who are working alone to study more thoroughly and understand Luke's message more clearly, and to check their own progress, they are in fact a real part of the commentary. They can also be used in the classroom, and provide

topics for group research and discussion. They are of three main sorts:
1. *Review of Content*: These are to help readers check the work they have done, deepen their understanding of important words used, and make sure they have fully grasped the ideas and points of teaching given;
2. *Bible Study*: These relate the ideas and teaching in Acts with ideas and teaching found in other parts of the Bible;
3. *Discussion and Application*: These are intended to prompt readers to recognize the links between the Church of Luke's time and the Church today, and to think out the practical application of Luke's message to their own lives as Christians. They are especially suitable for use by groups.

The best way to use these Study Suggestions is: first, re-read the Bible passage; second, read the appropriate section of the Guide once or twice; and then do the work suggested, either in writing or group discussion, without looking at the Guide again unless instructed to do so.

The *Key to Study Suggestions* (p. 233) will enable readers to check their work on those questions which can be checked in this way. In most cases the Key does not give the answer to a question: it shows where in the text an answer is to be found.

Map and Time Line
The map (p. 120) includes all place-names mentioned in Acts; the time line (p. 231) shows the approximate order of the events which Luke describes, in so far as their dates can be established.

Further Reading
The bibliography on p. x lists some books which readers may find useful for further study of Acts.

Bible Version
The English translation of the Bible used in the Guide is the *Revised Standard Version Common Bible (Ecumenical Edition)* (RSV). Other translations used in a few cases where they show the meaning more clearly are the *New English Bible* (NEB), *Good News Bible* (GNB), *New International Version* (NIV), and that by J. B. Phillips. The *Authorized Version* (AV) is also mentioned.

Index
The *Index* includes only the more important names of people and places mentioned and subjects which occur in Acts. Bold-type page references show where particular subjects are treated in detail.

FURTHER READING

ACTS

Barclay, William *Acts of the Apostles* (Daily Study Bible). St Andrews Press, 1976

Bruce, F. F. *The Acts of the Apostles.* IVP, 1991

—— *The Acts of the Apostles Today.* Manchester University Press, 1982

—— *Book of Acts.* Eerdmans, 1988

Hanson, R. P. C. *The Acts* (New Clarendon Bible). Oxford University Press, 1975

Marshall, Howard *Acts.* JSOT Press, 1992

Neil, William *Acts of the Apostles* (New Century Bible). Marshall Pickering, 1982

ST PAUL

Pollock, J. *The Apostle.* Lion Publishing, 1987

The Plan of *The Acts of the Apostles*

Introduction

WHY DID LUKE WRITE ACTS?

From time to time there are political revolutions in one country or
another, and radios and newspapers report them. The author of Acts
was also reporting a revolution, but it was a revolution of a different
sort. He was telling of a very great change in the way that people
thought about God as the result of the coming of Jesus. The author,
Luke, was a Greek who realized that God loved and cared about all
races and not about the Jews alone. This was such good news for Luke,
and was such a new and revolutionary idea to him, that he spent the
rest of his life in making it known. He probably helped Paul to preach
this good news to Jews and non-Jews, and he was certainly the author
of a two-part book.

The first part of Luke's two-part book is his Gospel, the second part
of it is Acts. In both parts he had this special purpose: to show that
God's Spirit inspired Jesus and the followers of Jesus to break down
barriers, i.e. those things which separated people of different religions
and races and countries. What took place, and what we read in Acts,
was so remarkable that to describe it as 'the Church spreading' is not
enough. It would be more accurate to say that the Church was
'exploding'.

We see Luke's purpose in his Gospel from such passages as the
following (passages which are not in the other Gospels): 'A light for
revelation to the *Gentiles*' (i.e. the non-Jews, Luke 2.32), or 'One of
them fell on his face at Jesus' feet, giving him thanks ... he was a
Samaritan' (Luke 17.16).

We find the same message in Acts, e.g. 'You shall be my witnesses ...
to the end of the earth' (1.8). Then, from ch. 2 to the end of the book,
Luke shows us the stages through which the Christians passed, as they
reached new groups or individuals and bridged the divisions which
separated Jews from others. He describes the sort of people whom the
Christians reached: the 'proselytes' in Jerusalem (the non-Jews who
were attached to the Jewish synagogue, 2.10), the Samaritans (8.5–25),
an 'Ethiopian' (8.26–40), Paul receiving a commission to carry God's
name to the Gentiles (9.15), Roman Gentiles (10.1—11.18), Gentiles in
Asia Minor (13.46), Gentiles whom the Jewish Christians admitted to
the Church at the Jerusalem meetings (15.19), Gentiles in Europe
(15.36—18.38). Finally Luke triumphantly records how Paul arrived in
Rome, the centre from which missionaries could reach every part of the

1

Roman Empire (28.14). (For an outline summary of this central message which Luke declared, see the Plan of the Book of Acts, p. xi.)

Although this was Luke's chief purpose in writing, he seems to have had three other aims also:

1. To show that God's Spirit was active in the lives of the first Christians, just as He was active in the life of Jesus. Luke wrote: 'All that Jesus *began* to do . . .' (Acts 1.1), meaning that Jesus continued His work in the lives of His followers. For this reason, many people call Acts the 'Acts of the Holy Spirit' rather than 'Acts of the Apostles'.

2. To defend Christians against those Romans who accused them of being disloyal to the Empire, and to show that Christians were grateful to the Roman authorities for their protection (see note on 1.1a).

3. To encourage Christians at a time when the Apostles were no longer there to lead them (Luke was probably writing between AD 80 and AD 90).

WHY DO WE READ ACTS TODAY?

We study Acts chiefly in order that we may be open to the same Spirit who inspired the first Christians and moved them to action, and in order that we may be directed by Him. Naturally God's Holy Spirit will lead us to do many of the things which He led the first Christians to do, and especially to break down the very serious barriers between nations and races in our own generation, and to create unity and fellowship among the many branches of God's Church.

But the first Christians lived in a different sort of world from ours. They had no radios or buses, no trade unions or United Nations Organization. We do not study them in order to imitate exactly what they did. God's Spirit is a living Spirit, and can lead us to do what is fitting in our own situations. So we should not expect to find answers in Acts to all the difficult questions which we face today, e.g.: whether women should be ordained as pastors or bishops, or how rich nations can share their riches with the poorer nations. We must find the answers to these questions for ourselves, and we shall do so mainly by trusting the promise which Jesus made: 'When the Spirit of truth comes, He will guide you into all truth' (John 16.13).

Acts is specially interesting and important to Christians who today are members of *new* congregations, or are members of Churches which are beginning *new* work. The first Christians learned to depend on God's Spirit because they faced *new* situations, and could no longer depend on traditions. Of course traditions are important, and it is foolish to disregard them. But many events take place today for which traditions cannot give guidance. So those who face new situations in this century read Acts to see how the first Christians lived, and by reading it they can find courage to grow in faith.

A further reason for reading Acts is that we see in it how the followers of Jesus *lived* the teaching of which we read in the Gospels (this is why the book is called 'Acts'). The good news is not only what Jesus said and did, but what He enabled and still enables believers to *do*. The gospel is about events rather than ideas.

Note: In this Introduction we have considered two questions only. Some other questions which readers will ask are considered in the Special Notes, such as: 'Was Luke reliable as a historian?', 'What is the background of the events recorded in Acts?'.

STUDY SUGGESTIONS

REVIEW OF CONTENT

1. Why do we need to study Luke's Gospel along with Acts?
2. (a) What was Luke's special purpose in writing his two-part book?
   (b) Study the Plan of the Book of Acts (p. xi). In what way does this plan show Luke's special purpose in writing?

BIBLE STUDY

3. Read Luke 4.25–29.
   (a) Why did Jesus refer to Elisha and Naaman (4.27)?
   (b) Why were Jesus's hearers angry with Him?
   (c) What is the connection between this passage and Acts?

DISCUSSION AND APPLICATION

4. 'The same Spirit who inspired the first Christians . . . will lead us to break down barriers which separate people'—and to carry the gospel across those barriers (p. 2). Three sorts of 'barriers' which separate people today are: (1) barriers between groups or classes of people, (2) barriers between nations and races of people, (3) barriers between different Churches and congregations.
   (a) What other sorts of barriers are there between people, which prevent the spread of the gospel?
   (b) What, if anything, is being done by Christians in your Church to break down any of these barriers? What more do you think could be done?
5. We have considered one chief reason why people read Acts (p. 2). Suggest another good reason.

1.1–11

The Commands and Promises of Jesus

OUTLINE

1.1–3: Luke reminds readers of what he had said about Jesus in his first book (i.e. his Gospel).
1.4–11: The commands and promises of Jesus.

INTERPRETATION

Many people, after reading through this passage, chiefly remember the detailed account of the Ascension in v. 2 and vv. 9–11. But, from a more careful study, we see that Luke did not put his emphasis on that story. What he did was to share with his readers three special thoughts:
   1. *There is a close connection between the events recorded in the Gospels and those recorded in Acts.* The Jesus who was active during His earthly ministry ('all that Jesus began to do', v. 1), was the same Person who was also active in the lives of His followers after the resurrection. As we have seen, (p. 1 above), Luke emphasized this truth by writing one book which had two parts, but which described the work of the one Person, Jesus.
   2. *Jesus gave commands to His disciples.* These commands were: (a) to wait patiently in Jerusalem (v. 4), (b) to be witnesses to Jesus (v. 8b), (c) to carry on witnessing across national boundaries (v. 8c).
   3. *Jesus made promises,* namely that those whom he had told to be witnesses would be given the power to do it, 'when the Holy Spirit has come upon you' (v. 8). God does not give us work to do without providing the power to do it. In these introductory verses Luke was chiefly pointing to what the first Christians were about to do (as recorded in Acts):
   (a) They based their lives on Jesus, whose activity was for them both past and present (2.22–24 and 3.6).
   (b) They carried out the command to be witnesses (2.14).
   (c) They were able to do this because they received the Spirit (2.4).

NOTES

1.1a: Theophilus. Luke dedicated both parts of his book to Theophi-

4

lus. Perhaps he was a Roman official ('most excellent', Luke 1.3), and Luke hoped that he would urge the Roman authorities to treat Christians well. The name Theophilus means 'Lover of God'.

1.1b: Jesus began to do. In these words Luke was referring to the events which he recorded in his Gospel. By saying 'Jesus began' he meant 'that was only the beginning of His ministry'. So Christians today do not follow Jesus who *was* once active, but Jesus who *is* active in the lives of His followers.

1.2a: When he was taken up. See also vv. 9–11. Luke is the only Gospel writer who recorded the 'ascension' of Jesus (24.51), and is the only New Testament writer who interpreted it as something which people actually saw.

The other New Testament writers pointed to the ascension as the 'exaltation' of Jesus in the Spirit. They emphasized two truths: (1) that Jesus had triumphantly completed His work in the world, handing over power and authority for continuing it to the Apostles. He no longer needed to be visible to human beings (see Heb. 12.2); (2) that God had received Him to sit at His right hand', i.e. to share the authority of God Himself (see 1 Pet. 3.22).

We see from Acts 2.33 and 5.31 that Luke also held these beliefs. But how should we interpret Luke's record of Jesus being 'lifted up' in the presence of the disciples? Here are some of the various explanations which have been suggested:

(a) That this is picture-language. 'Going up' is something that a first-year student does when he is promoted to the second year, and no one thinks that he leaves the ground. When we talk of God, we cannot help using picture-language, but the truth behind the picture is the important part of the record.

(b) That Luke's picture-language is not helpful, because it suggests that God is situated above us in space, that 'heaven' is a place above the clouds, and that Jesus rose upwards like a space-rocket. But God is Spirit. He is everywhere. He is not more 'up' than He is 'down' or 'around'. And 'heaven' is 'where God is' (it is not a territory).

(c) That the ascension was a miracle. If we say that it is only picture-language, we are saying that God does not do miracles.

1.2b: The apostles whom he had chosen. When Luke used the word 'Apostles' in Acts, he meant 'the Twelve', except in 14.4 and 14.14 where it refers to Paul and Barnabas.

But the Greek word translated 'Apostle' means 'someone who has been sent'. So other writers use the word for other Christian leaders, especially those who carried the gospel into new places (see 2 Cor. 8.23, where it is translated 'messengers' in RSV, and Acts 4.33.).

1.3a: Appearing to them during forty days. Luke recorded some of these appearances in his Gospel (ch. 24), and there are other accounts in the other Gospels and in 1 Cor. 15.5–8. Luke calls these appearances 'proofs' that Jesus really was alive after being killed.

If we ask what sort of body it was that 'appeared' there is no complete answer. In 24.43 Luke suggests that it was a 'flesh and blood' body ('he ate fish'), but according to John 20.19 it was not, because it passed through 'locked doors' (NEB). But our ignorance about the appearances does not mean that there were no appearances.

We read here that Jesus appeared for 'forty days', but in Luke ch. 24 it seems to be one day. Perhaps the word 'then' in Luke 24.44 and 24.50 means 'at another time' rather than 'on the same day'.

1.3b: Speaking of the kingdom of God. See note on 28.23. God's Kingdom is His sovereignty or rule over mankind. It does not mean an area or territory. It exists already ('is in the midst of you', Luke 17.21) but will one day be completed ('Thy kingdom come!', Luke 11.2). This activity of God is what Jesus preached. The first Christians carried on Jesus's preaching about the 'kingdom' (see Acts 8.12), but much more often they preached about Jesus Himself.

1.4a: While staying with them. The Greek word translated 'staying' really means 'taking salt', i.e. eating meals with them. This was the way Jesus often used to meet and teach His disciples (see Mark 2.15). Meals have always been important in creating fellowship among Christians, fellowship where learning also can take place, e.g. in monasteries and some colleges.

1.4b: Wait for the promise of the Father. The disciples were excited at what had happened and found it difficult to wait. They were only able to do so, (a) because they trusted Jesus, and (b) because they knew that they had not yet received the power which they needed.

Many new Christians feel that they must rush out and take some action rather than wait until they are equipped to act effectively. 'Waiting' means hoping in God and trusting Him (see Psalm 130.5; Heb. 11.1).

The minister of a Church in Sri Lanka died and the congregation had to wait four years before a suitable new minister could be found. They did not find it easy to wait and trust God. But during that time they did discover to their joy how many members there were who could give valuable service.

Promise. See note on 13.23.

1.5: Baptized with the Holy Spirit. This is part of Jesus's promise that His followers would be given power to witness to Him (see Luke 3.16).

Some Christians teach that in these words Jesus intended all His followers to go through two stages: first, conversion, with water baptism; secondly, baptism by the Spirit. But according to v. 5 Jesus did not speak of 'two stages', He only promised 'baptism with the Holy Spirit'. See Additional Note, 'Baptism', p. 79.

1.6: Will you at this time restore the kingdom to Israel? The disciples made two mistakes in asking this question:

1. They still hoped that Jesus might lead a political attack on the Roman authorities, so that the Jews could be a free nation. But this was not Jesus's work. (This does not, of course, mean that members of the Church should never join political activity to gain freedom from an unjust form of government.)

2. They wanted to know the future. Jesus said it was not for them to 'know times or seasons' (v. 7, see also Mark 13.32). It is natural to want to know what will happen next, e.g. in order to prepare for it. But the duty of Christians is to try to shape the future by their actions, rather than to predict it.

1.8: You shall receive power when the Holy Spirit has come upon you; and you shall be my witnesses in Jerusalem ... and to the end of the earth. This one verse sums up the whole contents of Acts.

Holy Spirit. The coming of the Spirit, which Jesus promised, took place continually and not only on the day of Pentecost (see note on 2.4a).

Witnesses, i.e. those who proclaim, by their words and behaviour, what they themselves have experienced or seen. This is what the Apostles did. See 1.22 and note on 23.11.

In Jerusalem ... and to the end of the earth. This is what took place. The Apostles witnessed to Jesus first in Jerusalem, then in the surrounding country, then (to people's surprise) in Samaria, and finally (after witnessing further and further from Jerusalem) Paul gave his witness in Rome. But the task of the Church in every age is to witness to the 'end of the earth', i.e. crossing all national and racial boundaries, as we saw on p. 1.

Power. See note on 3.12.

1.9–10: A cloud took him ... two men stood by them. Throughout the Bible, writers use a cloud as a sign that God Himself is present in His glory, e.g. Luke 9.34; Rev. 11.12. So Luke meant that at this time Jesus shared in the glory and authority of God Himself.

The 'two men' are angels (as in Luke 24.4), and in the Bible angels are a sign that God is communicating a message to human beings. So Luke was saying here that the message in v. 11 was from God (see note on 5.19).

Many readers will ask 'Were the cloud and the two men visible, or are they picture-language?' As we have seen, this is a question about which scholars disagree. But a far more important question is this: 'Is it true, (a) that Jesus shares God's authority, and (b) that God communicates with human beings? On both these points the writers of the New Testament agree in saying 'Yes'.

1.11a: Why do you stand looking into heaven? I.e. 'Why do you gaze at

'To break down the barriers between nations and races . . .' (p. 2).

The last sections of this bridge are being put in position and the bridge will eventually cross the river which at present separates the people of one country from those of another.

the sky instead of doing on earth what Jesus told you to do?' Here is a warning against making our prayers an escape from meeting the needs of those around us.

1.11b: This Jesus, who was taken up from you into heaven, will come. The 'coming' of Jesus (or 'Second Coming' as some Christians call it) means the time when God will have completed all that He is doing in the world. In this verse we learn that God has a purpose and that there is an end to which He is leading us. We are not in the hands of Fate, but in His hands.

Jesus warned the disciples not to ask, 'When will it happen?' (v. 7). If we also ask that question we are not trusting God.

Heaven. See note on 1.2a.

STUDY SUGGESTIONS

REVIEW OF CONTENT

1. Why did Luke refer to his 'first book' at the beginning of Acts?
2. Why did Jesus tell the disciples to wait in Jerusalem?
3. What mistake did the disciples make, according to this passage?
4. In what way does 1.8 sum up the whole book of Acts?
5. What does a cloud signify in the Bible?

BIBLE STUDY

6. 'Appearing to them' (1.3). Make a list of the people or groups of people to whom Jesus appeared, according to: Matt. 28.1–9 and 28.16–17; Luke 24.13–15 and 24.33–37; John 20.11–16 and v. 19; 1 Cor. 15.5–8.
7. Read the two accounts of the Ascension which Luke gives in Luke 24.45–53 and Acts 1.1–12. What are the chief differences between them?
8. What phrases concerning the Ascension do the following passages contain?
   (a) Acts 2.33   (b) Acts 5.31   (c) Rom. 8.34   (d) Eph. 1.20
   (e) Heb. 4.14   (f) Heb. 12.2   (g) 1 Pet. 3.22

DISCUSSION AND APPLICATION

9. Read the three different explanations in the note on 1.2a of Luke's account of the Ascension.
   (a) With which of them do you agree, and why?
   (b) If you do not agree with any of them, give your own explanation, with reasons.

10. What would your feelings have been if you had been one of the disciples when Jesus was 'taken out of their sight' (1.9)? How do you interpret Luke 24.51–52?
11. 'Staying with them' (1.4a) probably means 'having meals with them'.
    (a) What were some of the occasions (apart from the Last Supper) when Jesus had a meal with his friends? Give references, and read through one or two of the passages.
    (b) When and how do 'fellowship and learning' take place at shared meals in your experience?
12. 'It is not for you to know the times or seasons' (1.7).
    (a) Why did Jesus say this?
    (b) Give an example of some present-day religious person or group that claims to predict the future.

1.12–26
A Successor to Judas

OUTLINE

1.12–14: The disciples return to Jerusalem.
1.15–22: Peter's speech about Judas.
1.23–26: The choosing of the twelfth Apostle.

INTERPRETATION

In these verses Luke tells of two events: the return of the Apostles to Jerusalem and their choosing of Matthias to take the place of Judas Iscariot.

THE APOSTLES' RETURN

The Apostles had been on the Mount of Olives with Jesus, and then suddenly they could see Him no longer, and could only look back on His ministry with them. They then walked to the Upper Room in Jerusalem and there began a new life as they waited for the gift of the Spirit. In just the same way, Christians are right to look back to the past, to the earthly ministry of Jesus, but right also to live in the present as day by day they receive the gift of the Holy Spirit.

THE CHOOSING OF THE TWELFTH APOSTLE

There were twelve tribes of Israel and Jesus chose twelve Apostles to be the first members of the new Israel (see Gal. 6.16, where Paul calls the Church the 'Israel of God'). For this reason they believed that it was necessary to choose another Apostle when Judas died.

The names of the eleven listed in v. 13 are the same as the list in Luke 6.13–16.

NOTES

1.12: A sabbath day's journey, i.e. about one kilometre. Jews kept the fourth commandment by not walking further than this (see note on 13.14). The Apostles went down from the Mount of Olives, crossed the Kedron Valley, and climbed the steep hill into Jerusalem.

1.13: To the upper room. Most likely this was the room where Jesus had had the Last Supper with them (Luke 22.12), and was in the home of John Mark (Acts 12.12). Today the Syrian Church of St Mark probably occupies the place.

1.14a: Devoted themselves to prayer (or 'were constantly at prayer together'—NEB, a better translation) probably at the Temple or a synagogue (see also 2.42).

In this Gospel Luke records more examples of people praying than the other Gospel writers do, and there are many in Acts. Notice especially: (a) prayer as a regular practice (e.g. Luke 11.1; Acts 10.9), (b) prayer before taking decisions (e.g. Acts. 1.24; 13.3), (c) prayer as a chief way of receiving God's spirit. Unless Christians receive His Spirit, they cannot do His will.

1.14b: With the women . . . and with his brothers.

1. That women were included shows what a revolution had taken place among Christians as the result of Jesus's attitude to women. Although all the Apostles were men, women had an important place among the 'brethren' (see note on 16.14). These women may have been the Apostles' wives or the women of whom we read in Luke 8.2 and 24.10. One was Mary, Jesus's mother.

2. Jesus's own brothers had at first been against Him (John 7.5), but came to believe in Him. What changed them? Surely it was the fact that Jesus was made alive after His death.

1.15a: Peter stood up. As soon as the Apostles returned to Jerusalem Peter became their leader. It is strange that Luke does not mention him after ch. 15 (see note on 15.7).

1.15b: About a hundred and twenty. The number of people who followed Jesus was many more than the Twelve disciples (see Luke 10.1), and now 120 of them were brave enough to risk being arrested and to come out of their homes.

But they were a very small number out of the three-quarters of a million Jews who lived in or around Jerusalem. Yet it was through them that the Church grew.

1.16a: The scripture had to be fulfilled. The Apostles were so troubled by Judas's betrayal of Jesus and by His death that they looked for some explanation. Peter gave them an explanation by saying that if they read Psalms 69 and 109 they would not be surprised at such events. These events 'fulfilled' what was written in those psalms.

In what way were those events a 'fulfilment'?

1. Both those psalms refer to the sufferings and betrayal of the people of Israel (not of one person only), e.g. Pss. 69.1–5; 109.6–9. So Peter was saying, 'We see from these psalms that to be Israel is to be betrayed and to suffer. Because Jesus was the new and true Israel, it "had to be" that He would be betrayed and suffer (and that His betrayer would be brought low).'

We may add that whenever good people are betrayed and suffer it is in a way a 'fulfilment' of what was written in the Psalms.

2. Peter probably also believed that the writer of those psalms intended them to be predictions, although they seem to us to be mainly cries for help or curses on enemies. From Acts 2.16 and 3.18 we see that the first Christians did interpret much of the Old Testament as predictions.

But we should note that, (a) Judas was not 'fated' to commit sin. Like all of us, he was free to choose between right and wrong. (b) There is no evidence to show that the writer of those psalms knew that there would be a person called Judas who would betray the Messiah.

1.16b: By the mouth of David. It was the custom to call all the psalms 'Psalms of David' (see 2.25; 4.25) although many were written after David's time, e.g. Ps. 137 which refers to the Exile (400 years after David). But it may be that these Psalms, 69 and 109, were indeed by David himself.

1.16c: Judas who was guide to those who arrested Jesus.

1. *Judas's death.* Luke gives one account in vv. 18 and 19, and there is a different account in Matt. 27.5–8 ('he hanged himself'). When there are different accounts of the same event in the New Testament, it does not mean that the event did not occur.

2. *Judas's wrong-doing.* First he betrayed Jesus, secondly he failed to ask for God's forgiveness. Peter denied Jesus, repented and was forgiven: Judas betrayed Him and despaired.

1.17: Share in this ministry. See note on 21.19, 'ministry'. Here ministry is said to be 'shared', i.e. among the rest of the Apostles. It is sad when, in today's Church, ministers fail to share their ministry and try to work independently (see note on 6.2a).

1.22: A witness to his resurrection

1. The person taking the place of Judas had to: (a) have been with Jesus since the beginning of His ministry (v. 21), and (b) be able to say that he personally had seen Jesus after His resurrection (to report what others said was not enough).

We see here what the first Christians believed (what their first 'creed' was), i.e. that Jesus had been a man ministering in our world, but that He was unlike other men and rose after death.

2. According to the New Testament (and especially in Acts) it was the resurrection of Jesus which His first followers preached above everything else, e.g. in Acts 2.24; 1 Cor. 15.14. None of the Bible writers has explained *how* Jesus rose, and they give differing accounts of His appearances (see note on 1.3). But if there had been no resurrection there would have been no Church.

1.26: They cast lots. The way in which the Apostles chose a successor to Judas was much more than casting lots: (1) Peter decided what sort of person was needed (vv. 21,22); (2) the hundred and twenty nominated two candidates (v. 23); (3) they all prayed (v. 24), (4) Only then did they cast lots. (They wrote each name on a stone, and shook the stones in a pot until one fell out.)

Churches today use other methods of choosing their leaders, but their methods are not always better than the way which the Apostles used, e.g. in Sweden the Government appoints the bishops; in Japan the clergy and one lay member from each congregation vote for a new bishop.

STUDY SUGGESTIONS

REVIEW OF CONTENT

1. How far is a 'sabbath day's journey'?
2. What do we know about the brothers of Jesus?
3. Why did Peter quote the Psalms (1.20)?
4. Why was it important to find a successor to Judas?
5. What sort of person were the Apostles looking for, to take Judas's place?

BIBLE STUDY

6. 'Were constantly at prayer together' (1.14, NEB, see p. 11).
Read the following verses in Acts and say in each case who was praying, and, if possible, why they were praying:
(a) 4.31 (b) 6.6 (c) 16.25–8 (d) 21.5
Then read the following passages in Luke's Gospel and say what you discover about praying in each passage:

(a) 3.21   (b) 6.12   (c) 18.1–8   (d) 22.31–32

7. What belief do we find expressed in Acts 1.16 and also in 2.16 and 13.33?

8. 'The followers of Jesus preached the resurrection above everything else' (p. 13).

(a) What words are repeated in 2.24; 3.15 and 4.10?

(b) What did the speakers or writers in the following passages say about the resurrection? Acts 10.40–41; 1 Cor. 15.4–5.

(c) How would you answer people who said they could not believe in the resurrection because the accounts of it in the Gospels do not agree?

DISCUSSION AND APPLICATION

9. 'Prayer as a regular practice' (p. 11). What in your experience helps you to pray regularly and with perseverance?

10. The 120 men and women (v. 15) were a very small minority of the population, yet through them the Church grew.

(a) Describe any experience you have had, or that you know about, of a few dedicated Christians achieving important results.

(b) What are the advantages and disadvantages of being a small Church congregation?

11. 'Judas was not fated' (p. 12)

(a) Why did Judas betray Jesus? (John 12.6 only provides one possible answer).

(b) What effect would it have on you if you believed that your behaviour was fated?

(c) What would you reply to someone who said that Christians should thank Judas, because without him there would have been no crucifixion and, therefore, no salvation?

12. Ministry was 'shared . . . among the Apostles' (note on 1.17).

(a) Why should ministry be shared?

(b) Why, in your opinion, do some ministers fail to share ministry?

13. 'They cast lots' (v. 26).

(a) How does your Church choose its leaders?

(b) What are the advantages and disadvantages of the method?

2.1–13

The Outpouring of the Spirit

OUTLINE

2.1–4: The Holy Spirit fills the Apostles.
2.5–13: The crowd is astonished.

INTERPRETATION

Many Christians regard this event as the most important of all the events which Luke recorded in Acts, because in it the Church was being re-born or re-created, beginning a new stage. We need to remember that the Church was 'born' when God called Abraham (Gen. 12.1) and that it was re-created when Jesus called the Twelve. So it is more accurate to say that Pentecost is the story of the re-birth rather than 'the birth of the Church'. But certainly we read here of a totally renewed Church, with clearly re-newed members.

The chief way in which the Church was renewed was that its members had a new power and courage which came from outside themselves. Luke emphasized this in order to explain the fact that the gospel reached Rome, the centre from which it could spread to the rest of the world. Without a new power that could never have happened (see note on 3.12). This was the power called the Holy Spirit in them, just as it had been in Jesus (Luke 3.16). But this power was not given on this occasion only. God gave them His power continually, and offers to present-day Christians the same power.

NOTES

2.1a: The day of Pentecost. There were two Jewish harvest festivals: Pentecost, the grain harvest, when they baked the first barley loaves and offered them in thanksgiving; and Tabernacles, the fruit harvest which took place later in the year.

Pentecost was a public holiday (Lev. 23.21), and Jerusalem was full of pilgrims. Because the winter was over they could come by sea from such parts as North Africa, Italy, etc. (see vv. 9–11). So being in Jerusalem at that time was in some ways like being in a modern city when an international festival or sporting event is taking place.

2.1b: They were all together in one place. All means either the Twelve with the women and Jesus's family (1.14), or the hundred and twenty (1.15), or the Twelve (2.14).

Together. They were ready for God's gift in three ways, all of which are important:

1. They were in the same place.
2. They were in fellowship with each other. The words 'in one place' may mean in John Mark's home (1.13), or in a big courtyard surrounded by a number of living rooms. But the Greek words can also mean 'as one company', i.e. in fellowship.
3. They were sitting quietly, waiting (v. 2). God comes to those who have made themselves ready. Preparation is necessary. A plane cannot land on an airstrip in the rainy season (even with modern instruments) until the water from recent storms has been cleared away.

2.2–3: A sound ... like the rush of a mighty wind ... tongues as of fire. When people have a deep experience of the presence of God, they cannot find words to describe it. So here Luke can only report that it was '*like*' a wind and '*like*' fire. Wind and fire are both tremendously powerful natural forces, and Luke uses the words to indicate the power which God was giving to the Apostles.

They experienced the presence of God in a way that everyone could see. It was extraordinary. But God's power may be just as much present in us when there is nothing extraordinary to see or hear (see note 3 on 2.4a).

2.3: Resting on each one. Although the Apostles met as a fellowship, each of them individually experienced the presence and power of God.

2.4a: They were all filled with the Holy Spirit. Luke refers to the Holy Spirit more than the other New Testament writers do. He sees almost every action of the Apostles as being directed by the Holy Spirit.

From his writings we notice that:

1. The Holy Spirit is *God Himself*. We may speak of receiving from God His 'gift' of the Holy Spirit, provided we remember that that gift is God giving Himself. The Spirit is not 'something' that He gives.
2. When people were 'filled' with the Spirit, they experienced God *in* them. They were accustomed to thinking of God as being above them ('high and lifted up'. Isa. 6.1). It was a new experience to know Him as being in them.
3. They also experienced God as being *actively* in them (not simply *being* in them). He was active in two special ways: (a) giving them power: 'Filled with the Holy Spirit' they 'spoke with boldness' (4.31); (b) guiding them: 'The Spirit said "Go ..."' (8.29).

In some religions people believe that it would be 'beneath God's dignity' to intervene in the lives of human beings. But a Christian's experience of God's Holy Spirit is that He does actively intervene.

Sometimes the result is extraordinary (as in 2.1–13). At other times we experience Him as actively moving us in ordinary events. A social worker in a big city said, 'In my work I have difficult decisions to take all day. When I take a little step I find that I am part of a movement of God and that I am carried forward. I make many mistakes, but He is working away in me.' We see the results of the Holy Spirit's activity as much in ordinary events as in the extraordinary ones.

4. Luke knew very well that the Holy Spirit had been at work in the world long before Pentecost, e.g. inspiring people to 'prophesy' (see 28.25), and, of course, inspiring Jesus (Luke 4.1). But his activity at Pentecost was a new sort of event. First, it was shared among all sorts of people and no longer confined to special classes of people, such as kings or prophets or hermits. And secondly, His activity brought a continuing power and not only power for a special occasion.

5. Not all who claim to be led by the Spirit are really led by Him. Alice Lakwena in 1984 believed that she was guided by the Spirit to lead an anti-Government army in Uganda. She said that the Spirit had told her to provide magic oil to protect her soldiers from bullets, and they believed her, and many were killed.

2.4b: They began to speak in other tongues. See also 'in his own language' (v. 6), 'in his own native language' (v. 8), 'in our own tongues' (v. 11).

Were the Apostles speaking in 'ecstasy' (that is, with sounds but without ordinary words) or in foreign languages? Scholars differ in their opinions about this. Here are three of the opinions most widely held:

1. That it does not matter. The important event was that they somehow communicated to others what had happened to them; 'tongues' and 'languages' are only signs of sharing. This event is an example of the 'breaking down of barriers' between people of which Luke was writing throughout Acts.

2. That they spoke in foreign languages. Christians today who have the same sort of experience of being filled with the Holy Spirit do sometimes utter words which are words from a foreign language, although they themselves do not know that language. This is a miracle, and in Acts 2.1–13 Luke describes a miracle. Believing in God means believing that He does miracles.

3. That they spoke in ecstasy, and not in other languages. Some reasons for this opinion are:

(a) People in the crowd would not have said that they were drunk (v. 11) if they had spoken in foreign languages.

(b) In other passages in Acts 'speaking in tongues' clearly means ecstasy (see 10.46; 19.6).

(c) They did not need to use foreign languages. All the pilgrims who came to the Feast spoke at least one of the languages which the Apostles spoke, i.e. Aramaic and Greek.

(d) Luke was not present at the event and had to rely on reports (as he said in Luke 1.1–4) which were perhaps not accurate concerning the language used.

2.5: From every nation under heaven. Again Luke shows that the followers of Jesus were reaching people across national boundaries, and that this is what He calls Christians to do in every generation. Although Luke wrote 'every nation' he had in mind only the countries around the eastern Mediterranean where Jews lived. See vv. 9–11 for the names of those countries.

2.6: Each one heard. See also vv. 8 and 11: 'we hear'. What did they hear? Luke does not tell us. But he does tell us that those who had received the Holy Spirit were able to communicate with other people. They shared their convictions. Evangelism takes place only when Christians have learnt how to share what is important to them with others.

2.10: Both Jews and proselytes. There were a great many non-Jews who admired the Jews' teaching about God and their family life and their worship, and who wanted to be associated with their religion. If they were willing to keep the Jewish 'Law', including circumcision, they were baptized and became 'proselytes' (see also 13.43).

Other non-Jews who wanted to be associated with the Jewish religion, but less closely than 'proselytes', are called in Acts God-fearers (10.1) or worshippers of God (16.14).

It was chiefly non-Jews like these (proselytes and others) from Judea and surrounding countries who became Christians.

ADDITIONAL NOTE: 'TONGUES'

Speaking in tongues took place frequently in the early years of the Church and has continued from time to time up to the present. Paul could speak in 'tongues' (1 Cor. 14.18), but told the Corinthians that there were dangers in it (1 Cor. 14.9, 23).

What is the right way?

1. Its object is to glorify God, not to achieve a position of honour (1 Cor. 14.2).

2. It is chiefly for personal worship. When it is used in public it must be interpreted (1. Cor. 14.13).

3. It is a gift, and it is not given to all Christians, however Spirit-filled they may be.

4. It is not a proof that the worshipper is filled with the Holy Spirit.

The followers of the Greek god Dionysius spoke in tongues, and so do many 'diviners' throughout the world.

5. Most Christians who speak in tongues say that by doing so they feel they are praying more 'fully' than in ordinary prayer when they are using their minds. Others say that it is an alternative, rather than a fuller way of worshipping.

In recent years, the number of Christians for whom 'speaking in tongues' is usually a part of their worship has increased very rapidly all over the world. Their worship is often remarkable not only for their 'speaking in tongues', but their freedom from set forms, their close fellowship, their joyfulness, and their expectation that God will give bodily healing through prayer. Some, but not all, believe that members who have been converted need to have a 'second baptism' (or baptism of the Spirit) during which they will usually speak in tongues (see note on 8.16).

Some of the Christians who speak in tongues belong to the 'Pentecostal Churches' (at the time of writing, 22 million members in the world), some to Independent Church groups, especially in Africa (82 million members), and some, usually called 'Charismatics', who belong to the main traditional Churches but also meet in groups where worship is of this sort (11 million).

This sort of worship, like the worship of the Church in Corinth, has its dangers as well as its glories. Members may become separated from other Christians and believe that they are superior to those others, and some may be graded higher than others, e.g. because they speak in tongues. Or they may become so much concerned with their own experiences that they neglect their duties as citizens; they may be so deeply aware of the working of the Spirit at the present time that they neglect the guidance which the Spirit gave in the past and for all time; they may claim to be guided by the Spirit when really they are expressing their own wishes. We need to notice such dangers while at the same time taking very seriously Paul's words, 'Do not quench the Spirit' (1 Thess. 5.19).

STUDY SUGGESTIONS

REVIEW OF CONTENTS

1. What is the most important teaching which Luke was giving his readers in these verses?
2. What sort of feast was Pentecost?
3. In what two ways was this coming of the Holy Spirit a new event?

4. For what two reasons do many people believe that the Apostles spoke in 'ecstasy' and not in foreign languages?
5. Who were the proselytes?

BIBLE STUDY

6. 'The Holy Spirit had been at work in the world long before Pentecost' (p. 17). According to each of the following Old Testament passages, in whom was the Spirit working and with what result?
   (a) Exod. 31.1–5 (b) Num. 11.25 (c) Judg. 6.34–35
   (d) Ezek. 2.1–2
7. 'The Holy Spirit was active in two special ways: giving them power ... guiding them' (p. 16).
   Read the following passages in Acts and say in each case who received the gift, and whether the Spirit gave 'power' or 'guidance'.
   (a) 4.31 (b) 8.29 (c) 10.44 (d) 11.28 (e) 13.1–3 (f) 19.1–6

DISCUSSION AND APPLICATION

8. To what extent can everyone have the experience which the Apostles had at Pentecost?
9. How would you answer someone who asked you: 'I am a Christian and I believe that any good which I can do is God at work in me, but I have had no special experience of being "filled"; am I missing something?'?
10. Three different interpretations of 'speaking in tongues' (2.4 and similar phrases in 2.6; 2.8; 2.11) are given in the note on 2.4b.
    (a) Which interpretation do you accept, and why?
    (b) If you do not accept any of the three, what is your own interpretation?
11. There are at present about 115 million Charismatic or Pentecostal Christians in the world (see p. 19)
    (a) Why do you think they have increased?
    (b) What are the advantages and disadvantages of their freedom from set forms of worship?
    (c) How can this sort of worship unite Christians, rather than dividing them?

2.14–41
Peter's First Speech

OUTLINE

2.14–36: Peter's sermon:

(a) I will interpret these events (v. 14–15).

(b) They are part of God's purpose and Joel predicted them (vv. 16–21).

(c) They are the result of Jesus's coming (vv. 22–24).

(d) His resurrection was part of God's purpose, and David predicted it in Ps. 16 (vv. 25–32).

(e) It is Jesus who gave us the Holy Spirit (v. 33).

(f) Jesus is the Messiah and David predicted his coming in Ps. 110 (vv. 34–35).

(g) It is the Messiah whom you have killed (v. 36).

2.37: The crowd's question.

2.38–40: Peter's answer.

2.14: The crowd's response.

INTERPRETATION

Peter stood up in the open air, facing a huge crowd; some were pilgrims from other countries, some were inhabitants of Jerusalem. Round him stood the other Apostles. So began the very first sermon ever preached by the followers of Jesus.

1. HOW DID LUKE KNOW WHAT PETER SAID?

Luke was writing a long time after the events that he was recording. Where did he get his information?

Someone who was present may have given him a written account of it in Aramaic (the language which Peter spoke); phrases such as 'give ear to my words' (v. 14), 'pangs of death' (v. 24), 'the heavens' (plural, v. 34) are translations of Aramaic phrases. *Or* various groups may have told Luke what the earliest preaching was like, and he gave a summary of it. As it appears here it only takes four minutes to speak, and vv. 14–41 are clearly a summary and not the complete sermon. Also, according to v. 40 Peter said much more than Luke recorded here.

2. THIS SERMON AND OTHER SERMONS IN ACTS

This sermon is very like the others, and so we can see the sort of preaching that was done in the time that followed Pentecost. If we compare this one with the six other chief sermons (from among the 21 sermons in Acts) we see the same plan in nearly all of them:

(a) *Fulfilment*: In the events concerning Jesus and the gift of the Spirit God's purpose has been fulfilled (see 3.12–26; 10.43; 13.23–34; 26.22; also 1 Cor. 15.3–4; Rom. 1.2).

(b) *Jesus*: Jesus the Messiah, risen and exalted, is the centre of our preaching (see 3.13–18; 5.30; 10.36–40; 13.23–37; 17.31; 26.23; also Rom. 1.3–4; Phil. 2.9–10).

(c) *Experience*: We preach from experience–'we are witnesses' (see 3.15; 5.32; 10.39–41; 13.31; 26.9–23; also 1 Cor. 15.5–9).

(d) *The Future*: God has a plan for the future, which includes judgement and His final defeat of evil (see 3.21–23; 10.42; 13.40; 17.31; also 1 Thess. 1.9–10)

(e) *Repentance*: Change the direction of your life (see note on v. 38).

3. THESE SERMONS AND OTHER NT WRITINGS

When we compare these sermons with later writings such as Paul's letters, John's Gospel, and the Letter to the Hebrews, we notice differences. We see that some teaching is missing from these sermons, for example:

(a) *Jesus*: Here He is called by such titles as 'man' and 'Lord' and 'Messiah', but not 'Son of God' except in an account written by Luke (9.20).

(b) *The cross*: Here the death of Jesus is a crime, but there is no teaching that He 'died for us' as in Rom. 5.6.

(c) *Faith*: The people were urged to 'repent' but not to 'have faith' (compare Rom. 5.1).

(d) *Sin*: Here the Jews of Judea are 'sinners', but it is not said that 'all have sinned' as in Rom. 3.9.

When we study these differences it seems that Christian preaching and teaching changed and developed after the first period and in the centuries that followed. What are we to think about such development? Where do we find the truth? Here are three out of many opinions which Christians hold:

1. That the early preaching is the true gospel because it was nearest in time to Jesus Himself, and that later preaching and the Church's creeds contained unnecessary additions.

2. That God intended and still intends development to take place under the guidance of the Spirit (see John 16.13).

3. That God intended development to take place when all branches

of the Church agree on such development, but that if there is no agreement there must be no development. (According to this view the Creeds were a good development but no development is permitted today.)

One reason why Christians are divided today is that they cannot agree concerning 'development'.

NOTES

2.16: This is what was spoken by the prophet. In the past Peter had many special experiences which had changed his life, e.g. he had realized that Jesus was the Messiah (Luke 9.20), he had seen the risen Jesus, and he had received the gift of the Spirit. His aim in this sermon was to explain these facts to his hearers. But they did not have his experience and so he needed to support his statements in a way that they could understand. This is why he quoted three Old Testament passages. He interpreted these passages as predictions of the future, since this was the way in which Jewish teachers ('Rabbis') very often interpreted the Old Testament.

The first passage which Peter quoted (2.17–21) was from Joel ch. 2, which he interpreted as a prediction of the coming of the Holy Spirit.

The second (2.25–28) was from Psalm 16, which he interpreted as a prediction of the resurrection of Jesus.

The third (2.34–35) was from Psalm 110, which he interpreted as a prediction of the Messiahship of Jesus.

What are we to think about Peter's statement?

(a) We certainly *can believe*: that the events to which Peter referred really took place; that these events were part of God's purpose; and that they fulfilled the writings of prophets and psalmists.(b) But it is *not necessary* for us: to follow the Jewish Rabbis' methods of interpretation, nor to believe that the prophets and psalmists knew in what way their writings would be fulfilled.

2.17: All flesh. Peter did not have in mind the non-Jews when he said this, because at this time he had not discovered that the Spirit was for them (see ch. 10). 'All flesh' means all God's creation, so he was thinking not only of special groups of people such as prophets and hermits and kings, but all who seek Him. So today God offers His Spirit to everyone, not only to educated people or the rich or Church leaders.

2.18: They shall prophesy. 'Prophesying' has many meanings (see note on 15.32). Here it means 'speaking in tongues' (ecstasy). But in v. 30 'prophet' means someone who predicts the future.

23

'Those who received the Holy Spirit were able to communicate with others ... they shared their convictions—and their possessions. Christian Basic communities are sharing this sort of fellowship today' (pp. 18 and 31).

Members of this 'basic community' in Mexico, like others in many parts of the world, meet to worship together and to share their ideas for future action.

2.22: Jesus of Nazareth, a man attested to you by God with mighty works.
  1. Luke calls Jesus 'a man'. Christians are sometimes so keen to call Jesus 'God' that they forget that He was a real human being. On the other hand those who are not Christians usually see Jesus as nothing more than a man (see note on v. 36).
  2. 'Attested to you by mighty works', i.e. proved to be God's servant by the miracles which He did. But Jesus Himself did not want to be 'proved' by His miracles. We see from Luke 11.15 that His casting out demons did not at all prove that God had sent Him. It needed more than miracles to persuade people to believe in Him as God's Messiah (see Additional Note, Miracles, pp. 189, 190).

2.23a: This Jesus, delivered up according to the definite plan . . . of God, you crucified. These words show us two important truths about the cross:
  1. It was not surprising. Suffering is part of the nature of God, and when He became man of course suffering and death followed. Peter had to explain this, because the Jews thought that it was impossible for someone who was Messiah to suffer and die.
  2. It was a crime, and those who were responsible for it were guilty. Some people say that God 'sent Jesus into the world in order to die', i.e. in order that God should receive a sacrifice for the world's sin. But if this is true, it is unfair to blame those who killed Him.

2.23b: You crucified. Who crucified Jesus? Who was responsible? When Peter said 'you' in this verse, and when he called them 'Men of Israel' (2.22 and 3.12), he was referring to the Judeans of Jerusalem (see v. 14, 'Men of Judea'). (Peter himself was a Galilean.) Later he showed which Judeans he chiefly accused of killing Jesus: the rulers (4.8–10) and 'the council' (5.27–30). Perhaps also there were people to whom Peter was speaking who had been present when Jesus was being tried and who did nothing to save Him.

But it is entirely wrong to accuse the whole Jewish nation of killing Jesus. Christians have often made this unjust accusation, and as a result have committed many terrible crimes against the Jews, even in the 20th century. According to Acts, the only guilty Jews were some of the Judeans.

However, it was Pilate, the Roman, who was really responsible. He alone had the power to release Jesus or to condemn Him (13.28).

2.24: God raised him. In his preaching, Peter emphasized the resurrection (rather than the birth of Jesus or the death of Jesus or His ascension or the coming of the Spirit).

The clear statement 'God raised him' is an example of all good Christian preaching, that is, it declares events (rather than ideas) and proclaims good news (rather than good advice). Other marks of good preaching which we see in Peter's sermon are: (a) He put himself alongside his hearers by referring to something which he and they had in common, in this case the events recorded in vv. 5–13. (b) He used language which his hearers also used, e.g. his references to David's 'prediction' in v. 31. (c) He spoke from his experience: 'We are witnesses' (v. 32). (d) He invited a response and a changed attitude from his listeners (vv. 37–41).

We should especially note the words 'God raised Him', not 'He rose'. This is the wording in v. 32 and in nearly all the NT verses which refer to the resurrection.

2.29: I may say to you confidently. 'Confidently' is an important word, showing the extraordinary way in which Peter had changed. Compare it with Luke 22.60. Peter could now speak 'confidently' because Jesus had risen and because he was 'filled' with the Spirit. The Greek word translated 'confidently' is also translated 'openly', 'plainly', 'boldly' in other NT verses (e.g. John 10.24; Acts 4.13).

2.31: David . . . foresaw and spoke of the resurrection of the Christ. See note on 2.16 for 'David foresaw' and on 2.36 for the title 'Christ'. The whole book of Psalms had the title 'Psalms of David' in Hebrew, even though David himself may have composed only a few of them.

2.33: Being . . . exalted at the right hand of God. See note on 1.9. NT writers were not much interested in *how* Jesus 'ascended'. The truth that He *is* now 'exalted', i.e. shares the authority of God, was far more important to them.

2.36: God has made him both Lord and Christ. According to the sermons in Acts, the first Christians used at least eight names or titles for Jesus. 'Lord' and 'Christ' are two of them.

Lord. See also 10.36 and 20.21, i.e. the one to whom total loyalty is due, the one whom we obey even above Caesar. It is a translation of the Greek work '*Kyrios*' which people used when speaking about God. But in the early days of the Church the Jews probably were not meaning to call Jesus 'God' when they called Him 'Lord'.

Christ. See also 3.18; 10.36; 20.21; 26.23. Today we often use this name as if it was Jesus's surname, but it is a title. It means 'the anointed Messiah', the messenger from God for whom the Jews had waited for centuries. He was the one who would 'restore the kingdom to Israel' (Acts 1.6). Some people thought that he would be a military leader, others that he would be a spiritual head (Luke 2.25–32). Jews today, except for the few who have accepted Jesus as Messiah, are still waiting for their Messiah.

The other names for Jesus which we find in Acts are:

Man (2.22; 17.31). See note on v. 22 and 1. Tim. 2.5.

Servant (3.13), the servant of God. See Luke 22.27.

Holy One (3.14) and **Righteous One** (3.14; 7.52).

Leader or **Author of life** (3.15; 5.31).

Saviour. See note on 5.31.

In addition Luke uses the title 'Son of God' (9.20) when describing the preaching of Paul in Damascus (see also note on 8.36).

2.37: What shall we do? Peter had preached in such a way that at the end of the sermon his listeners were hungry for changes in their lives, however uncomfortable the changes might be. Any preacher who hears members of the congregation saying this knows that he has achieved something.

2.38a: Repent. It was the Jewish religious leaders of Judea who had caused the death of Jesus. Most of the people who listened to Peter had had nothing to do with His death. So why were they 'cut to the heart' (v. 37)? Probably because they had done nothing to prevent His death. To do nothing when evil is being planned is to share in the evil. Sin is not only what we do wrong, but the good which we fail to do.

What is 'repentance'?. It is chiefly changing direction in our lives, having a fresh object in living. (It is not the same as the feeling of misery which we may have after doing wrong.) There are four stages: (1) turning away from past evil (3.19); (2) trusting God that He fully forgives us and gives us a new start (5.31; 11.18); (3) intending to behave in a new way; (4) being open to receive the Holy Spirit who makes it possible to live in this new way. See the final words of this verse.

2.38b: Be baptized in the name of Jesus. See note on 8.12 for 'baptism', and on 3.6b for 'in the name of Jesus'.

2.39: The promise is to you and to your children and to all that are far off, every one whom the Lord calls.

Your children, i.e. future generations. (This verse does not prove that the baptism of infants is God's will or that it is *not* His will.)

Those far off, i.e. others, not only those who hear this sermon.

Everyone whom the Lord calls, i.e. 'all of us'. It has the same meaning as 'all flesh' in v. 17, i.e. all sorts of people. It does not mean that God calls some people to salvation and leaves others to perish.

2.41: Three thousand souls. This does not mean that they were all baptized that day or in one place. It means that from that day large numbers of people accepted Jesus as Messiah and were eventually baptized.

STUDY SUGGESTIONS

REVIEW OF CONTENT

1. Who was guilty of the death of Jesus, according to Peter?

2. What sort of people heard Peter's sermon?
3. What shows that vv. 14–40 are a summary and not a full report?
4. Mention two ways in which the teaching of the sermons in Acts is different from the teaching we find in later writings.
5. (a) What does the title 'Christ' mean?
   (b) What *three* other words are used in these verses as names and titles of Jesus?
6. Give two results of Peter's sermon.

BIBLE STUDY

7. The Greek words which are translated 'confidently' in 2.29 are translated in various ways in the New Testament. Read the following verses and say in each case what the translation is and what action is referred to.
   (a) Mark 8.32 (b) John 16.25 (c) Acts 9.27 (d) Acts 28.31
   (e) Eph. 6.19 (f) Hebrews 4.16
8. 'There are four stages in repenting' (note on 2.38a). Read the following passages and say in each case which stage (1, 2, 3 or 4) the author was referring to:
   (a) Ezek. 14.6 (b) Ezek. 36.25 (c) Ezek. 36.26
   (d) Mark 1.15b (e) Luke 3.8 (f) Acts 5.31 (g) Acts 13.39
   (h) Acts 26.20

DISCUSSION AND APPLICATION

9. In section 3 of the Interpretation we noticed differences between the sermons in Acts and later Christian teaching.
   (a) Three opinions are given on pp. 22, 23 concerning these differences. Which of the three do you agree with, and why?
10. 'This Jesus delivered up according to the plan of God' (2.23).
    (a) What does this verse mean?
    (b) How far in your experience, do present-day preachers talk about the 'fulfilment' of prophecies?
    (c) What is your opinion of the following comment on Acts 2.23: 'If God sent Jesus into the world in order to die, it is unfair to blame those who killed Him' (p. 25)?
11. When you next hear someone preaching a sermon, note which of the five 'marks of good Christian preaching' listed on pp. 25, 26 you have found in that sermon. What other marks of a good sermon were *not* listed on pp. 25, 26?
12. 'We all are witnesses'. (2.32) How can modern preachers preach 'as witnesses', i.e. out of their own experience, without drawing attention to themselves?

13. Read Peter's speech again.

(a) What passage in it do you consider is most needed by the congregation of which you are a member, and why?

(b) What do you think people find most puzzling in the speech?

2.42–47
The Character of the First Christian Groups

OUTLINE

2.42a: The first Christians followed the Apostles' teaching.

2.42b (with 44,45): They lived in fellowship.

2.42c (with 46b): They broke bread together.

2.42d (with 46a, 47a): They prayed together.

2.43: They healed the sick.

2.44–45: They shared everything they possessed.

See also 4.32–35; 5.12–14.

INTERPRETATION

A WAY OF LIVING

These verses refer to the way in which the first Christians lived. Note the three parts of ch. 2:

vv. 1–13: what *happened* at Pentecost,

vv.14–41: how Peter *explained* it,

vv. 42–47: how the early Christians *lived* it.

For Christians what has happened under God's direction is important, and the explanation of those events (in preaching and creeds) is important. But it is not enough merely to remember events or to accept explanations. Christians need to join a group of people who are *living* in a way that fits the events and explanations. What we hear, we forget; what we see, we remember; what we do, we know (see note on 'the Way' on 22.4).

THEN AND NOW

What can present-day Christians learn from these verses? Certainly we need to live in the same Spirit in which the first Christians lived (as the notes that follow suggest), so it is important to study vv. 42–47 carefully.

But Luke did not write this as a guide for our generation, and indeed circumstances have changed in a number of ways: (a) The Apostles, unlike ourselves, had all lived and worked with Jesus in Palestine and had seen Him alive after His death. (b) They and those whom they taught believed that Jesus would return to the earth very soon, so they did not expect to live in this way for very long, and probably did not do so. (c) In the early days of the Church, all the members were Jews. When non-Jews came into the Church, it became far more difficult to live in fellowship, as we see from such passages as 1 Cor. 1.10–13.

NOTES

2.42a: They devoted themselves to the Apostles' teaching.
They. Was Luke referring to the 3,000 or the Apostles? Probably 'they' were the Apostles together with the men and women who lived in the same part of Jerusalem. Perhaps they had formed a new synagogue (Jews were allowed to do this if there were at least ten men).
Devoted. See NEB: 'They met constantly to hear . . . .'
Apostles' teaching. For 'teaching' see note on 20.20. The Apostles handed on what Jesus had taught and what they believed about Jesus, and the ways in which the Old Testament had been fulfilled. What they handed on was much later collected, joined with other records, and became the written Gospels which we have today.
2.42b: Fellowship. See also 'were together' (v. 44a), 'had all things in common' (v. 44b), 'together' (v. 46a). What is 'fellowship'? The word is one translation of the Greek word '*koinonia*', which is also translated 'sharing', 'community'. In the New Testament it has several meanings:

(a) Christians having fellowship with God: 'Our fellowship is with the Father and with His Son Jesus' (1 John 1.3b);

(b) As a result of their fellowship with God, they have fellowship with each other: 'You may have fellowship with us' (1 John 1.3a);

(c) The service of Holy Communion in which worshippers express both (a) and (b) above (see 1 Cor. 10.16).

(d) A collection of money for people in need, which is a sign of the fellowship which the givers have with the receivers (see 2 Cor. 9.13).

How did they express fellowship? They did so in several ways, e.g. (a) by meeting in the same place together (vv. 44a; 46a); (b) by praying together (vv. 42b; 46a; 47a); (c) by voluntarily sharing their possessions and selling what they had in order to have something to share. At this time they probably shared with each other rather than with the poor people of Jerusalem (see 4.32; 4.36–37). The Qumran Community, who lived near the Dead Sea until AD 70, shared their possessions with each other. But this was a rule of the Community, it was not done individually.

Jesus taught His followers to share their possessions, and Luke records this teaching far more often than do the other Gospel writers (see Luke 12.33: 'Sell your possessions and give alms').

In what other ways do Christians express 'fellowship' today? They share their thoughts and feelings with other members. They give time to one another. They listen as well as talk. They receive as well as give; they share themselves. They share the gospel with one another (and with anyone who is willing to listen). The many 'Base' or 'Basic Christian Communities' in Brazil and elsewhere are experiencing this sort of fellowship today. But see also note on v. 44 'had all things in common'.

2.42c: The breaking of bread. See also v. 46b. Jews often took bread and broke it and shared it as part of a fellowship meal. As they broke it they said (and still say) the prayer, 'Blessed be Thou, O Lord God, who didst make bread to be on earth.' Jesus 'broke bread' on many occasions, e.g. at the Last Supper (Luke 22.19) and at Emmaus (Luke 24.30).

In this verse Luke is probably referring to three sorts of 'breaking bread': (a) eating their meals together in fellowship; (b) a very simple form of the service which we call the Lord's Supper or Holy Communion or Eucharist; (c) the 'Love-Feast' or *Agape*, the fellowship meal which ended with the Lord's Supper (referred to in Jude v. 12).

2.42d: The prayers. See also v. 46a; 47a and 5.12. Again Luke is here referring to three sorts of prayer: (a) in their homes (v. 46a), (b) in a synagogue, (c) in the Temple courtyard. They probably attended the 3.00 p.m. service of prayer at the place where the priests offered a burnt sacrifice. Christians still did this because they were loyal Jews. It was only later that they realized that Jesus Christ had made possible a new relationship with God, and that they had to choose between the old and the new.

2.43b: Wonders and Signs. See note on 3.12.

2.44: Had all things in common. Some people who read this say that the first Christians were 'Communists' because they shared their property, and that modern Christians should do the same. But this 'sharing' was different from the life of modern Communists.

The first Christians (a) believed that Jesus would return very soon, so they did not intend to live in this way for ever (Paul had money of his own; he paid for his own food, see note on 18.3); (b) shared their possessions voluntarily, chiefly in order to relieve the needs of their very poor members; (c) did not force others to live as they did.

Modern Communists (a) also share their property; but (b) in a Communist State sharing is a law, and all members are forced to obey it; (c) they intend to enforce this law permanently.

Modern Christians have much to learn from all those, in the past and in the present, who practise what they believe and who, at a cost to themselves, share what they have with those in need. What Christians possess is not their own, but God's, and is therefore to be shared. The following are some of the ways in which present-day Christians 'have all things in common':

(a) By belonging to a group whose members 'tithe'. They all agree to give away a tenth each year of what they earn, following Deut. 14.22.

(b) By being a member of a Christian Co-operative, whose members share their wages. One of these is the 'Daily Bread' group in the north of Britain. There are twelve members from different Churches, who grow food and sell it. There is daily worship and a weekly meeting at which each member has an equal vote. Everyone, including the manager and the newest assistant, receives the same wages. After wages have been paid, profits are sent to people in other places who are in special need.

(c) By joining a community which has a rule which all members promise to keep. Some are groups of a few people who live together in 'cells' or 'ashrams', others are huge institutions. In some groups members join for life, in others they are free to leave when it seems right. In all of these groups members share their lives with each other and with God. This has been true from the time of St Antony (with his tiny group in Egypt in AD 300) up to the present time. There are now at least 25,000 Christian communities connected with the main Churches.

2.46a: In their homes. At that time it was in private houses that Christians usually met each other and worshipped together. So far as we know, special church buildings did not exist until after AD 300. There are many references to such 'households' in the New Testament, e.g. 'Greetings to Prisca and Aquila ... also to the church in their house' (Rom. 16.3–5). In the same chapter of Romans Paul mentions other 'house churches' (vv. 14;15;23).

When we think of a 'house church' we should think of quite a large group of worshippers, because the household itself usually contained other people besides the parents and children, e.g. grandparents, married sons, slaves and trading partners, etc.

An advantage of meeting in someone's home was that it was private. But there were disadvantages too, e.g. the Christians were split into different groups, and it was often difficult for the various groups to work together in fellowship (see 1 Cor. 1.10–12).

Very many Christians today worship in private houses rather than in church buildings. In Zambia there are 'hut churches'. The worship is less formal than in church, and worshippers have more opportunity to participate and take responsibility. But, as in the first century, there are disadvantages: a house church often becomes isolated from other groups; or too much depends on the leader. Healthy house groups are those whose leaders are answerable to someone or some group beyond themselves.

2.46b: Partook of food with glad and generous hearts.
Glad. One thing that people noticed about Christians was their joy. Joyful people are those who are so sure that God holds them for ever in His love that they remain joyful even when trouble comes. Joy is not the same as laughter or joking or optimism.
Generous. The Greek word here translated 'generous' would be better translated 'sincere' or 'free from pretence' (see 2 Cor. 1.12).
2.47a: Praising God. Praise is a special sort of prayer, and means rejoicing in God because of who He is rather than because of what He has done. It is an important part of public and personal worship.
2.47b: Having favour with all the people. People respected them. As far as possible Christians need to gain the good opinion or 'favour' of those who do not belong to the Church. If people find that Christians are good neighbours they are more likely to join them. To give one example, this is the reason why Paul said that women should wear a veil in public worship (1 Cor. 11.5). It was necessary because at that time and in that place bare-headed women were regarded as immoral.
2.47c: The Lord added to their number. See also 5.14. The Church grew. Indeed, the way in which the Church grew in numbers in its first 300 years was a miracle. From twelve Apostles it grew until it was the official religion of the Roman Empire. In a similar way today the Church in South Korea and Kenya is growing in numbers very rapidly indeed.

(a) *What is the value of numerical growth?* If a congregation expects to gain new members and does succeed in increasing, this is encouraging to the members, and they may be able to serve the community better. But a bigger congregation is not always a better one. A small group of committed Christians is more able to serve God and their fellow human beings than a big crowd of half-committed members can.

Also, a congregation sometimes becomes so big that members cannot know each other nor can its leader know them. In such a case it may be wise for it to divide into two congrgations.

(b) *What is real numerical growth?* Sometimes a congregation grows by people transferring from another church, sometimes by the return of lapsed members, and sometimes by parents having more children. But God's Church is not really growing unless unbelievers come to believe in God as He is shown to us in Jesus Christ, so that *new* members are joining His Church.

33

Note: Of course numerical growth is not the only sort of growth.
2.47d: Those who were being saved. See note on 4.12 on the meaning of 'saved'. Here we notice that, according to Luke, 'being saved' is a continuous process rather than an event that occurs on one special occasion.

STUDY SUGGESTIONS

REVIEW OF CONTENT

1. In v. 42 we read of 'the Apostles' teaching'. How can we today find out what that teaching was?
2. Name two ways in which the first Christians expressed fellowship with each other.
3. What is a 'love-feast' or 'agape'?
4. Who was St Antony?
5. (a) Why did the Christians attend the Temple worship?
   (b) What sort of worship was it?
6. What is the difference between joy and joking?

BIBLE STUDY

7. 'Fellowship' is one translation of the Greek work '*koinonia*' which has several meanings in the New Testament (p. 30). What is its meaning in each of the following passages? (You may find it helpful to use more than one translation.)
   (a) Rom 15.26   (b) 1 Cor. 1.9   (c) 1 Cor. 10.16   (d) Gal. 2.9
   (e) Phil. 1.5   (f) Phil. 3.10
8. 'Breaking of bread' (2.42).
   According to each of the following passages, where was bread broken and why was it broken?
   (a) Luke 9.12–16   (b) Luke 22.12–19   (c) Luke 24.28–30
   (d) Acts 20.7–8
9. 'In their homes' (2.46).
   To whose homes or household do the following passages refer?
   (a) 1 Cor. 1.11   (b) 1 Cor. 1.16   (c) 1 Cor. 16.19
   (d) Rom. 16.11   (e) Rom. 16.23   (f) Col. 4.15

DISCUSSION AND APPLICATION

10. How far can, or should, Christians today copy the sort of fellowship described in 2.42–47?
11. (a) What was the main cause of 'fellowship' among the first Christians?

(b) Where there is real fellowship in a present-day congregation, what do you think are the two main causes?

12. Some groups of present-day Christians 'have all things in common' (note on 2.44). What groups of this sort, if any, exist in your area, and what are their aims?

13. 'In their homes' (2.46). What are the advantages and disadvantages of Christians worshipping in private houses?

14. 'The Greek word translated "generous" in 2.46 would be better translated "sincere"' (see p. 33). How is it translated in : (a) another English translation? (b) another language which you know?

15. 'The Church grew in numbers' (p. 33).
    (a) If your congregation is growing numerically, what are the reasons? (See note (b) on 2.47c). If it is not growing, what are the reasons?
    (b) 'Numerical growth is not the only sort of growth' (p. 34). In what other ways can a congregation grow?

3.1–26

The Healing of a Lame Man

OUTLINE

3.1–8: Peter and John heal a cripple.
3.9–16: People are astonished, so Peter explains the healing to them.
3.17–26: Peter speaks about the blessings which God will give to those who repent.

INTERPRETATION

The first Christians, as we have seen, regularly attended prayers in the Temple. On this occasion they left John Mark's house and were going up to the higher part of the city where the Temple was (see v. 1 'went up'). The word 'Temple' is sometimes used to mean the building which contained the 'Holy of Holies' and the 'Holy Place', which only priests could enter. But usually (and in this passage) 'Temple' means the whole area in which were many buildings, courtyards and porticos (see diagram, p. 197). As Peter and John came through one of the entrances a cripple with a begging-bowl stopped them and asked for money. Instead of giving him money they miraculously gave him his health.

This healing is important because it shows that Jesus was as active and as powerful in the world after His ascension as He had been during His visible ministry. Peter made this plain (v. 16). This power of Jesus to heal is still true (see Additional Note, Healing, pp. 40–42).

Just as Peter made a speech to the people to explain the event of Pentecost (ch. 2), so in this speech (3.12–26) he explained the healing to those who saw it. He repeatedly appealed to his listeners to repent of the sin of killing the Messiah.

NOTES

3.1: Up to the Temple. See also vv. 2, 3, 8, 10, 11. The Christians continued to worship at the Temple because they remained loyal and religious Jews. Jesus had told His followers that He had completed and fulfilled the traditional religion, but not abolished or contradicated it (Matt. 5.17).

3.2: Gate called Beautiful. This was probably the gate leading from the Gentiles' courtyard to the Women's Courtyard. But some scholars think that it was the Shushan Gate or the Nicanor Gate (see diagram, p. 197).

3.6a: I have no silver or gold, but I give you what I have. Peter had no money, and instead gave the cripple God's power, which was more precious than money. If Peter and John had possessed money and had put some of it into his bowl, he would not have been healed. Does this mean that when the members of a Christian congregation are poor, like Peter, they are more likely to meet the real needs of the poor and others who are not its members? St Francis of Assisi said 'Yes', and encouraged his followers not to own property. Should Christians follow his advice today? If not, what enables a congregation who have a credit balance in the bank to have concern for the real welfare of those who are in great need?

3.6b: In the name of Jesus ... walk!

Name of Jesus. New Testament writers used the phrases 'Name of Jesus' and 'Name of God' with three different meanings:

1. The *power or authority* of Jesus. That is its meaning here: 'By the authority which Jesus gave me, walk.' See also 2.38, which means 'Be baptized according to the authority which Jesus gave us.'

2. The *character or nature* of Jesus as God's Son. Jesus's words in John 14.13, 'Whatever you ask in my name, I will do it', refer to praying in accordance with the spirit and character of Jesus (see also Phil. 2.10–11).

3. *God Himself.* In the Lord's prayer 'Hallowed be thy Name' means 'May you, Lord, be honoured and reverenced'. And in the Ten Commandments 'You shall not take the name of the Lord your God in vain' means 'Do not treat God, the One who has power and authority, as if He was of no effect.' See note on 3.16.

Walk! Followers of Jesus, like Peter and John, are concerned for people's bodies, including their 'feet and ankles', as well as for their souls. This means that they are also concerned for the material things that affect people's bodies, e.g. their houses, their work, their wages, their food. Some religious people teach that souls are important but that bodies are not. But Jesus was concerned for the whole of a person.

3.11: Portico called Solomon's. One of the long covered passages in the Temple, called porches or porticoes, was called Solomon's. This is where Jesus debated with Jews (John 10.23), and where His followers often met together (Acts 5.12, see diagram, p. 197).

3.12: As though by our own power ... we had made him walk. Peter explained that it was God's power which had healed the cripple. He himself was only a channel or 'agent' of God. Every modern doctor is a channel of God's power, although many doctors do not know this.

New Testament writers use three different words to describe miraculous healings like this one:

1. The Greek word *dunamis*, here translated 'power' (and from which we get our words 'dynamo', 'dynamic', etc.), means 'the power of God at work'. In Acts 19.11 it is translated 'miracle'.

2. 'Sign', which (like 'power') means a sign that the loving God is at work just as He was in the miracles that Jesus did during His visible ministry (see Acts 8.7).

3. 'Wonder'. Writers use this word when they are chiefly thinking of the onlookers, who are astonished at an unusual event. The Gospel writers used it only three times, but they used the words 'sign' and 'power' forty times. This is because they wanted their readers to look to God as the creator of healing, rather than to marvel at the unusual nature of an event.

3.13: His servant Jesus. (AV 'son' is incorrect.) In his first speech Peter called Jesus 'Lord', 'Man', 'Messiah'. In his second speech he used four more titles for Jesus:

1. *'Servant'* (also in 4.27; 30). The word does not mean a slave. It means the special person who, according to Isaiah's predictions, would come to 'restore the preserved of Israel' (49.5, 6; 53.12), i.e. the one who would rescue others through his own suffering. According to Luke 22.37 Jesus Himself said that He had fulfilled those predictions of Isaiah.

2. *'Holy and Righteous'* (v. 14). Peter used these words to show the

37

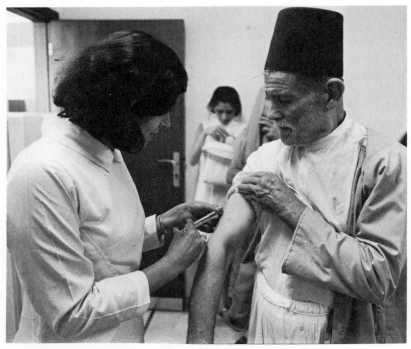

'The power of Jesus cured the man' (p. 39).

When this elderly man went to an out-patient clinic in north Africa for an injection, the healing power of Jesus was at work, just as much as it was when the cripple was healed through the faith of Peter.

contrast between the character of Jesus (perfectly just) and the character of those who killed Him.

3. *'Author of life'* (v. 15), i.e. pioneer. Dr Aziz, a Pakistani scientist, discovered a new way of growing wheat so that it gave three crops a year, and so people called him a 'pioneer'. Jesus was 'pioneer' because he opened up a new way of living for all mankind (see 5.31 and Hebrews 2.10; 12.2).

4. *'Prophet'* (vv. 22, 23, see note on 3.22).

3.16: His name, by faith in his name, has made this man strong. The language of this verse is confusing, but its meaning is clear: The power or 'name' of Jesus cured the man, and did so because there were people who had faith in Him (see note on 20.21).

1. Whose faith? The cripple, it seems, would not have been healed unless someone had faith (i.e. confidence or trust) in the power of Jesus. Some think that the cripple had faith, just as many of those whom Jesus healed had faith. Luke 8.48: 'your faith has made you well' (see Acts 14.9). But it seems more likely that it was Peter and John who had faith, just as it was the man's friends who had faith according to Luke 5.20, and not the paralysed man himself. Luke does not say that the cripple showed any sign of having faith.

2. Is faith necessary for miraculous healing? It is clear that either the patients themselves or other people usually need to have faith in order that the illness may be miraculously cured. But when illness is not cured, Christians should not say, 'If the patients and their friends had had more faith, the patients would not have died.' There are other reasons why patients die: the lack of faith is not the only reason.

Also when patients are cured, the reason is not always because they or others had faith in Jesus. There can be other reasons, such as medical treatment, why patients are cured. Luke mentions that the patient 'had faith' in only one of the miraculous healings in Acts.

3. What is the difference between 'miracle' and 'magic'? In this verse we see *one* difference between doing miraculous healing in Jesus's name and doing magic: (a) Peter and John had faith in Jesus's power and gave Him the praise when the man was cured. This was a 'miracle'. (b) But many people try to use the name of God as a magic spell, as if making the sound of His name produces a result, just as pouring water on a fire puts it out (see note on 19.11).

3.17–19: I know that you acted in ignorance ... repent.
Peter was saying, 'At the time you killed Jesus, you did not know what you were doing (Luke 23.34). But now that you know that it was the Messiah whom you killed, you must repent.'

Repent. In this speech Peter called his hearers 'guilty' more strongly than in his other speeches (see especially vv. 13–15; also 4.10; 5.30; 7.52; 13.28).

In vv. 19–26, Peter used three ways of urging them to repent: (1) He said that the time between Jesus's resurrection and His future return was their opportunity to repent. (vv. 19–21). (2) He called Jesus the expected 'prophet' and quoted Moses's words (Deut. 18.15–19), that those to whom the prophet comes will no longer belong to God's people if they do not repent (vv. 22–23). (3) He reminded them that God sent Jesus to the Jews before any other nation. Therefore, they should respond to this privilege by repenting (vv. 24, 25). See notes on 2.23b and 2.38a.

3.18: What God foretold by the mouth of all the prophets, that his Christ should suffer. As in his first speech (2.14–41), Peter here tells the people not to be astonished that their 'Christ', i.e. Messiah, had suffered. The events were a fulfilment of old predictions. But in spite of what Peter says, no prophet expected the Messiah to suffer. Isaiah expected the 'servant' to suffer, but not until Jesus came did anyone see that the 'servant' and the Messiah were the same.

3.22: Moses said, 'The Lord God will raise up for you a prophet'. See Deut. 18.15. There were various interpretations of this verse, and some Jews said that Moses was referring to one special person who would be born one day in the future, e.g. 'Are you *the* prophet?' they asked Jesus (John 1.21). After Jesus had come His followers said that Moses was referring to the Messiah, i.e. Jesus.

3.23: Every soul that does not listen ... shall be destroyed from the people.' In this sentence Peter combines Deut. 18.19 with Lev. 23.29. He was not saying that those who did not repent would be destroyed, but that they would no longer belong to the people of the true Israel.

3.25: You are the sons of the covenant. See note on 7.8.

3.26: God, having raised up his servant, sent him to you first. Peter was still appealing to them to accept the blessings which God was offering them through His 'servant' Jesus: 'God has made His offer to you before making it to other races' ('to the Jew first, and also to the Greek', Rom. 1.16). But most Jews did not accept the offer (see 13.46).

ADDITIONAL NOTE: HEALING

ACCOUNTS OF MIRACULOUS HEALING IN ACTS

There were many different sorts of 'sickness' which the disciples were able to heal, such as lameness (e.g. 3.1–10), blindness (e.g. 9.18), dysentery (e.g. 28.7–8), 'unclean spirits' (e.g. 5.16). There were also three other events which some readers do not call 'healings' (9.36–43; 16.16–18; 20.7–12).

Luke says that healers 'spoke the name of Jesus' on four occasions, 'laid their hands on the patient' twice, and 'prayed' twice.

WHAT ENABLED THE FIRST CHRISTIANS TO HEAL PEOPLE?

1. They believed that God is a loving God and a strong God, who wants human beings to have 'wholeness', and who can give it to them. So they relied on His power to heal, and praised Him when healing took place.

2. They believed that God usually gives His healing through human agents or channels, and so they offered themselves to be those agents.

3. They believed that 'healthy' people are healthy in the whole of themselves—in their bodies and in their thinking and in their feeling; and that healing is, therefore, a healing of the whole person, not of one part only.

4. They usually healed as members of a team, rather than as individuals (see 2.43; 5.12; 14.3).

WHAT ENABLES CHRISTIANS TO BE HEALERS TODAY?

1. Present-day Christians can be healers if they work in the ways in which the first Christians worked, i.e. if (a) they have the same belief in God's love and power; (b) they offer themselves to be His agents; (c) they work together (e.g. a medical doctor with a priest and a Christian counsellor).

2. But, especially, present-day Christians have to rediscover the truth that each person is a unity. Our thinking and feeling and doing all belong together and affect each other. The Jews and the first Christians all understood this truth. Today many Christians, especially members of the newer 'independent' Churches, are rediscovering it. A headmaster had stomach pains and his doctor found that he had an ulcer. The doctor said, 'People often get stomach ulcers through worrying. Have you been worrying instead of trusting God and your fellow-teachers?' The man said that he had been worrying. His wife was very ill, and he was afraid that he was not able to spend enough time in his school. He thought he might lose his job. The doctor said, 'Then we must treat your fears as well as your ulcer.' That doctor was treating the whole person.

3. Modern Christians also need to know the difference between three sorts of sickness. Each sort produces its own sort of pain, and for each there are suitable ways of healing.

(a) Sickness of the *spirit* is caused by a person's sin, often resulting in feelings of great guilt, and sometimes in bodily sickness.

Healing is given through *prayer*, *loving support*, and through the declaring of *God's forgiveness by absolution*.

(b) Sickness of the *feelings* is often caused by the sins of other people who have hurt the patient in the past, or by events such as bereavement or a sudden change. The result is often *sickness of the body*.

Healing is given through *prayer, loving support, skilled counselling* or by the *'laying on of hands'*.

(c) Sickness of the *body* is caused by disease or bad habits or accidents or wrong diet. Or it may be the result of sickness of the feelings or of guilt.

Healing is given in the *ways referred to above*, and also through *anointing* in Jesus's name, or *medical care*, or *changed diet*.

(d) Many people would include another sort of sickness, namely *demon-possession*, which leads to sickness of the feelings and of the body. This needs an *exorcist* to heal it (see note on 16.16).

Note: The above paragraphs refer only to one sort of sickness, that of an individual. But God offers healing and reconciliation *wherever there is bitterness and division*, e.g. in a family or a congregation or between nations. Healing is given through *prayer* and through the *active work* of Christians.

STUDY SUGGESTIONS

REVIEW OF CONTENT

1. What was meant by 'the Temple'?
2. Why do New Testament writers usually refer to miraculous healings by the words 'sign' and 'power', and only occasionally by the word 'wonder'?
3. (a) What are the seven titles for Jesus which Peter used in his two sermons (chaps. 2 and 3)?
   (b) Which of them do you use most often, or hear others using?
4. Peter's speech in this chapter is like his speech in ch. 2. What *two* statements do we find in both speeches?
5. What are the 'three sorts of personal sickness' (pp. 41, 42)?

BIBLE STUDY

6. 'Either the patients themselves or other people usually need to have faith in order that the illness may be miraculously cured' (p. 39). Read the following passages and say in each case who if anyone, had faith.
   (a) Luke 5.18–24   (b) Luke 8.46–48   (c) Luke 18.35–43
   (d) Acts 3.2–6   (e) Acts 14.8–10

7. Read the following passages and say in each case what the healer did before performing the healing.
   (a) Luke 4.40   (b) Acts 9.17–18   (c) Acts 9.33–34
   (d) Acts 14.8–10   (e) Acts 28.7–8

DISCUSSION AND APPLICATION

8. Why do you think Peter and John healed this cripple?
9. 'Followers of Jesus are concerned for the material things that affect people's bodies' (note on 3.6b) What are Christians doing in your neighbourhood which shows that they share this concern? What more, if anything, do you think they could be doing?
10. What sort of person is able to heal in the way in which Peter and John healed?
11. 'Our thinking and feeling and doing all belong together and affect each other' (p. 41). Give an example of this from your own experience.
12. (a) To what extent is it necessary for a patient to have faith in order to be healed?
   (b) What could you say to a man whose young wife had just died after an illness, although she was a strong Christian for whom many people had prayed?

4.1–31

The Arrest of Peter and John

OUTLINE

4.1–4: The arrest.
4.5–12: Peter's explanation.
4.13–22: The release of Peter and John.
4.23–31: The Apostles pray together.

INTERPRETATION

OPPOSITION

This is the first of the many passages in Acts where Luke tells of Christians being opposed or persecuted, and of how the Christians responded. Christians who are being persecuted in different ways in many parts of the world at the present time know from passages such as this that they are enduring the same sort of suffering which the Apostles and Jesus Himself suffered (see Additional Note, Persecution, pp. 48, 49).

THE EVENTS

On this occasion it was the Jewish 'Council' who opposed Peter and John, and they did so out of fear. Council members feared that the number of Christians would increase as a result of the healing of the cripple, and that this would lead to disorder in Jerusalem. They knew that if there was serious disorder the Roman government would take away the power which it had given to the Council; but they did not know what to do with Peter and John. They could not accuse them of committing a crime, and they could not say that the man had not been healed. So they locked them up, as it was late in the day, and held a trial the next morning. The Council members sat in a half-circle and made Peter and John stand in the middle. But the only action the Council took was to tell them to stop speaking in Jesus's name, and then let them go.

Peter, with great courage, gave a clear answer, first as we find it in vv. 8–12, and later in vv. 19 and 20: 'we cannot but speak' (v. 20). Then he and John joined the other followers of Jesus in a song of praise to God (vv. 23–31).

NOTES

4.1: The priests and the captain of the temple and the Sadducees ... These people, and those mentioned in vv. 5, 6 and 23, were the members of the Jewish Council or 'Sanhedrin' (v. 15). This was the chief Jewish Law court and had 71 members. It had power over the whole nation, although it had to answer for its actions to the Romans. The members were:

Priests (v. 1), called 'chief priests' in v. 23;

The captain of the temple (v. 1), a priest who was next in rank to the High Priest and who was in charge of the whole Temple area;

Sadducees (v. 1): they were the most influential and wealthy members; they collaborated with the Romans (and this is the reason why they wanted to prevent disorder in Jerusalem);

Rulers (v. 5): ex-High Priests, and members of the High Priest's family;

Elders (v. 5): other members of the Sanhedrin who did the work of judges (see note on 14.23),

Scribes (v. 5): most of them were *Pharisees*, teachers and interpreters of the 'Law'; unlike the Sadducees they were concerned to apply the Law to everyday life;

The *High Priest* (v. 6): two are named: Annas had actually ceased to be High Priest, but Luke gave him the title because he was the most influential of all the ex-High Priests; Caiaphas, son-in-law of Annas, was the ruling High Priest and President of the Sanhedrin.

No-one knows who John and Alexander were (v. 5).

4.4: Many ... believed. Although the Sanhedrin had arrested Peter and John, the number of Christians increased. Some readers find this very surprising, but people joined the followers of Jesus because they could see clearly the courage which Jesus had given to Peter and John (see Additional Note, Persecution, pp. 48, 49).

4.11: This is the stone which was rejected by you builders. In the first few verses of Peter's speech he repeated what he had already been saying (e.g. in 3.12–16). In this verse, by quoting Psalm 118.22, he said something new and extraordinary: that the person who had been hung on a cross as a common criminal was the most important person in the whole world. He was 'the one stone at the top of the corner which holds together the two walls at the place where they meet'.

4.12: There is salvation in no one else.

1. Peter may have been referring to the healing, i.e. 'Only through Jesus can anyone do these healings'. The Greek word translated 'healed' in v. 9 is the same word which is translated 'saved' in v. 12.

2. But he may have had in mind the whole Jewish nation. Note the word 'we' at the end of v. 12. If so, then he meant, 'No one but Jesus the Messiah can deliver our nation of Israel from our enemies.'

Although Peter most probably had in his mind one of those two interpretations, Christians know that God's 'saving' is far more than the saving of someone from sickness or the saving of a nation from slavery. These 'savings' are only part of a greater saving which includes God's saving us *from* being separated from Himself by our sins, and saving us *for* eternal fellowship with Him, and thus for wholeness of body, mind and spirit.

If we remember this, how do we interpret these words 'salvation in no one else'?

(a) Some Christians say, 'No one can have *any* fellowship at all with God unless their fellowship is through Jesus' (and often they quote John 14.6, 'No one comes to the Father but through me'). They may add that all who are not members of the Church are condemned to eternal separation from God.

(b) Other Christians say, 'No one can have *full* fellowship with God unless they come to Him through Jesus.' But they are unwilling to say that there are limits to what God can do. They believe that God may

45

have other ways of being in touch with all human beings. They point to 10.35, where Peter says that Cornelius (who had never heard of Jesus) was 'acceptable to God'. They point also to 14.17; 17.28 and Rom. 1.19–21.

Neither group of Christians can prove that their interpretation is the right one from v. 12 alone. We must reach our conclusions from other parts of the Bible and from our experience, as well as from this verse. See Additional Note, Christians and Other Religions, pp. 165, 166.

Salvation. We have seen that in Acts 'salvation' means the saving of the whole person (our doing, our thinking, our feeling), and we saw in the note on 3.6b that 'healing' has the same meaning. We notice now that writers use the word 'save' in this way throughout the Bible: (a) They include the saving of people or a nation from evils such as sickness (Ps. 6.4) or captivity (1 Sam. 4.3) or poverty (Ps. 72.13) or death (Matt. 8.25). (b) But the saving that God offers and gives is more. It is a saving *from* the results of sinfulness (Matt. 1.21) and *for* 'fullness' of life (John 10.10). (c) It is God's gift and we cannot earn it (Exod. 14.30; Eph. 2.8). (d) We can receive this gift now (2 Tim. 1.9). (e) But the complete gift may not be ours till 'the last day' (Rom. 5.9).

4.13a: When they saw the boldness of Peter and John, and perceived that they were uneducated ... they wondered. Luke uses the word 'boldness' three times in this passage (vv. 13, 29, 31; see note on 2.29).

They 'wondered' at his boldness for many reasons:

(a) Peter had been a very different sort of person before Jesus rose (Luke 22.60).

(b) He and John were not trained, as Pharisees were, in the interpretation of Scripture. The Sanhedrin members did not believe that the Spirit of God could work actively in uneducated people. They were like some highly educated people today, including some Christian ministers whose college learning had made it more difficult for them to communicate the gospel to their congregations.

(c) The place where Peter was speaking was the same place where the Sanhedrin had tried and condemned Jesus only a few weeks before (Luke 22.66ff).

(d) Peter was attacking the most powerful council in the nation: '*You*' crucified (v. 10).

The Sanhedrin 'wondered' but Luke could explain it: 'He was filled with the Holy Spirit' (v. 8), just as Jesus had promised (Luke 21.14–15).

4.13b: They recognized that they had been with Jesus. The Sanhedrin saw that Jesus had trained Peter and John and that they were speaking with the same sort of authority with which Jesus spoke at His trial.

What they did not understand was that the Apostles were constantly in touch 'with Jesus', who was present in spirit. Anyone who today has a living fellowship with Jesus speaks with some of that 'authority'.

46

4.16: What shall we do ...? ... a notable sign has been performed. The Sanhedrin members were afraid, and they opposed the Apostles not because of what had been *said*, but because of what had been *done* ('a sign'). When Christians speak, e.g. about the need for mercy and justice, some people respond, others may not. But when the speakers follow up their words with actions, then two results usually follow: (1) Some people, like the Sanhedrin, are afraid of the influence which the speakers will now have, and therefore attack them. (2) Others begin to believe the preaching.

There was a time when 'white' preachers in the USA taught that 'all men are equal in God's sight', but did not welcome black people into their churches. Then they did open their doors to blacks, with the result that some of the richest members resigned their membership and called the ministers 'Communists'. On the other hand, some who had never been to a church before, began to attend.

4.20: We cannot but speak. The disciples had to be loyal to God before being loyal to the leaders of their nation (see v. 19). Jesus had commissioned them to be witnesses (1.8), and they had to witness to His power.

How do modern Christians follow Peter and John?

(a) Many Christians since Peter and John have said these same words, or something like them, at the risk of their lives. In recent times, we think of Janani Luwum of Uganda and Desmond Tutu of South Africa, but the list of such people grows every day.

(b) Many preachers base their preaching on these words. They say what they feel compelled to say because of their loyalty to God and His Son Jesus, rather than what they think political or religious leaders would approve (see Ezek. 2.1–5).

4.24: they lifted their voices together to God. They responded to the threats of the Sanhedrin by praying. They prayed in great faith in God that He would in the end overcome the opposition of the Sanhedrin, quoting Psalm 2, and asking for further power to speak and heal.

4.25: Who by the mouth of our father David didst say by the Holy Spirit. The Greek words of this verse are confused, and no one knows what Luke originally wrote. But the meaning seems to be as RSV gives it.

Once again Peter (a) said that they should not be surprised at the opposition, and that it was a 'fulfilment' of what had been said long ago; (b) assumed that it was David who had written Psalm 2 (see notes on 2.23a and 3.18).

4.27: There were gathered together against ... Jesus, whom thou didst anoint, both Herod and Pontius Pilate ... and the peoples of Israel. Jesus whom thou didst anoint can also be translated 'Jesus whom thou didst make Messiah' ('Messiah' means 'the anointed'; see v. 26b).

Herod. There are four Herods mentioned in the New Testament, who held their position under the Roman government:

(a) The Great, who began to build the Temple in 20 BC and died before it was finished.

(b) Antipas, son of the Great. This is the Herod to whom Peter referred in this verse. He ruled over Galilee and Peraea from AD 4 till 39 (see Luke 3.19 and Acts 13.1).

(c) Agrippa I, grandson of the Great (see 12.1).

(d) Agrippa II, great grandson of the Great (see 25.13).

Pontius Pilate. Usually it seems as we read Acts that it was only Jews who were to blame for Jesus's death. But here Peter names Pilate, the Roman Governor, as being 'against Jesus' (see note on 2.23a).

4.28: To do whatever thy ... plan had predestined. This does not mean that from the time of their birth God had chosen those who killed Jesus to commit sin and to be permanently excluded from fellowship with Him. Throughout the Bible writers make it plain that God has given us all freedom to do right or to do wrong.

This is another verse in which Peter is saying that 'what has happened is not surprising' (see note on 3.18).

4.31: The place ... was shaken; and they were all filled with the Holy Spirit. Did the walls really shake as they do in an earthquake, or did the walls seem to the Apostles to shake because they themselves were so deeply aware of the Spirit of God in them (see Isa. 6.4)?

ADDITIONAL NOTE: OPPOSITION AND PERSECUTION

AS RECORDED IN ACTS

Luke describes more than thirty occasions when Christians were opposed or persecuted. He also tells us of the many different opponents, and gives details of what they did to the Christians. It is important to note the Christians' response, e.g. they gave answers in defence (4.1–3), they continued preaching (5.17), they prayed (12.3), and sometimes they had to escape (e.g. 9.23).

AT THE PRESENT TIME

Although in some countries Christianity is the 'official' religion, Christians are still opposed or persecuted in many places and for many different reasons.

1. Who are the *persecutors or opposers* Christians have to face today? They may be: (a) Members of another religion, as in Iran, where the head of Islam has been the head of State (as was the Jewish High

'Luke describes thirty occasions when Christians were opposed or persecuted. Christians are still opposed and persecuted in many places and for many reasons' (p. 48).

This church in Torit, southern Sudan, was destroyed by anti-Christian government forces.

Priest); (b) Another branch of the Church, for example in countries where a Roman Catholic or Protestant majority does not treat the minority with justice (e.g. in the law courts), (c) The people of the country who treat the gospel as an ancient tradition which is of no interest in the present age; this is common in Europe today.

In some countries the laws of the state are oppressive. To give some examples at the time when this book is being written: they may forbid citizens to change their religion (e.g. the law in Malaysia that Malays must remain Muslim); or forbid preaching or holding a meeting in public (e.g. in Turkey and Afghanistan); or forbid all evangelism, even in private (e.g. in Tunisia); or forbid the sale of Christian literature (e.g. in Saudi Arabia).

2. What are the *reasons for the opposition or persecution*? Some newly-formed governments regard the Christian gospel as 'foreign' (e.g. as European or American) and are afraid that it will weaken the nationalism of their country.

Some of the great non-Christian religions have had a revival during the last twenty years, e.g. Buddhism and Islam.

Some states are politically connected with communism and accept their official anti-God philosophy, e.g. Vietnam, Cuba, North Korea.

Sometimes Christians bring opposition upon themselves, e.g. because the Church is still divided between different denominations and even within individual congregations. Governments do not want the Church to cause divisions among their people in the same way, and therefore, try to suppress any conflict.

3. What happens *after persecution*? In some cases a Church is destroyed by persecution. This happened in many parts of N. Africa when Muslims invaded them during the 7th century AD.

In other cases the Church seems to grow in numbers *because* of persecution. During the 'cultural revolution' in Communist China, Christians were forbidden to meet for worship. But when the law was changed thirty years later (in 1982), and Christians were free to worship, the Roman Catholics found that they had twice as many members as before. A new Christian church building is opened every day.

At other times it is difficult to know whether the Church has grown *because* of persecution or *in spite of* it, e.g. in Russia there had been anti-Christian propaganda for seventy years, yet groups of Baptists were chosen to share in the re-housing of Armenians after the 1988 earthquake. When Ethiopia was a communist country there were so many people wanting to worship God that every church in Addis Ababa had to hold a number of services each Sunday.

STUDY SUGGESTIONS

REVIEW OF CONTENT

1. What was the Sanhedrin?
2. Who were the most influential members of the Sanhedrin?
3. Why did the Sanhedrin arrest Peter and John?
4. Give two reasons why the Sanhedrin members were surprised at Peter's words in Acts 4.8–12.
5. Give one example of a modern state preventing Christians from publicly witnessing to Jesus.

BIBLE STUDY

6. In the note on p. 46 we saw that writers use the words 'save' and 'salvation' in five different ways. In which one (or more) of those ways was the writer using the word in each of the following passages?
   (a) 1 Sam. 7.8   (b) Luke 9.24   (c) John 3.17   (d) Acts 2.47
   (e) 2 Tim. 1.9   (f) 1 Pet. 1.5
7. What is the truth which is contained in Ezek. 2.1–5 and Acts 4.20?
8. In what way is the prayer in Acts 4.24–30 like the prayers in 2 Kings 19.15–19; Jonah 2; and Daniel 3?
9. 'Luke describes occasions when Christians were . . . opposed, and tells of the many opponents' (p. 48).
   According to each of the following passages in Acts, who was being persecuted or opposed?
   (a) 4.1–3   (b) 12.3   (c) 16.23   (d) 19.29
   According to each of the following passages, who were the opponents?
   (e) 5.17–18   (f) 12.1   (g) 16.23   (h) 24.1

DISCUSSION AND APPLICATION

10. Some Christians interpret 4.12 to mean that 'no one can have *any* fellowship with God at all unless the fellowship is through Jesus' (p. 45). What is the teaching of your own Church on the subject? What is your own opinion, and what are your reasons?
11. We see from 4.13 that Peter could preach convincingly although he had no college education such as the scribes had. What do you see as the advantages and the disadvantages for a Christian preacher of (a) having had a college education, and (b) not having had a college education?
12. (a) How much opposition or persecution is there to the Church of which you are a member, and who are the opponents?

(b) How do the members respond to this opposition?

13. Read the paragraph about Christians in China on p. 49. Why do you think the number of Roman Catholics increased during the time when public worship was forbidden?

4.32—5.42

The Christians and the Jewish Council

OUTLINE

4.32–37: The fellowship of believers.
5.1–11: The hypocrisy of Ananias and Sapphira.
5.12–16: The growth of the Church.
5.17–26: The arrest and escape of the Apostles.
5.27–32: The second arrest.
5.33–39: Gamaliel's speech.
5.40–42: The release of the Apostles.

INTERPRETATION

The above outline shows that, apart from the reference to Ananias and Sapphira and Gamaliel, this part of Acts is very like an earlier part. In 4.32—5.42 we see (as we saw before) how they did signs and wonders (compare 2.43b), how they increased in numbers (compare 2.47b), how the Sanhedrin arrested them (compare 4.3), how Peter gave his sermon (compare 4.8–12 and 3.12–16), and how they were released (compare 4.21b).

Why are the two parts so alike?

It may be that incidents very similar to those recorded in the earlier chapters did occur, perhaps several times, over the period of two or three years. Or perhaps Luke (who had to rely on reports given to him by others) received two accounts of the same series of events and wrote down both of them, side by side (2.1—4.31 alongside 4.32—5.42).

Whatever the true explanation is, three facts are plain: (a) the early Church grew in numbers; (b) it remained united in spite of trouble within it; (c) the Sanhedrin continually threatened to destroy it.

NOTES

4.36–37: Barnabas ... sold a field. Barnabas was one of the believers who voluntarily sold something that he possessed so that the Church could give help to its poorer members. (Luke's pointing to his action shows that not all the members did this.)

Barnabas was a cousin of John Mark (Col. 4.10). His fellow-Christians must have given him the nickname 'son of (i.e. man of) encouragement' because of the great support he gave to others, e.g. to Paul after Paul's conversion (9.27), to the newly converted believers in Antioch (11.22 and 23), to Paul after his absence in Tarsus (11.25) and on the many journeys he and Paul made together until their disagreement (15.39). See note on 11.22.

5.1: Ananias with his wife Sapphira. They did wrong, not in stealing but in pretending that they had given a part of what they owned. Their sin was 'hypocrisy'—the sin of pretending to others, and often to ourselves, to be different from, or better than, we really are. Jesus regarded this as a very serious sin (Luke 6.42). Also, by deceiving the others they committed another sin, that of breaking the fellowship in which members trusted each other (see 4.32).

Some readers feel that Luke wrote about the early Church as if its members were holier than they really were. But in this passage he reminds us that people inside the Church committed sin. Of course they did, being human, and of course Christians, both members and leaders of the Church, are often guilty of hypocrisy, now as then. Church members sometimes break away from the congregation they belong to because of the sinfulness they see in it. But as soon as they start up a new one, sin and hypocrisy are there all over again. The most serious sin that Christians can commit is to think that they have no sin.

Luke has also shown the importance of distinguishing between right and wrong. If the early Christian group had not made this distinction clearly they might not have blamed Ananias and Sapphira at all. When a USA Minister of Finance in 1980 was found guilty of fraud, a foreign journalist said 'What a corrupt country!' Wiser people said 'If he had not been taken to court *that* would have shown that the country was corrupt.'

5.3: Why has Satan filled your heart? Why did Ananias and Sapphira do it? Was it because they wanted to be important and to have the reputation of being generous?

Satan. See note on 26.18.

5.4: You have not lied to men but to God. There is no difference between sinning against other people and sinning against God. All sinning is sinning against God (Matt. 26.25).

5.5: Ananias fell down and died. Readers of this verse have many questions to ask, e.g. 'Were Peter's words too harsh? Did he give them no opportunity to repent?' Luke does not tell us. Different interpretations have been suggested:

(a) That Ananias and Sapphira both died from shame and the shock of realizing that they had been found out. This seems probable.

(b) That Peter put a curse on them and that this is shown by the harshness of his words in v. 9. But there is no evidence that those words were a curse. Surely Peter would never have cursed them, knowing that he himself had committed the sin of denying Jesus and that Jesus had given him a fresh start.

Certainly those who first read these verses learnt from them how important it is that members of a congregation are honest with each other and without hypocrisy.

5.11: Fear came upon the whole Church. The word 'Church' appears here for the first time in Acts (see note on 9.31).

5.15: As Peter came by, at least his shadow might fall on them. It seems that the crowds were regarding Peter as a magician and as so powerful that even his shadow could heal the sick. But Luke does not say that anyone was actually healed in this way.

5.19: An angel of the Lord opened the prison doors. Was the 'angel' a supernatural being, or a human being who opened the doors, perhaps a secret follower of Jesus? Who or what are 'angels'?

Most Jews believed that angels were unseen spirits who were different from God Himself and who were His personal agents. They saw angels as bringing warnings (Matt. 2.13), or support (Dan. 3.28), or guidance (Gen. 22. 11–12), or judgement (2 Thess. 1.7–8), or as waiting on God and worshipping Him (Isa. 6.6).

When we read of 'angels' in Acts: (a) we seem sometimes to be reading about God Himself giving guidance (27.23–24); (b) sometimes 'angel' may mean a human being whom God is using as His messenger; (c) but some Christians believe that 'angel' always means a separate spiritual being, and they interpret this verse and 12.7 in that way. (The word 'angel' is used to translate Hebrew and Greek words which mean 'messenger').

5.20: The words of this Life. In the RSV, life is given a capital letter to show that it means the full Life which Jesus has made possible. Compare the word 'Way' which in Acts means 'the way in which Christians live'. See note on 22.4 and note John 14.6: 'I am the way, the truth, and the life'.

5.34: A Pharisee in the council named Gamaliel.

A Pharisee. In the Sanhedrin the Pharisees were a smaller group than the Sadducees, but (unlike the Sadducees) they were popular with the ordinary people of Jerusalem. They had never been so violently against Jesus as Sadducees had (see Luke 7.36), and did not take part in condemning Jesus to death. Some of them later became Christians (Acts 15.5; 23.6).

Gamaliel was their leader in the Sanhedrin. He was the most learned and respected religious teacher at that time, and (as we see from vv. 38 and 39) was willing to listen carefully to other people, and took their opinions seriously. According to 22.3 he was tutor to Paul.

5.36–37: Before these days Theudas arose ... after him Judas the Galilean. Gamaliel was saying 'If you leave trouble-makers alone, they will die out', and gave Theudas and Judas as examples.

The statements about Theudas and Judas in these verses are not quite correct. First, Theudas led his revolution against the Romans *after* Judas's revolution and fifteen years *after* Gamaliel's speech. Secondly, Judas's movement (which began in AD 6) lasted for 60 years and out of it grew the important Zealot revolt. At the time when Gamaliel spoke (AD 29 or 30) it was not true that 'all who followed him were scattered' (v. 37).

Some readers may ask, 'How reliable is Luke as a historian?' See Special Note below, Luke as a Historian.

5.41: Rejoicing that they were counted worthy to suffer dishonour for the name. Because Jesus could not complete His work without suffering, it follows that His followers must also expect to suffer. But according to this verse they did not simply endure suffering, they rejoiced to be allowed to follow Jesus in this way (see 1 Pet. 4.13).

STUDY SUGGESTIONS

REVIEW OF CONTENT

1. Find one incident described in 4.32—5.42 which is also described in ch. 2 or 4.1–31.
2. Why did the Christians call Barnabas 'son of encouragement'?
3. In what *two* ways did Ananias and Sapphira do wrong?
4. Who was the leader of the Pharisees in the Sanhedrin?

BIBLE STUDY

5. What do we learn about the Pharisees from the following passages?
   (a) Luke 11.37   (b) Luke 11.42   (c) John 3.1–2
   (d) Acts 15.5   (e) Acts 23.7–9   (f) Phil. 3.5
6. In what way is the message in 5.41:
   (a) like the message in Col. 1.24 and James 1.2?
   (b) *un*like the message in Luke 9.23 and Phil. 1.29?

DISCUSSION AND APPLICATION

7. 'Christians, both members and leaders of the Church, are often guilty of hypocrisy' (p. 53).

(a) What is hypocrisy?

(b) A girl was asked to become a Church member, and replied, 'No, I don't want to belong to a society whose members pretend to be holier than they are.' If that girl had been your friend, what would you have replied? How much truth is there in her remark?

8. Two interpretations of the deaths of Ananias and Sapphira are given in the note on 5.5.

(a) Which interpretation do you accept, and for what reasons?

(b) In what way(s), if any, does Peter's treatment of Ananias and Sapphira show a modern Church leader how to treat wrongdoers in the Church?

9. 'An angel of the lord opened the prison doors' (5.19). Do you think that the 'angel' was a human being or a supernatural being? Give your reasons.

10. According to 5.38 and 39 Gamaliel said 'If God is not with them, they will fail. If He is, you cannot stop them.' To what extent is this good advice today, e.g. when a Church council is discussing some of the Church members who are planning to break away and form a new Church?

Special Note A
Luke as Historian

1. Some people find it difficult to rely on the information which Luke gives us in Acts for such reasons as the following:

(a) He did not have first-hand information about any events that took place before AD 50 (when he joined Paul, see 16.10). As a result he had to rely on other people's reports.

(b) Acts contains some incorrect information, e.g. 5.36.

(c) In several places Luke's information differs from the information which Paul gives in his letters, e.g. according to Acts, Peter and Paul were always on friendly terms, but according to Paul this was not so (Gal. 2.11). In such cases we should usually accept Paul's report, because Paul wrote about events in which he himself had taken part and wrote soon after those events.

2. On the other hand there is much information which Luke gives in Acts which we can safely believe to be accurate, because it is supported by evidence from first century inscriptions and the writings of others (see introductory note to Time Line, p. 231). For example:

(a) Luke's information about the titles of Roman officials is always correct, even though those titles were often changed, e.g. the 'proconsul' of Cyprus (13.7) and of Achaia (18.12), the 'strategoi' of Philippi (16.19), the 'politarchs' of Thessalonica (17.6), the 'protos' of Malta (28.7). He even knew the correct title of the town-clerk of Ephesus— 'asiarch' (19.31).

(b) Luke describes Roman legal procedure accurately, e.g. when Paul is before Gallio (18.12–17), before Felix (23.26–35; 24.22–23), before Festus (ch. 25).

These facts show that, on such matters, Luke took great trouble to obtain correct information. So it seems probable that he took as much trouble as possible to report other matters accurately.

Although Luke hoped that through his writing of Acts the Roman authorities would treat the Church with understanding, he does not hide the sins and weaknesses of Christians, e.g. in 5.1–10; 6.1 etc. We can see that he aimed at describing the Church as it really was, not as he would like it to have been.

3. To sum up:

We need to know as accurately as possible what really happened among the early Christians, because the Church is founded on events. So it is important to find out how reliable Luke was as a historian.

Some people (as we saw above) think that Luke was less reliable as a historian because he wrote with special aims and had a special message to proclaim. But no human beings have ever written history without interpreting it. All write from their own point of view. It is also clear that Luke had to rely on others for his information in many cases, and may sometimes have been misinformed.

So long as we take into account such points as these, we can read Acts as a book which, taken as a whole, gives us a faithful record of the growth of the Church and of the Spirit who inspired it.

STUDY SUGGESTIONS

1. (a) Give one reason why some people find it difficult to rely on Luke as a historian.

   (b) Give two examples from Acts which show that Luke took trouble to obtain correct information about the events he was describing.

2. How much do you yourself think that it matters whether Luke is reliable as a historian or not? Give reasons for your opinion.

6.1–15

The Appointment of the Seven

OUTLINE

6.1–6: The Apostles commission Stephen and others.
6.7: A note on the growth of the Church.
6.8–15: Stephen speaks in public.

INTERPRETATION

A NEW STAGE

From 6.1 to 9.31 Luke is writing about a new stage in the life of the Church.

In the early days recorded in chs 1—5, most Christians lived in Jerusalem, and kept fairly closely to their Jewish traditions. They were, with some exceptions, a united body, and their leaders did not need to organize them. The people of Jerusalem respected them.

But as the Church grew in numbers and entered on a new stage, there were changes. Many Christians were living outside Palestine. They began to think and act differently from Jewish traditions, and before long they welcomed non-Jews into the Church. There was disagreement among members (6.1), and then leaders had to organize them (6.2–4). Meanwhile the ordinary people, and not only the chief priests, began to oppose the new teaching (6.9).

This is the first 'new stage' of which we read. But in later chapters of Acts Luke records other 'new stages'. Indeed every Church from time to time has to enter into a new stage, and to use new methods in order to do what God calls its members to do at that time.

STEPHEN

More than anyone else, Stephen brought about this 'new stage'. He was the first to see that Christians had to make a break with the traditions of the past. In vv. 9–14 we see the beginning of this break. It may be that Stephen also saw that the gospel was for non-Jews as well as for Jews, but this is not certain.

NOTES

6.1a: Hellenists murmured against the Hebrews. The 'Hellenists' were Jewish Christians who spoke Greek (the word comes from 'Hellas'. i.e. Greece), and many of them lived outside Palestine, in other parts of the Roman Empire. The 'Hebrews' here means Jewish Christians who spoke Aramaic (the everyday language which Jesus spoke), and who lived in Palestine. Long before the coming of Jesus these two groups had found it difficult to understand each other. The Hebrews thought that the Hellenists were too much influenced by Greek ways of living; the Hellenists thought that the Hebrews were too unwilling to adopt new ideas.

Murmured. The leaders of the Hellenists in Jerusalem sent a deputation to the Apostles to make a complaint on behalf of their widows. They said that the Hebrews were giving less food and money to the Greek-speaking widows than they gave to those who spoke Aramaic.

The Hellenists needed to express their disagreement with the Hebrews in this way in order that their widows should be treated justly. Christians sometimes feel that it is right and necessary to express serious disagreement with other Christians. They damage the fellowship among members only when they quarrel. Christians today do not all agree, for example, about the best way of obtaining justice for the very poor people of South America. But sharing their different opinions will help them to achieve their aims. In the same way Christians do not all have the same ideas about God or about the Bible, but they will more fully see the truth by sharing their different convictions. A congregation which never has controversy is not necessarily 'at peace'. It is either being suppressed by its leaders or is not really interested in God's will. It does not become united by hiding the disagreements.

6.1b: Their widows were neglected in the daily distribution. Widows were some of the poorest people among the Jews, and the authorities employed full-time workers to take care of them as well as other people who were in need. Indeed, Jews in all countries have always taken special care of their poor members, and they do so with great generosity today.

When the Church began to grow in Palestine, its members also took special care of their widows, probably distributing food and money, called 'tables' in v. 2.

How well do Christians treat widows today? Often widows are treated as people of no importance after the death of their husband. In some countries they are prevented from inheriting any property, or are blamed for the death of their husbands unless they can prove that they are innocent.

Distribution. The Greek word which is translated 'distribution' in this verse is *diakonia*, which is usually translated 'service' or 'ministry'. Here it means the ministry of giving aid to widows. In v. 4 it means the service or ministry which the Apostles gave by preaching (see note on v. 6b and on 21.19).

6.2a: The twelve summoned the body of the disciples. The Twelve Apostles did not attempt to settle the dispute by themselves. They consulted Church members, and they and the members shared in finding suitable people to look after the widows. They had a meeting together (v. 2a), and the Apostles explained what sort of people were needed (v. 3b). When the seven had been chosen the Apostles prayed for them, and then publicly gave them authority to do this work (v. 6).

Present day Church leaders have a ministry to perform, as the Apostles had their ministry. But they also have a duty to share it. This is true, whether they are the leaders of a whole nation's Christians or are the leaders of a village congregation (see 1.17).

6.2b: It is not right that we should give up preaching ... to serve tables. Here and in v. 4 Luke mentions two ways in which the Church did its work, and in which every Church in every age must do its work: (1) By preaching and praying (see v. 4, 'We will devote ourselves to prayer and to the ministry of the word'); (2) By practical caring for those in need ('serving tables'). The Apostles could not themselves do both tasks, but they made sure that both tasks were done.

Christians go wrong if they preach and pray but pay less attention to caring for the poor. If a city congregation spends $200,000 on an organ which would help the members to worship, but gives much less in supporting poor congregations and poor people in the country, then it is not following the example of the Apostles. But Christians also go wrong if they care for the poor but pay less attention to preaching and praying.

6.3: Pick out seven men of good repute. The Apostles said that they would give authority to seven men on condition that they were of the right sort, i.e. (a) those whom other Christians could trust ('of good repute'); (b) those who were open to the guidance of the Holy Spirit and did not depend only on their own ideas ('full of the Spirit'); (c) those who were able to administer the work of relieving the poor, and could keep accounts of the money received and spent ('full of wisdom').

6.5: They chose Stephen ... and Philip. We can see from their names that all the seven were Greek-speaking Jews, and thus well able to meet the needs of the Hellenist widows.

6.6: They prayed and laid their hands upon them. See note on 'laid their hands' on 13.3. On this occasion the Apostles laid their hands on the seven men in order to give them the authority to carry out special work.

They did this in the presence of other Christians so that everyone should know that the seven had been given authority. We should say today that the Apostles commissioned them to be 'social workers' or 'administrators', i.e. to do special work in Jerusalem and for that special period of time.

In times past some people have interpreted this verse in ways which scholars do not accept today; e.g.

(a) That the Apostles 'laid their hands' in order that the men should receive the Holy Spirit. But they were already 'full of the Spirit' (v. 3).

(b) That the Apostles gave them the authority which those 'deacons' had who assisted the bishops at the end of the first century (see 1 Tim. 3. vv. 1 and 8; Phil. 1.1) and were later part of the 'ministry team' of 'bishops, priests, and deacons'. But Luke does not call them 'deacons' in this chapter, and in 21.8 he calls Philip 'one of the seven', not 'Philip the deacon'.

(c) That the Apostles ordained the seven to be Apostles like themselves or to be 'presbyters'. But no one produces evidence which supports this interpretation.

6.7a The word of God increased, i.e. the will of God was increasingly understood and acted upon.

This verse is just a short report of progress. The Apostles had helped to heal the split between the 'Hellenists' and the 'Hebrews' and as a result the Church grew.

6.7b: A great many of the priests were obedient to the faith. It seems from this verse that the Christians were still in close touch with the Temple in Jerusalem and that they still attended its worship. But many of these priests probably ceased their connection with the followers of Jesus when they heard Stephen speak.

The faith. These words do not have the same meaning as 'faith' (see note on 20.21). Here (and in 14.22) 'the faith' means 'the gospel which we preach' or 'what Christians believe'.

6.9: Some of those who belonged to the synagogue of the Freedmen ... disputed with Stephen. There were a great many 'Freedmen' in Jerusalem. These were Jews who had been taken prisoner by the Romans and enslaved. Later they were set free, and those of them who lived in Jerusalem (or their descendants) formed themselves into a Freedmen's synagogue. This was one of the very many synagogues in Jerusalem, places which were mainly used for the reading and interpreting of the Jewish Scriptures. Stephen spoke in this synagogue, probably a long time after the events referred to in vv. 1–6. The Freedmen were Hellenists, like Stephen, and so they listened to him and (as often happened in synagogue worship) debated with him. But later (v. 11) they thought that he was rejecting Jewish traditions, so they arrested him and took him to the supreme 'council'. This 'council' was the

Sanhedrin, which met in their hall very near the Temple (see note on 4.1).

6.10: They could not withstand the wisdom and the Spirit with which he spoke. The Apostles commissioned Stephen to be a 'social worker', but now he had become an outstanding speaker, and soon afterwards he became a martyr. In the same way, Philip became an evangelist (see 21.8).

They allowed Stephen to develop and to grow so that he was able after some time to give the service to God and to the Church which he was capable of giving. If the Apostles had not encouraged him in this way, he might never have led the Church into the 'new stage' of its life. All Church leaders have this responsibility—to encourage the members in their care to develop and to see what new and greater service they could give to God and to the Church in the future.

6.13: This man never ceases to speak words against this holy place and the law. This 'holy place' was the Temple.

Several groups of Jews now joined together to make the accusations against Stephen: the 'Freedmen'; the false witnesses whom they employed (v. 11); some people from the street; and the elders and scribes who were Pharisees (v. 12).

These Jews seem to have made the same two accusations against Stephen which the chief priests had made against Jesus:

1. They accused him of saying that Jews need no longer obey the laws of Moses: 'blasphemous words against Moses' (v. 11); speaking 'words against the Law' (v. 13); saying that Jesus 'will change the customs which Moses delivered' (v. 14).

But it seems unlikely that Stephen spoke 'against the Law'. Probably he spoke, as Jesus did, against customs or traditions which some Pharisees had added to the Law (see Matt. 15.3, 6; Mark 2.27.)

2. They accused him of saying that they no longer needed the Temple: 'blasphemous words against God' (v. 11); speaking 'words against this holy place' (v. 13); saying 'that Jesus will destroy this place' (v. 14).

For most Jews the Temple and the sacrifices which were performed there were the chief sign that God lived among them. Saying that it was no longer needed was like saying that God was no longer necessary. But what did Stephen really say? He probably did not say that Jesus would destroy the Temple (nor did Jesus say that, see Mark 14.58, 59). But he probably did follow the teaching of Jesus which we find in Mark 12.1–7, namely that showing mercy to people in need is as important as offering Temple sacrifices (and perhaps more important).

6.15: His face was like the face of an angel. In the Sanhedrin the accused person stood in the middle and the members sat in a half-circle facing him. One of them (perhaps it was Paul and perhaps he told this to Luke) saw that Stephen's face was like an angel's face, i.e. that it was shining or 'transfigured'. Why did Stephen experience ecstasy at this point of his trial, so that his face shone? Was it because at that moment he was totally putting his life into God's hands, believing that he would not live much longer?

STUDY SUGGESTIONS

REVIEW OF CONTENT

1. Describe two ways in which, according to this passage, the Church had entered on a 'new stage'. In each case quote words from the passage to illustrate your answer.
2. Who were the Hellenists and why did they have a dispute with the 'Hebrews'?
3. What is meant by 'serving tables'?
4. Why did the Apostles lay their hands on the seven?
5. Who were the 'Freedmen'?

BIBLE STUDY

6. 'Church leaders have a ministry to perform ... they also have a duty to share it' (p. 60).
   In what way or ways did each of the following share their ministry according to the passages listed?
   (a) The Apostles (Acts 6.2–6)   (b) Moses (Exod. 18.13–26)
   (c) Jesus (John 6.5–13)   (d) Paul (Phil. 2.19–27)
7. 'The accusations which they made against Stephen were like the accusations which the chief priests brought against Jesus' (p. 62). Read the following passages together with Acts 6.14, and say in each case how they support that statement.
   (a) Mark 7.1–7   (b) Matt. 15.3–6
8. Read Acts 6.15 together with Exod. 34.29–30 and Matt. 17.2.
   (a) Suggest a reason in each case why that extraordinary event took place.
   (b) If you have ever seen anyone 'shining' in that way, describe what happened and suggest a reason for it.

DISCUSSION AND APPLICATION

9. 'From 6.1—9.31 Luke is writing about a new stage in the life of the Church' (p. 58).
   What events and changes (if any) are taking place in the life of your

Church which lead you to believe that your Church is experiencing a 'new stage'?

10. 'Christians sometimes feel that it is right and necessary to express serious disagreement with other Christians' (p. 59).
    (a) Give an example of any serious disagreement among Christians which you witnessed or experienced.
    (b) Say if you think it was right or necessary, or could have been avoided, giving your reasons.
    (c) What was the result of the disagreement?

11. 'How well do Christians treat widows today?' (p. 59).
    (a) What is your opinion?
    (b) Ask any widows whom you know well, and who have been widowed for some time, what their feelings are about being widows.

12. 'There were two ways in which the Church did its work . . . :
    (1) Preaching and praying; (2) Practical caring for those in need' (p. 60).
    (a) Does the congregation to which you belong regard both these ways as equally important? Give examples to explain your answer.
    (b) If not, which does it regard as the more important? (Give examples). Why does it do so?

7.1—8.1a

Stephen's Speech and his Death

OUTLINE

7.1–43: The first part of Stephen's speech, concerning the deliverers whom God had sent to deliver the Jews: Abraham (vv. 2–8); Joseph (vv. 9–16); Moses (vv. 17–43).

7.44–50: The second part: concerning the Temple.

7.51–53: The third part, repeating briefly what Stephen said in Part 1, but also passing judgement on his listeners.

7.54–8.1a: Stephen's prayer and his death watched by Saul.

INTERPRETATION

THE SPEECH

In this speech Stephen did not defend himself directly against his accusers. They had accused him of saying that Jesus rejected the Law (6.13–14) and of wanting to destroy the Temple (6.14). Instead of defending himself he accused his accusers, saying that (1) Their own forefathers had always rejected the deliverers whom God had sent and had thus rejected God (vv. 2–43, 51–53). (2) They were talking as if God was present only in one place, i.e. the Temple (vv. 44–50).

Why did Stephen oppose them in this way? Because, being a Hellenist (see note on 6.1), he realized, as most Christians did not, that there must be a break between the followers of Jesus and those who kept to the old ways. When he decided to say this publicly, he must have known that he would be killed.

Luke gives a whole chapter to this speech, because it makes clear the chief message of the book of Acts. As we saw in the Introduction, this message was that the gospel was not for the Jews alone, and that the Holy Spirit was moving the followers of Jesus to take it to non-Jews, however difficult this might be.

Luke was not present at this speech, and there is no evidence that anyone recorded it at the time. So Luke could not report every word that Stephen said. He probably gives us here the sort of speech which Stephen made, according to the reports which he received.

STEPHEN'S DEATH

At the end of his speech Stephen said (v. 53) that it was not he, but those who had accused him who had rejected the Law. It was surely then that the seventy-one members of the Sanhedrin agreed that they must put him to death. Their chairman was Caiaphas, the same High Priest who had condemned Jesus not long before. But Luke does not make clear what they did. Under Roman law they could condemn Stephen to death if they had permission from the Governor. But the Governor was away in Caesarea at the time, so there was a delay. Probably it was during this delay that people in the crowd threw Stephen down into a deep pit outside the city walls and killed him by stoning.

Verses 55–60 not only describe Stephen's death, but also the way in which he died: his vision (vv. 55–56), his prayer of commitment to Jesus (v. 59), and his prayer of forgiveness (v. 60a).

NOTES

7.2: The God of glory appeared to our father Abraham, when he was in Mesopotamia. In his speech Stephen was chiefly reminding his Jewish listeners of the story of their ancestors, beginning with Abraham. His aim was to show that the story was an incomplete story unless it included the coming of Jesus as Messiah.

Stephen referred to Abraham because he was the 'father' of all Jews, and for another reason also: Abraham was willing to move into a new life at God's call. He came out of the land of the Chaldeans (v. 4). Obedience to God is more important than living in the place we have always known. Stephen declared that his listeners also should move into a new stage of life and no longer regard the Law and the Temple in the old way.

7.8: Abraham ... circumcised him on the eighth day. Those nations and tribes who use circumcision use it for different purposes. In many parts of Africa they circumcise teenage boys and girls as a way of initiating them into full membership of their tribe. Among Jews it was by circumcision that a person entered into the special covenant which God had with His Chosen People. Jesus was circumcised like other boys on the eighth day (Luke 2.21).

Being circumcised was what made the Jews different from most other nations. That is why some Jewish Christians said that Gentiles should keep the same rule when they were baptized. But after the meetings in Jerusalem (ch. 15) they did not enforce the rule.

Paul taught that cutting away anything that prevented Christians from following Christ was more important than physical circumcision (Gal. 6.15).

7.9: The patriarchs, jealous of Joseph, sold him into Egypt. Joseph was hated by his brothers and made a slave, and yet God used him to be a great saviour. Clearly God uses people whom others have despised.

Stephen saw Joseph as a sort of illustration or 'type', whose life pointed forward to Jesus. Joseph was a saviour and so was Jesus. Joseph was rejected and so was Jesus. Since the time of Stephen many preachers have spoken about great Hebrew leaders in this way, e.g. some have said that reading about them helps us to understand Jesus, others say that God Himself caused these things to happen to them in order to teach what sort of Messiah would come (see also note on v. 20).

7.15–16: Jacob ... and our fathers ... were carried back to Shechem and laid in the tomb that Abraham had bought. According to Gen. 50.13 Jacob was not buried in Shechem but in Machpelah, near Hebron (where guides show his tomb to visitors today). According to

Gen. 33.19 it was not Abraham but Jacob who bought the tomb at Shechem.

There are other statements in Stephen's speech which do not agree with statements in Genesis (see note on v. 2). This may be because Luke did not receive an accurate report of the speech. Or perhaps Stephen used a version of Genesis which is different from the version which we have today.

But some readers are troubled by all this, and ask how the Bible can be reliable or 'inspired' if it contains contradictions. We should note that: (a) the Bible is the result of God's activity: He inspired it, i.e. He influenced the minds of those who wrote it; (b) it is also the result of the activity of human beings; (c) human beings sometimes make mistakes and they do not always agree with each other; (d) God inspires those who read the Bible today, including its 'contradictions', and He guides them to discover His message from it.

7.20: At this time Moses was born. Like Abraham, Moses led his people out of what was known and familiar to them (Egypt) into what was unknown (v. 36). Like Joseph, he was rejected by his own people (vv. 23–29 and v. 39).

7.37: Moses ... said ... 'God will raise up for you a prophet ... as he raised me up'. Stephen quoted Moses (Deut. 18.15) because he saw Jesus as that 'prophet'. God sent Him to deliver His people and lead them into a new age, just as He had sent Moses to lead his people into the promised land (see Luke 24.19 and note on 15.32, 'prophet').

7.38: The angel who spoke to him at Mt Sinai ... and he received living oracles to give to us. The 'living oracles' or 'messages' were the Law. Stephen was accused of despising the Law, but here he is giving it great honour, describing it as a gift from God that is 'living', i.e. leading people to fullness of life. See Additional Note, Law, p. 72.

7.41: They made a calf in those days. (see Exod. 32.4). The Sanhedrin members were getting more and more angry, as they realized that, by referring to the golden calf, Stephen was accusing them of making the Law and the Temple into idols. We make things into idols when we give them the reverence which belongs to the living God. Present-day Christians do sometimes turn forms of worship or Church traditions or a church building or even the Bible into idols.

7.42: God turned and gave them over to worship the host of heaven. This does not mean that God punished them by making them do wrong and worship the sun instead of worshipping Himself. God does not make us sin. But we have free wills, and He allows us to follow the wrong path if we insist on doing that (see Romans 1.24–32).

7.44: Our fathers had the tent of witness in the wilderness. Stephen told his accusers that they had forgotten that the Tabernacle was a tent which was movable. It was for the travelling Israelites who discovered that God was present in each new place which they reached. They learned to serve God in new circumstances wherever they went. The Christian Church, too, is a 'tent Church', i.e. it is for people who can, like the Israelites, find God everywhere. In the early days of the Church in Ireland the bishop had no central cathedral. He moved from one congregation to another, as a symbol of the truth that God does not reside in one place.

7.47–48: But it was Solomon who built a house for him. Yet the Most High does not dwell in houses made with hands. Stephen contrasted the 'tent' with the Temple, and was saying that Solomon had done wrong in building a permanent Temple. By having a Temple instead of a tent their ancestors had fallen into two errors. First, they had ceased to look forward to new opportunities, and as a result were not ready to accept Jesus when He came. And secondly, although they, like Solomon himself (1 Kings 8.27), knew that God did not really live in the Temple, they behaved as if He did. They forgot that He was active and present wherever people were ready to find Him.

How can Christians who use church buildings avoid the mistakes which the Jews made concerning their Temple? Most Christians (but not all) need a building where members can worship God together and where they will not be disturbed. But there are dangers in using a church building. For example, members may think that God is only to be found in that building, and forget that God is Lord over them when they are at work or at home or in a foreign country. They may turn the church into an idol, i.e. give to it the respect which they should give to God, and spend so much money on the building that they have nothing left to contribute to the needs of the poorer Churches or to poor people. Or they may give the impression that Christians wish to 'keep themselves to themselves' and exclude other people. When a village church in India burnt down and the congregation had to worship out of doors for a time, they found that many of the other villagers came to see what was going on, and eventually joined in and became Christians themselves.

7.52: Which of the prophets did not your fathers persecute? Stephen was saying, 'By persecuting prophets, as your ancestors did, you are resisting God's Spirit who inspires prophets. You have killed the Prophet-Messiah, just as your ancestors persecuted those who predicted His coming, the coming of the Righteous One.'

Many prophets (although not all) were persecuted, and this is not surprising. A large part of a prophet's work is to question the way in which people are living, and to call on them to change their ways (see Additional Note, Persecution, pp. 48, 49).

7.53: You ... received the law ... and did not keep it. Stephen was saying 'You accuse me of dishonouring the Law. But it is you who are

'A large part of a prophet's work is to question the way people are living and to call on them to change their ways' (p. 68).

Dr Fritz Schumacher was a great 20th-century prophet. He was a watchman, he gave a warning that if nations put first the getting of power and profit, using up oil and land and forests in big commercial enterprises, there could be no future for human beings. In his book *Small is Beautiful* he showed that we shall survive only if we find peace with ourselves, with one another, and with God-given nature.

dishonouring it because you disobey it.' After that his accusers were certain that Stephen must be destroyed (v. 54).

Today the word 'law' usually refers to the rules which a government makes its citizens obey. But for Jews 'Law' meant the guidance which God had given them through the great leaders of the past (see Additional Note, Law, p. 72).

7.56: I see the heavens opened, and the Son of man standing at the right hand of God.

I see. Stephen was able to describe what he saw in his vision. Perhaps someone heard what he said and reported it to Luke (see note on 16.9, visions). Luke has interpreted it in v. 55.

The heavens opened. The way was open for Stephen to be in the presence of God's glory.

The Son of man. Jesus called Himself by this title, according to the Gospels. But it was an old title which came from a vision of Daniel (Dan. 7.13–14): 'I saw ... there came one like a son of man ... and to him was given dominion ... that all peoples, nations and languages should serve him.' If Stephen had this passage in mind, he was now seeing Jesus as the Saviour not only of the Jews, but of 'all peoples'.

At the right hand of God. Jesus had been condemned by Jews because He said that He would be 'at the right hand of Power' (Mark 14.62). Now Stephen was saying that he saw in his vision that this was true, and that Jesus did indeed share the glory of God. As they condemned Jesus for blasphemy, so for the same reason they killed Stephen.

7.58a: They stoned him. So Stephen became the first 'martyr'. The word 'martyr' means a witness. Christians witness by words and actions to the truth of the gospel (see note on 1.8). But usually the Church has used the word 'martyr' to describe people who, like Stephen, gave their witness by giving up their lives. Their self-sacrifice has led to the growth of the Church. Tertullian (3rd century AD) said, 'The more you cut us down, the more we grow.'

Many Christians have been martyred by the State, e.g. Polycarp in Smyrna in AD 155 because he refused to throw incense on a fire to show that the Roman Emperor was divine; Father Popieluszko in Poland was killed in 1985 because he taught that members of his Church living under a Communist government must be free to worship and speak in the name of Jesus.

Many have been martyred by fellow-Christians, e.g. Roman Catholics like Thomas More martyred by Protestants in 1535, Protestants like Archbishop Cranmer martyred by Roman Catholics in 1556.

Many, like Stephen, have witnessed to the gospel by what they said at the time of their death, e.g. Fung Mei Ts'en killed by Communists in China in 1930, saying 'I hear perfect peace in my heart'; Max Metzger, killed by the Nazis in Germany in 1944, saying 'I have offered my life for the peace of the world'; Miguel Pro, a young Jesuit priest shot by anti-Communists in Mexico in 1980, shouting 'Long live Christ the King!'.

Note: We should distinguish between martyrs like those mentioned above and: (a) Christians who have wanted to be martyred for wrong reasons, e.g. to draw attention to themselves, or because they were obstinate, or in order to obtain eternal life as soon as possible; (b) Non-Christians who have shown great courage in giving up their lives to witness to a truth in which they firmly believed, e.g. Japanese 'suicide squads' in World War II.

7.58b: The witnesses laid down their garments at the feet of a young man named Saul. Those who stoned Stephen took off their long robes in order to do the stoning. But Saul supported it (8.1a) because Stephen's speech seemed to him to be blasphemy.

But by being present, Saul heard Stephen's prayer, and it may be that he began to change his mind from that time on and to ask himself questions, e.g. 'What made Stephen able to pray in that way?' 'Is it possible that Jesus is what Stephen believes He is?' (This 'Saul' was, of course, Paul. See note on 9.4.)

7.59: Lord Jesus, receive my spirit. Stephen was able to pray at the very time when he was in agony, being crushed to death by the rocks that were thrown down. Jesus also had prayed at His crucifixion: 'Into thy hands I commit my spirit' (Luke 23.46).

What can we discover from this about prayer? (a) That if in the past we have made a relationship with God, then we are able to pray when we meet very great trouble; (b) that all prayer is prayer of committal, 'Lord, receive!'; we do not tell God what to do: we ask Him to 'receive' ourselves and others for whom we pray. (c) That at the time of death the chief prayer is one of trust, entrusting our spirits into God's hands, knowing that He will love us after death as firmly as He loves us now.

7.60: He knelt down and cried ... 'Lord, do not hold this sin against them'. It may be that Stephen knelt in submission to the will of God. But Jews stood to pray, so Stephen probably fell to his knees as a result of the stoning. We can, of course, pray in any position.

By asking God to forgive those who injured him, Stephen was following Jesus, 'Father, forgive them ...' (Luke 23.34). Perhaps that was the most difficult thing that he had ever done in his life. How can we learn to forgive others? (1) By taking trouble to forgive the many little injuries that we experience, so that when we are badly injured we know how to do it; (2) by loving those who have done the injury while hating what they have done; (3) by realizing that we ourselves need to be forgiven; (4) by telling God Himself when it seems too difficult to forgive someone. A woman whose husband had left her in order to live with someone younger said, 'At first I was so angry that I did not want to forgive him. Then I wanted to, but I could not do it. Later I said a prayer, "God help me because I can't do it myself." After some time I prayed, "God, I see that you can forgive him just as Jesus forgave his murderers." At last, I said, "God, alongside you, I can begin to forgive him." '

ADDITIONAL NOTE: LAW

1. To the Jews 'Law' meant the will of God, the teaching which He gave through priests and prophets (see Exod. 24.12; Rom. 13.8). It was not a burden but a light and a signpost for which Jews were very grateful.

2. After the Exile (586 BC) 'Law' meant the Pentateuch, the first five books of the Bible, and this is its meaning in most of the Bible (Psalm 119; John 1.45). In the New Testament 'Law' sometimes means the whole Old Testament, e.g. in Rom. 3.19.

3. Jews honoured the Pentateuch almost as if it was God Himself, and thus were tempted to make it a sort of idol. Stephen, in his speech, was accusing his listeners of doing this. He honoured the Law but he believed that it was incomplete until Jesus came to perfect and interpret it (compare Matt. 5.17).

4. For Paul, as for Stephen, the Law was very important, but as a preparation for Jesus (Gal. 3.24). He saw that many Jewish Christians thought that by trying very hard they could keep the Law and so earn God's approval. He called this 'living by the Law' (Rom. 3.28), and added that it was a useless attempt because no one could fully keep the Law. Christians must instead entrust themselves to God's forgiveness, and ask to be accepted because Jesus has made that possible. He called this 'living by the Spirit' or 'by faith' (Rom. 3.30).

STUDY SUGGESTIONS

REVIEW OF CONTENT

1. What were the two main accusations which Stephen made against his judges? Quote words from his speech.
2. (a) What great Hebrew leaders did Stephen refer to?
   (b) Why did he tell their stories?
   (c) According to Stephen which of them were rejected by their people?
3. (a) What was the 'tent of witness' (7.44)?
   (b) Why did Stephen refer to it?

4. What did he see in his vision (7.55–56)?
5. What were the prayers that he made as he was dying?

BIBLE STUDY

6. 'God gave ... the covenant of circumcision' (7.8). The following passages all refer to 'circumcision'. Say in each case whether the writer refers to (i) physical circumcision or (ii) an attitude of the spirit.
   (a) Gen. 17.14   (b) Jer. 4.4   (c) Luke 1.59   (d) Rom. 2.29
   (e) Phil. 3.3   (f) Phil. 3.5
   What does 'circumcision of the heart' mean?
7. The following passages refer to the persecution of 'prophets' (see v. 52). Say in each case, wherever possible, who was the prophet, and who persecuted him.
   (a) 1 Kings 19.10–14   (b) 2 Chron. 24.20–21
   (c) Jer. 26.20–24   (d) Jer. 32.1–3
8. In the Bible the word 'Law' has different meanings. Which of the four chief meanings given in the Additional Note, Law, does the word have in each of the following passages?
   (a) Josh. 8.31   (b) Isa. 5.24b   (c) Matt. 5.17   (d) Rom. 6.14
   (e) Gal. 3.24   (f) Phil. 3.9

DISCUSSION AND APPLICATION

9. 'There are statements in Stephen's speech which do not agree with statements in Genesis' (note on 7.15–16, and see Gen. 33 and 50).
   (a) Give one example.
   (b) How would you reply to people who say that because of such 'disagreements' it is useless to read the Bible?
10. Christians should be like the 'tent' or Tabernacle of the Israelites rather than the Temple (see p. 68). In what ways does a congregation show that it is like (a) the tent; (b) the Temple? Give examples.
11. What are the main lessons that we can learn about our own prayers from studying Stephen's prayers in vv. 59 and 60?
12. Why did Stephen choose to be martyred rather than save his life?
13. Find out all you can about one of the Christians martyred in the early days of the Church, and one martyred in modern times.
14. Write down what (in your opinion) Paul said to his friends among the Pharisees after the stoning.

8.1b–25

Persecution Results in a Mission to Samaria

OUTLINE

8.1b—3: The persecution of Christians in Jerusalem.
8.4–13: Philip preaches, heals and baptizes in Samaria.
8.14–17: Peter and John visit Samaria.
8.18–24: The story of Simon the magician.
8.25: Peter and John preach in Samaria.

INTERPRETATION

THE NEXT STAGE

In chs 6 and 7, Luke was describing how some of the Christians were beginning to think that perhaps they should take the gospel beyond the Jewish nation. In ch. 8 we see the next stage. Philip, and later two of the Apostles, took the surprising step of welcoming Samaritans into the Church.

THE SAMARITANS

The Samaritans were neither Jews nor Gentiles, but the Jews despised them more than they despised the Gentiles, and kept apart from them as far as possible (John 4.9). The reasons for this were that: (a) When Jews were taken into exile (586 BC), some of those who were left behind married non-Jews and after that were not pure Jews; (b) They later built their own temple on Mt Gerizim, about 50 kms north of Jerusalem, in Samaria; (c) When the exile was over, these Samaritans considered that, during the time of exile in Babylon, the Jews were no longer keeping to the traditional interpretation of the law. They believed (and the 200 Samaritans who live near Nablus still believe) that they, not the Jews, are the true descendants of Abraham.

In view of this separation of Jews from Samaritans the events which Luke records are very remarkable and very important.

PERSECUTION

The Christians' missionary activity, in fact, resulted from the persecution. When the persecution took place the Christians surely saw it as a disaster. But those who had to escape from Jerusalem and move to new areas shared the gospel with the people of those areas. As Paul wrote from his prison (Phil. 1.12), 'What has happened to me has really served to advance the gospel.' It was like a seed-pod being opened by the heat of the sun and the seeds scattering and taking root far from the parent tree.

NOTES

8.1b: They were all scattered ... except the apostles.
Scattered. Jews had been scattered into many parts of the Roman Empire, either because of persecution or trade, and they called this the 'Dispersion'. This verse refers to the dispersion of Christians because of persecution. An example of present-day 'dispersion' is the large number of Indian and Pakistani Christians who live in the Gulf States, and are an important witness to the gospel there.
Except the Apostles. Why were the Apostles not persecuted? *Either* because they went into hiding so that those who had been with Jesus should stay alive to witness to Him, *or* because their teaching was more traditional than that of the Hellenists, and therefore the Jewish persecutors were not afraid of them.
8.2: Devout men buried Stephen. They were brave to give Stephen a burial because, by showing that they were his friends, they risked being persecuted along with him. In the same way Joseph of Arimathea and Nicodemus were very brave to see that Jesus was buried with dignity (John 19.38–40). In many countries today it is dangerous to attend the funerals of those whom the State police have killed.
8.3: Saul was ravaging the church: This is the persecution to which Paul referred later in his life (see 26.10–11). The Greek word here translated 'was ravaging' really means 'tore in pieces', as for example a leopard or hyena tears a gazelle.
8.5: Philip went down to a city of Samaria, and proclaimed to them the Christ. This Philip was not the Apostle, but the Philip who was one of the seven social workers. These seven were all Greek-speaking Jews, i.e. Hellenists (see note on 6.1a). Philip, being a Hellenist, was far more ready to share the gospel with non-Jews than an Aramaic-speaking Jew would have been.
The 'Samaria' he went to was a district, not a town, and he visited one of the towns in that area.
Although the Samaritans did not usually mix with Jews, they, like

the Jews, were waiting for the Messiah to come (see John 4.25–29). So Philip 'proclaimed the Christ', i.e. he said 'The Messiah [the Christ] has already come!'

8.6: They heard him and saw the signs which he did. Luke notes three things that Philip did: (1) he preached the gospel to the Samaritans (v. 5). (2) he showed that he was concerned for their health, both in body and mind (vv. 6, 7). (3) he brought them joy (v. 8).

Members of one present-day congregation held a special month of 'mission' in their neighbourhood and chose these three phrases to describe their aims.

8.9: Simon who had previously practised magic. See note on 19.11, 'Magic'.

There were a great many magicians in the Roman Empire at that time. The reason is that people were losing faith in the traditional religions, such as the worship of the Greek gods and goddesses. They were looking for other ways in which they could be in touch with unseen powers. This is taking place today in countries where Christians are failing to share the gospel effectively, and as a result more and more people are putting their faith in magic and lucky charms. They put a curse on a political leader whom they oppose, or make a wax image of him and stick pins into it. They consult witches and fortune-tellers of all sorts, and 'mediums' who claim to be in touch with the dead, and they read newspaper 'horoscopes' which 'predict' each person's future from the movement of the stars.

Philip preached in the town where Simon had been doing magic 'for a long time', and where they called him 'God's Prime Minister' ('that power of God which is called Great' v. 10). Philip did not argue with Simon, nor did he say that Simon could not do magic. What he did was to proclaim the true Power which comes through Jesus. In the end the people turned away from Simon and were baptized, including Simon himself. Compare the way in which Moses and Aaron met the Egyptian magicians (Exod. 7.11–12).

8.12: When they believed Philip as he preached good news about the kingdom of God and the name of Jesus Christ, they were baptized.

1. Christians had to show that they believed in Jesus as 'Lord' before they could be baptized (see Additional Note, Baptism, pp. 78, 79).

2. Philip's preaching was about 'the Kingdom of God' and about 'the name of Jesus'. (a) The Kingdom of God is what Jesus preached about (e.g. Luke 4.43). (b) The name (or nature) of Jesus is what His followers preached about (e.g. Acts 4.10, 17). Christian preachers need to do what Philip did and combine the two, i.e. explain what Jesus *said* and what Jesus *is* for us.

8.14 the apostles at Jerusalem ... sent to them Peter and John. According to v. 1 it was not safe for the Apostles to travel, so v. 14 refers to a time after the persecution had become less severe.

The Apostles were anxious because they had heard that something extraordinary had happened: despised Samaritans had been admitted into the Church. So they delegated Peter and John to go and investigate. In spite of Stephen's speech most Christians in Jerusalem were not ready to welcome non-Jews into the Church.

This was only one of several occasions when the Apostles sent a delegation to see for themselves what was happening. Delegations from headquarters are helpful when they go to a place to see for themselves rather than depend on rumours, and when they listen carefully to the people who work there.

8.15–16: The Holy Spirit . . . had not yet fallen on any of them. How did anyone know that the Spirit had not yet fallen on the Samaritans? Perhaps at that time they thought that 'speaking in tongues' was the only sign that the Spirit had come. As we have seen, when Christians speak in tongues it is often (but not always) a sign that they have the Spirit (see 2.4 and 10.45, 46). But there are many other signs of the presence of the Spirit in Christians, e.g. when they preach with power (4.8; 6.10) or live joyfully (1 Thess. 1.6; Acts 13.52; 16.34). Note also that when Christians have been filled with the Spirit they do not always show it outwardly or audibly or immediately.

8.17: They laid their hands on them and they received the Holy Spirit. Why did the Apostles lay their hands on them? Why, as a result, did the Samaritans 'receive the Spirit'?

1. It seems that the Apostles laid their hands on them in order to show them that they were in fellowship with the Church in Jerusalem, and that when the Samaritans realized this they showed in some way that they had received the Spirit.

2. Some Christians say: (a) that the Apostles came because no one except an Apostle could enable the Samaritans to receive the Spirit; (b) that since that time bishops are the only successors of the Apostles who can perform this action; (c) that therefore in v. 17 we are reading about a 'Confirmation Service'.

'Confirmation' has been an important service for a very long time and is so for very many Christians today. But the New Testament does not provide evidence that v. 17 refers to Confirmation, or that it was necessary for the Apostles to lay their hands on people before they could receive the Spirit (see 2.38–41; 9.17).

8.18–19: Simon ... offered them money, saying, 'Give me also this power'. Simon was mistaken in three ways:

1. He thought that Peter and John had controlled the Holy Spirit by using the correct words and actions, and he wanted to control and use

the Spirit as he thought they had. Many Christians make this mistake in their prayers when they try to persuade God to do what they want Him to do.

2. Simon wanted to be a leader in the Church in order to have power over other members. Jesus had taught His disciples that they would be tempted in this way. 'Those who are supposed to rule over the Gentiles lord it over them.... But it shall not be so among you; but whoever would be great among you must be your servant' (Mark 10.42–43). It is excellent for Christians to be ambitious, if they are ambitious to use more and more fully their gifts of service to the glory of God. But often they are tempted to be 'career ministers', who are hungry for personal advancement and for power over other people's lives (see also 1 Pet. 5.2–3).

3. Simon thought that he could buy power from the Church leaders. Today we say that someone is guilty of 'simony' if he obtains a leading position in the Church by bribery. There was a man who wanted to be a bishop, and said to a builder, 'If you will collect votes for me as bishop, I will see that you get the contract for building the new senior school.'

8.20: Peter said to him, 'Your silver perish with you'.

Peter. We have noticed Peter's extreme severity with Ananias and Sapphira, and here he says to Simon, 'To hell with you and your money!' (J. B. Phillips's translation). Probably Peter was neither cursing him nor expelling him ('excommunicating him') from the Church. From v. 22 and v. 24 it seems more likely that he was giving Simon a severe warning.

Simon. Luke does not tell us whether (a) Simon had committed a sin by pretending that he was a believer in order to get the power which Philip and the Apostles had, *or* (b) he was ignorant rather than sinful, because he had not received proper instruction before baptism.

8.24: Pray for me. It is not clear what Simon was thinking as he said this. He may have been terrified of the curse that he thought Peter had put on him, or he may have been genuinely sorry.

ADDITIONAL NOTE: BAPTISM

1. Before Jesus came Jews did baptize people, but it was only for special reasons, e.g. when Gentiles wanted to be 'proselytes' or when Jews wanted to be ritually clean (Lev. 14.8).

2. John the Baptist was doing something unusual when he invited all Jews to be baptized as a sign that they repented (Luke 3.7–8).

3. After Pentecost all those who wanted to follow Jesus were baptized, and by being baptized they became full members of the Church.

4. It was a public event, and was a visible sign that they had made a break with the past, i.e. (a) as Jesus died so they 'died to sin'; going down into the water was a sign of this (see Rom. 6.4); (b) as Jesus rose to new life, so they began a new sort of life, having His Spirit in them; coming up out of the water was a sign of this (Rom. 6.11).

5. The five parts of baptism were: (a) repentance and the receiving of God's forgiveness (2.38); (b) believing in Jesus (8.12); (c) the use of water; usually candidates were dipped in a river or pool, but see note on 8.38; (d) 'in the name of Jesus' (10.48); (e) receiving the Holy Spirit (1 Cor. 12.13).

6. When we ask, 'What was the connection between these parts of baptism?' we find various different answers in the New Testament, not one single answer. For example: according to Acts 10.44–48 some people received the Holy Spirit *before* baptism; according to Paul, the Spirit was received *at* baptism (1 Cor. 12.13); according to this chapter (vv. 12–16 and 19.5–7) some received the Spirit *after* baptism. There are many Christians today who have had an experience of receiving the Holy Spirit apart from being baptized by water and *after* that baptism. They often call this experience 'Spirit-baptism'. This is an important experience, but (as we saw above) New Testament writers do not tell us that all Christians had this experience or should have it (see note on 19.2).

7. Christians are not agreed concerning the baptism of infants (see note on 16.33).

STUDY SUGGESTIONS

REVIEW OF CONTENT

1. Where was Samaria and what was it?
2. Give one reason why the Jews and the Samaritans did not live happily together.
3. Why did many people practise magic in the first century AD?
4. Why did the Apostles send Peter and John to Samaria?
5. Why did the Apostles lay their hands on the Samaritan Christians?
6. Describe one error that Simon made.
7. What were the five parts of baptism?
8. What is meant by 'Spirit-baptism'?

BIBLE STUDY

9. What was Jesus's attitude to the Samaritans, according to the following passages?

(a) Luke 9.52–56   (b) Luke 10.30–37   (c) Luke 17.11–19
(d) John 4.7–9

10. In the Additional Note on Baptism we saw that there was variety concerning what took place before baptism and what took place after baptism.
Read the following passages in Acts and say in each case what came *before* baptism.
(a) 2.38   (b) 2.41   (c) 8.12–13   (d) 9.17–18   (e) 10.44–46
(f) 16.14–15
In each of the following passages what came *after* baptism?
(g) 8.16–18   (h) 16.34   (b) 19.5–6

DISCUSSION AND APPLICATION

11. (a) What sorts of 'magic' do you find are the most popular in your area, and why?
(b) What is the official teaching of your Church concerning magic?
(c) What is the attitude of most Church members to it?

12. 'When Christians have been filled with the Spirit they do not always show it outwardly or audibly...' (p. 77). What signs (if any) are there that the Spirit is at work in your Church?

13. Simon wanted power (p. 78). Are there any ways in which in your experience Christian leaders are tempted to be more interested in gaining power than in giving service? Give examples.

14. 'Peter said to Simon ... "To hell with you and your money!"' (p. 78). In what ways, if any, do you think Peter or Philip could have given Simon more pastoral help?

15. (a) Find out from one or two people who have been baptized as adults in what ways baptism was important to them.
(b) A group of people in India have been influenced by Jesus's teaching and want to follow Him without being baptized. If such people consulted you, what would you say to them about baptism?

8.26–40
Philip and the 'Ethiopian'

OUTLINE

8.26–27: Philip is moved by God to take the Jerusalem–Gaza road, and meets the Finance Minister of 'Ethiopia'.
8.28–35: He interprets Isaiah to the 'Ethiopian'.
8.36–38: The 'Ethiopian' is baptized.
8.39–40: Philip travels to Caesarea.

INTERPRETATION

ANOTHER NEW STAGE

This is another passage in which Luke shows that, under the guidance of the Holy Spirit, Christians reached those who previously had been regarded as unreachable. On this occasion the man who was baptized was considered by the Jews 'unreachable' for three reasons. First, he was not a Jew. Secondly, he was a eunuch, so that, according to Deut. 23.1, he was an outcast. Thirdly, he lived a very long way from Jerusalem, even outside the Roman Empire. So Luke saw his baptism as another sign that the gospel was reaching Gentiles in the most distant parts of the world.

THE 'ETHIOPIAN'

At the time when Luke wrote, the name 'Ethiopia' was given to an area which is now part of the Sudan. This is the part called Nubia, between Aswan and Khartoum, whose people have suffered so much during the civil war in recent years. For this reason we should perhaps call this man a 'Sudanese'. He was the Finance Minister of the state whose capital was Meroe. Probably he was a 'God-fearer' (see note on 2.10) who had joined a pilgrimage to Jerusalem. Like present-day visitors to cathedrals or Church headquarters, he had bought some religious literature during his visit. When Philip met him he was on his way home, sitting in his carriage (not 'a chariot') and reading Isaiah aloud. He so much wanted to understand the passage that he invited Philip, a stranger, to sit with him. So Philip was able to explain that Jesus Christ had fulfilled the events of which he was reading in the passage. Eventually the eunuch was baptized in the name of Jesus. Philip was with Paul and Luke twenty years later and perhaps told them about this event (21.8).

PHILIP'S EVANGELISM

Philip, like Stephen, was commissioned to be a social worker, but he became an evangelist, and Luke calls him that in 21.8. In these verses we see some of the ways in which he did his evangelism:

(a) He was open to the guidance of God (see note below on v. 26a);

(b) He took the opportunity to talk about Jesus before the opportunity passed: he 'ran' (v. 30);

(c) He discovered something about the eunuch before he spoke about Jesus Christ: 'Do you understand . . .?' (v. 30);

(d) He made use of something which they had in common: 'reading Isaiah' (v. 30);

(e) He was able to interpret the Old Testament: 'beginning with this scripture' (v. 35);

(f) He made Jesus the centre of his interpretation: 'told him the good news of Jesus' (v. 35);

(g) He spoke in such a way that the eunuch wanted to respond: 'What is to prevent my being baptized?' (v. 37);

(h) He trusted God for what should happen next: 'the eunuch saw him no more' (v. 39).

OUR EVANGELISM

People describe evangelism in different ways, e.g. 'being able to say why we are Christians', or 'wanting to share with someone else what matters most to us' or 'one beggar showing another beggar where to find bread'. In whatever way we describe evangelism, in these verses Luke has given us an excellent guide to some ways of doing it. But we should note that Philip was doing person-to-person evangelism, and Luke has shown us in other parts of Acts that this sort of evangelism must be accompanied by the witness which the congregation as a whole gives (see e.g. 2.44-47). A congregation evangelizes by being a fellowship in which members know and trust each other and, therefore, show to the world what the gospel is and does.

NOTES

8.26a: An angel of the Lord said ... Perhaps it seemed to Philip at the time that it was by chance that he met the 'Ethiopian'. But according to

Luke God was actively guiding Philip. He refers to God's guidance by using the word 'angel' here (see note on 5.19, and the words 'the Spirit' in vv. 29 and 39). Some Christians today use the same words, for example, to explain why they paid someone a visit or wrote someone a letter. Others might say that they were in touch with God through regular prayer, and in this way knew that it was 'right' to do these things. The words are different, but the experience is the same.

Philip was open to God's guidance for him, and so he 'rose and went' (v. 27).

8.26b: The road that goes down from Jerusalem to Gaza. This is a desert road. The Greek words can also be translated 'the road ... to Gaza, which is a desert place', and this is probably what Luke meant. The trade route from Jerusalem to Egypt passed through Gaza, which is about 100 kms south of Jerusalem. As far as Gaza the road was not desert; the desert was south of Gaza. It was the *town* of Gaza that was desert, having been destroyed by an invading army. Today Gaza is desert of a different sort. There are half a million inhabitants, but at the time of writing 480,000 of them are Palestinian refugees, living in shanty huts with almost no drainage.

8.27: A minister of the Candace, queen ... had come to Jerusalem to worship. The Greek word here translated 'to worship' means 'to make a religious pilgrimage' and this is what the queen's Finance Minister was doing. Being a God-fearer he had joined a group of Jewish pilgrims to the Temple, and was now on his way home. Making a pilgrimage of this sort is what Jesus and His family used to do, (Luke 2.41–43).

8.30: Philip ... heard him reading Isaiah the prophet and asked, 'Do you understand what you are reading?'. Philip heard him because he was reading aloud. Reading a scroll of a Greek manuscript was very difficult, partly because there was no division between the words, and partly because it was hand-written, and most readers found it easier to read it aloud than silently.

By his question Philip shows that reading the Bible and being able to interpret it must go together. The words of the Bible are not magical words, and it is not the act of reading them aloud that gives the reader eternal life. Reading and understanding what the writer meant belong together. In our own generation the Bible Societies give us the Bible to read, and scholars and their publishers have the extremely important task of helping readers to understand it.

8.32: As a sheep led to the slaughter ... so he opens not his mouth. These verses 32 and 33 come from Isaiah 53.7–8. They are part of a long passage in which the prophet describes the 'Servant'. This 'Servant' suffers in silence and although he is innocent, he is killed. We do not know whether Jews interpreted the 'Servant' as referring to Isaiah himself, or to the people of Israel as a whole, or to some person who

'Do you understand what you are reading?' (8.30)

For this Christian couple in the Central African Republic, as for Christians everywhere, 'reading the Bible and being able to interpret it must go together' (p. 83).

would come in the future. But we see from 8.35 and many other verses in the New Testament that Christians taught that Jesus was the fulfilment of the passage.

We may notice that Luke omits the last part of Isaiah 53.8 'stricken for the transgression of my people' (i.e. 'died that we might be forgiven'). Why did Luke do so?

1. Perhaps these words were not in the Greek version of Isaiah which Luke or Philip used. This is the usual explanation.

2. But some scholars think that although Luke firmly believed that God forgives us and takes away our sins (e.g. see Luke 15), he may not have thought that it was necessary to connect God's forgiveness with the death of Jesus. They have also noticed other passages where Luke omits a reference to sinners being saved by Jesus's death, e.g. by comparing Mark 10.45 with Luke 22.25–27. They remind us that Paul, on the other hand, taught that it was only because Jesus died that God forgives us (Rom. 5.8–9; Gal. 2.21 etc.). If these scholars are right, then it shows that Christian leaders who did not hold the same opinions on important matters of belief were nevertheless able to accept each other as genuine Christians: Paul and Luke worked closely together for many years. Other scholars, however, point to 20.28b.

8.36: The eunuch said, ... 'What is to prevent my being baptized?'. Clearly Philip said much more to the man than Luke has reported in these verses, e.g. finding out if he really believed in Jesus and explaining the meaning of baptism. As a result of their conversations the man asked to be baptized. In some manuscripts there is an extra verse (v. 37): 'And Philip said, "If you believe with all your heart, you may." And he replied, "I believe that Jesus Christ is the Son of God." ' (see Special Note C, The Manuscripts of Acts, pp. 182, 183).

8.38: They both went down into the water ... and he baptized him. It seems that the water was deep and that Philip probably baptized the eunuch by dipping him under the water, rather than by pouring water over him. Luke does not tell us. It may be that at that time all baptism candidates were dipped under the water; the members of the Baptist Church believe that is how all baptisms should be done. This seems suitable in warm climates, or where people can afford to heat a pool, but not so suitable in cold climates such as Russia or Canada. New Testament writers do not give us a rule on the subject.

8.39: The eunuch saw him no more, and went on his way rejoicing. Good evangelists link people to God and to other Christians, not to themselves. They work in such a way that they are no longer needed. A minister saying farewell to his congregation said 'If you cannot do without me, then I have been a failure'. Evangelists can leave those to whom they have ministered by entrusting them to God, knowing that His Spirit will be at work among them.

Philip could not put this 'Ethiopian' in touch with fellow-Christians, but he had shown him the way to God through Jesus Christ. So when Philip left him, the eunuch did not feel lost or neglected. He rejoiced!

But he had a hard time ahead. When he returned home he was the only follower of Jesus in his community. The question is asked in many parts of the world today: 'Is it right to baptize someone who will have no support from fellow-Christians?' When a young Turkish student asked a Christian minister 'What is to prevent my being baptized?' (v. 36), it was a very difficult question to answer. Turkey is officially a 'secular' state, but 98 per cent of the people (including the student's family) are Muslim. (The student *was* baptized, and at the time when this is being written is still a firm member of the Church.)

8.40: Philip was found at Azotus and ... preached the gospel to all the towns till he came to Caesarea. The people of Azotus and of the towns and villages along the coast between Azotus and Caesarea were Greek-speaking Jews (Hellenists), and so were more likely to listen to Philip, who was a Hellenist. From 21.8 it seems that Caesarea was Philip's home.

STUDY SUGGESTIONS

REVIEW OF CONTENT

1. Why do we refer to the eunuch as a 'Sudanese' rather than an 'Ethiopian' in the notes?
2. For what three reasons did a Sudanese seem to be 'unreachable' to Jews?
3. Describe two sorts of evangelism.
4. Why did the eunuch want Philip to sit with him?
5. What sentence from Isaiah 53.8 is omitted from Acts 8.32–33?
6. (a) What were the eunuch's feelings when Philip left him?
   (b) Why did he feel like that?

BIBLE STUDY

7. Luke refers to God's guidance by using the words 'angel' in 8.26 and 'the Spirit' in vv. 29 and 39. What words does he use to refer to God's guidance in each of the following verses?
   (a) 8.26 (b) 8.29 (c) 8.39 (d) 10.3 (e) 10.19 (f) 27.23
8. The eunuch needed an interpreter.
   (i) Give an example, if you know one, of people getting wrong teaching from the Bible because they had no one to interpret it.
   (ii) Read the following passages and, if possible, say in each case what had to be interpreted and who was the interpreter.

(a) Dan. 4.19–24   (b) Luke 24.27   (c) Acts 8.35
(d) 1 Cor. 14.5

9. The eunuch was reading part of Isaiah 53. The writers of the following passages all refer to Jesus as the 'servant' of Isaiah 53. Say in each case whether the writer was referring to (a) His suffering and death or (b) His taking away the sins of others through his suffering and death.

(a) Mark 10.45   (b) Luke 22.37   (c) Luke 24.26
(d) Acts 7.52   (e) Rom. 4.25   (f) 1 Pet. 2.22–25

DISCUSSION AND APPLICATION

10. (a) What is evangelism?
(b) Should all Christians be evangelists? Give reasons for your answer.
(c) In what ways, if any, can a non-professional Christian be a more effective evangelist than a trained professional?

11. Discover what life is like for Palestinians in Gaza today and describe it.

12. It seemed to be by chance that Philip met the Sudanese, but later Philip believed that God had guided him. Describe any experience you have had of an event which seemed to occur by chance, but which later you believed was due to God's guidance. What are the words you would use in speaking with your friends about God's guidance?

13. What groups, either inside or outside your Church, are producing Christian literature in your area?

14. (a) In your Church is baptism done by pouring water on the candidates or by dipping them under the water?
(b) What are the reasons for using one way rather than the other?

9.1–19a

The Conversion of Paul

OUTLINE

9.1–2: Paul receives permission to arrest Christians in Damascus.
9.3–9: Paul's vision
9.10–19a: Ananias welcomes Paul.

INTERPRETATION

WHY DID PAUL GO TO DAMASCUS?

According to 8.1–3, Paul agreed with the stoning of Stephen, and after Stephen's death he organized the persecution of Christians in Jerusalem. As we have seen, Paul did so because the Christians were putting Jesus (rather than the 'Law') in the centre of their lives. In Paul's eyes, this was blasphemy (read again the notes on Stephen's speech (pp. 66–70) and on the word 'Law' in 7.53). And now Paul had news that some of Stephen's supporters had escaped to Damascus, where there had been a synagogue of Greek-speaking Christian Jews for some time. So he set out on the 270 kms journey to prevent the spread of the teaching that seemed to him to be so evil (see Special Note B p. 93, 'Paul's Background').

WHAT CAUSED PAUL'S CONVERSION?

(a) Some people think that ever since Stephen's death Paul had been questioning his own attitude to the Law; that the more he tried to obey it, the more he was failing to do so; that Romans 7.21,24 refer to this time; 'When I want to do right, evil lies close at hand . . . Wretched man that I am! Who will deliver me?', and that Paul was ready for a great change in his outlook.

(b) Others think that there is not enough evidence for the above interpretation, and that Paul's conversion was totally sudden and unexpected.

LUKE'S ACCOUNT OF THE CONVERSION

The conversion of Paul was so important for the Church, and for the whole world, that Luke reported it three times over, here and in chs. 22 and 26. We shall study all three passages in the notes below, and readers will notice two facts: ; first, that the accounts do not always agree (see note on v. 7), and secondly that they describe extraordinary and dramatic happenings. But neither of these facts are central. The central truth is that the change in Paul took place, and that God offers others also the experience of conversion.

WHAT IS CONVERSION?

Luke does not use the Greek word for 'conversion' here (but he does use it in 3.19, where RSV translates it 'turn again'). However, it is a suitable word, provided that we see the full extent of the experience:

(a) Conversion is an event, but it is not usually so dramatic as it was for Paul (see v. 3), nor is it usually sudden.

(b) It is both God's action and ours (see v. 5). When we are converted we are responding to God, and responding with trust in Him and with penitence for our own failures.

(c) We make a break with the past; thus it is often a painful as well as a joyful experience (see v. 9).

(d) After conversion we usually join a fellowship of believers (see v. 19). Sometimes a whole group or fellowship experience conversion at the same time.

(e) We begin to change the way we behave (see v. 20).

(f) Conversion is a beginning. But it should not be the only time in Christians' lives when change and renewal take place. For this reason it is a mistake for Christians to spend much time looking back to their conversion rather than looking to the Holy Spirit to show them what changes are needed in their lives, e.g. when their trust has grown weak, or their prayers have become formal, or if they are no longer concerned for the well-being of people in need. Paul himself knew that he needed to be continually renewed and redirected in order that he should grow and develop in his loyalty to Jesus Christ (see Rom. 12.2; Phil 3.12–14).

NOTES

9.2: If he found any belonging to the Way, men or women, he might bring them bound. The 'Way' was a name for the followers of Jesus (see note on 22.4).

Paul wanted to arrest women as well as men. Luke points out that men and women were equally effective as evangelists and, therefore, equally harmful, in Paul's opinion, to the Jewish religion.

9.3: A light from heaven flashed about him.

(a) Some scholars think that there was a thunderstorm with a flash of lightning; this would explain why Paul's friends also saw the light, as in 22.9. God, they say, used this ordinary event as a way of speaking to Paul. Paul was ready for a change in his life and was able to use the event. The event which was ordinary at first became an extraordinary and life-changing experience.

(b) But others point out that 'light' is a symbol of the presence of the glory of God which several writers in the Bible use, and that many people today who experience a sudden conversion have said afterwards that they saw light. It is useless to ask if a camera could have photographed the light which they saw. The light was as real to them as the conversion itself. Sometimes such people also fall down (see v. 4), or hear a voice (see v. 4), or are blind for a time (see v. 8), as the result of the shock.

Whichever interpretation we accept, we should note that for most people conversion takes place without any experience of a visible light or audible voice.

9.4: He ... heard a voice saying to him, 'Saul, Saul, why do you persecute me?'

Saul, Saul. This is the name by which Paul's family called him. So he experienced God calling him personally, and by his name. Since he was a child he had been called both Saul and Paul, Saul by those who spoke Aramaic and Hebrew, Paul by those who spoke Greek or Latin.

Perhaps the name was repeated because the call was urgent. See 'Abraham, Abraham' (Gen. 22.11), 'Moses, Moses' (Exod. 3.4), and 'Samuel, Samuel' (1 Sam. 3.10).

You persecute me. Paul realized that by persecuting the followers of Jesus he was persecuting Jesus Himself. Jesus's followers were His 'body' (1 Cor. 12.27). See Luke 10.16; Matt. 25.40. When we go astray we are not just breaking rules, we are breaking His heart (see also 26.14).

9.7: Hearing the voice but seeing no one. According to 22.9 Paul's companions saw the light but did not hear the voice. As we saw above, the details of the events are not important, nor are the differences between the accounts.

9.8: They led him by the hand. Paul the powerful persecutor was so blinded and helpless that his friends had to lead him the rest of the way like a child. Perhaps Paul had this in mind when he wrote 'When I am weak, then I am strong' (2 Cor. 12.10).

9.9: He neither ate nor drank. We cannot say whether Paul was unable to eat or drink because of the shock he had received, or because he was keeping a three-day fast as a way of dedicating himself to the service of Jesus Christ. See note on 27.9, fasting.

9.10: The Lord said to him in a vision 'Ananias'. After his experience on the road Paul needed to join with the Christians whom he had come to persecute. It was Ananias who helped him to do so. This Ananias was not the Ananias mentioned in ch. 5. Luke describes him as 'well-spoken of by all the Jews who lived there' (22.12), so probably he had lived in Damascus for some time. He was one of those of whom we read (in Acts and in Paul's letters) who were not officially appointed leaders, but were committed Christians without whom the Church could not have grown, e.g. Aquila and Priscilla (18.2). According to ch. 9 Ananias had a vision in which the Lord persuaded him to meet Paul, and Paul also had a vision about Ananias (v. 12). In 22.12–16 the account is simpler, and there is no reference to visions. See note on 16.9, Visions.

9.11: Go to the street called Straight. This street is still a main road in Damascus.

9.13: Thy saints at Jerusalem. 'Saints' means all the Christians (See note on 26.1).

9.15: He is a chosen instrument of mine to carry my name before the Gentiles and kings and the sons of Israel. Compare this with 22.14–15 and 26.16–18. These words well describe Paul's own conviction, (a) that God had chosen him for special work (Gal. 1.15), and (b) that God intended him to go to the Gentiles and to the Jews (Eph. 3.1).

9.16: How much he must suffer. No-one can follow Christ without sharing some of His suffering.

9.17a: Brother Saul. According to vv. 13 and 14, Ananias was unwilling at first to meet Paul, who was well known to be a persecutor of Christians. But he was also courageous, willing to forgive Paul, willing to trust him and determined to obey God. For all these reasons he was able to say 'Brother'.

9.17b–18: Be filled with the Holy Spirit ... he regained his sight ... and was baptized. All this happened after Ananias had 'laid his hands' on Paul (see note on 13.3).

1. Some Christians have interpreted these verses as a set of rules, as though everyone must first be converted, then have hands laid on them (v. 17), then be filled with the Spirit (v. 17), and then be baptized (v. 18). But Luke did not write in order to pass on rules for the future, he wrote in order to give a report of the events (see Additional Note, Baptism, p. 79.)

2. But many people also ask some questions about this verse, e.g.: (a) Do all Christians need to have a second experience after conversion, i.e. of being filled with the Spirit, as Paul had? After conversion Christians need *many* opportunities (not just one more) of being renewed in various ways by the Spirit. (b) Is it necessary for converted people to be baptized? Yes, because baptism is the time when those people become members of the Church and other members promise to support them (1 Cor. 12.13). (c) Is it necessary for baptized people to be converted at some time? Yes. Conversion can take place before, or during, or after baptism (Eph. 4.23,24).

9.19: He took food. Like the girl whom Jesus had cured (Mark 5.43), and like all of us, Paul needed food for the body as well as food for the spirit.

STUDY SUGGESTIONS

REVIEW OF CONTENT

1. Why was Paul so determined to suppress the Christian Church in Damascus?
2. Why do we sometimes read of 'Paul' and at other times of 'Saul'?
3. What do we know about Ananias who came to the help of Paul after his conversion?
4. What happened to Paul after Ananias had 'laid his hands' on him?

BIBLE STUDY

5. 'Light is a symbol of the presence of the glory of God' (p. 89). Who saw that light according to each of the following passages?
   (a) Luke 2.9   (b) Luke 9.29–32   (c) Acts 12.7
6. Read the following passages and say in each case who heard a voice and what message did they hear?
   (a) Exod. 3.1–6   (b) Isa. 6.1–9   (c) Luke 3.22   (d) Luke 9.35
   (e) Acts 10.13
7. What does Paul say about his conversion in each of the following passages?
   (a) 1 Cor. 9.1   (b) 1 Cor. 15.8–10   (c) Gal. 1.12–17
   (d) Phil. 3.6–8   (e) 1 Tim. 1.13–14

DISCUSSION AND APPLICATION

8. Find out from some of your Christian friends how many of them can say when and where they were converted, and how it happened. What is the value of being able to do so, and what is the danger?
9. What would you reply to someone who said 'I was born and brought up in a Christian family, so I do not need to be converted'?
10. 'Conversion should not be the only event in the life of Christians when change and renewal takes place' (p. 89).
    (a) What evidence is there that Paul experienced renewal at times other than his conversion?
    (b) What can you do to ensure that you, like Paul, can be renewed or 're-directed' during your life?
11. If a village chief or other group leader asked to be baptized and then the whole community asked for baptism, what advice would you give them if you were a neighbouring pastor?
12. Tell the story of Paul's conversion as if you were Ananias telling his friends about it.

Special Note B
Paul's Background

HIS HOME

Paul was born in Tarsus, in the mountainous south coastal area of the country we now call Turkey (then the Roman Province of Cilicia). His family belonged to the tribe of Benjamin, he had a sister (23.16), and he himself probably got married (1 Cor. 9.5).

HIS LANGUAGE

Paul spoke Aramaic (the everyday language of Jews at that time), also Hebrew and Latin. He also wrote and spoke in Greek, which was the main language of the Roman Empire.

HIS NATIONALITY

Paul's father was a Roman citizen. When people living in the Roman Empire had given special service to the Empire, they were often made Roman citizens. Such people had privileges, e.g. they could not be imprisoned without a trial. A West Indian said recently that being a Roman citizen in the first century was like having a British passport in the twentieth century. One of the extra privileges that such citizens had was that their sons inherited citizenship, and that is how Paul the Jew became a Roman citizen.

The enormous Empire of which he was a member included many different tribes and languages, and had thousands of miles of well-built roads. This is the reason why Paul knew about other religions than his own, and why he was able to travel widely.

HIS RELIGION

Paul was educated at the synagogue school at Tarsus, and later he became a student in Jerusalem under the famous Jewish theologian Gamaliel. He then became a 'Rabbi' (an official religious teacher) and, as it was the rule that Rabbis should have a trade, became a tent-maker. He belonged to the Pharisees' group (Phil. 3.5), the group who aimed at strictly applying the 'Law' to everyday life. After his conversion, however, Jesus (rather than the 'Law') was the centre of his life. In spite of this, Paul always thought like a Jew and always spoke reverently about the 'Law' (Romans 7.12).

'Paul was born in Tarsus, in the mountainous south coast of the Roman Province of Cilicia' (p. 93).

This is the present-day road that leads from Tarsus, through these narrow 'Gates of Cilicia', into the wild regions to the north. Paul did much of his travelling for the sake of the gospel in country like this (but without modern transport!).

HIS APPEARANCE

In 2 Cor. 10.10 Paul wrote that people call him 'weak in bodily presence', and in other letters he refers to his ill-health (e.g. in Gal. 4.13). An unknown writer in AD 160 said he was 'a sturdy little bald-headed man, with meeting eyebrows and a rather prominent nose'.

STUDY SUGGESTIONS

1. What do we know about Paul's family?
2. What languages did he speak?
3. What religious group did he belong to?
4. Paul was a Rabbi, a tent-maker, and a Roman citizen. In what particular ways do you think each of these 'qualifications' helped him in his work of carrying the gospel to 'Gentiles and kings and the sons of Israel' (9.15)?

9.19b–31

After Paul's Conversion

OUTLINE

9.19b–30: Paul's movements after his conversion.
9.31: A description of the Church at that time.

INTERPRETATION

WHAT FOLLOWS CONVERSION?

When people have had an experience which changes their lives as powerfully as Paul's life was changed, what comes next?

After their astonishment at what has happened, life is often difficult. Some people are tempted to feel superior to those who have not had that experience (and even to tell them that they are not real Christians). Or they may want humbly to tell other people what God has done, though the others may not want to hear. Friends are not always sure how to treat them and sometimes cease to be friends.

PAUL'S EXPERIENCE

During the fifteen years after his conversion, life was at times very difficult for Paul, and he bravely endured loneliness and persecution. But what took place was very important, because during that time he was preparing (and God was preparing him) for the great missionary work which he did later.

However, we do not have much information, and the accounts which we do have are rather different from each other. They are different because Luke and Paul had different aims in writing. Luke's aim (vv. 19b–30) was to show that the Church was growing, but Paul in Gal. 1.17–21 wished to explain that God had commissioned him *directly* and not through the apostles.

It seems that the events were as follows:

1. For a few days Paul remained in Damascus (v. 19b).

2. For two years or so he was in the Arab kingdom of Nabataea and later moved to Damascus. The Arab kingdom included the trade route from the East and such cities at Petra and Philadelphia (the modern Amman).

No one needed passports or visas in those days to pass from one kingdom to another. In Gal. 1.17 Paul calls it 'Arabia', but the area is what we now call the southern part of Syria and the northern part of Jordan. Only part of it was desert. We do not know what he was doing there. Perhaps he went to think and pray, just as Jesus went into the desert after His baptism. But Paul may, on the other hand, have immediately carried out the commission which God had given him to preach the gospel, and have tried to make converts along the trade routes and in the towns.

3. In Damascus many people strongly opposed Paul's teaching, and he had to escape (vv. 23–25).

4. After that he was in Jerusalem, but again had to escape (9.29; 2 Cor. 11. 32–33).

5. Then for about 13 years he lived in his own home town of Tarsus and in other parts of the Province of Cilicia (Gal. 1.21; Acts 9.30).

NOTES

9.20: He proclaimed Jesus, saying 'He is the Son of God'. At this time (AD 34) 'Son of God' meant the 'royal Messiah' (see note on 2.3b). This is what it meant to Jews, as we see from v. 22: 'proving that Jesus was the Christ', i.e. Messiah (see also Ps. 2.7; Matt 16.16; Luke 22.67,70). Christians did not give Jesus the other and different title of 'God the Son' until much later.

9.23: When many days had passed, the Jews plotted. This happened during Paul's second visit to Damascus and after he had been in the Nabataean kingdom. We learn from 2 Cor. 11.32 that the King of the Nabataeans (as well as Jews in Damascus) wanted to kill Paul, perhaps because Paul had been trying to evangelize his people, the Nabataeans.

Paul escaped by being let down in a basket from a window in the city wall, looking more like a load of dried fish than God's 'chosen instrument' (9.15). It was not a dignified way to travel, and he found it difficult to bear, (see 2 Cor. 11.29–33).

9.26: When he had come to Jerusalem he attempted to join the disciples. Whom did Paul meet in Jerusalem?

1. According to vv. 27–29a Barnabas helped him to meet the Apostles and many other Christians, although at first everyone had been afraid of him.

2. But in Gal. 1.18 and 19 Paul says he met no one except Peter and James.

3. As the reports are not the same we do not know exactly who Paul met. But we know that he spent two weeks with Peter, and this was surely a very important meeting indeed. The two men had different backgrounds: Peter had been a fisherman, Paul a Rabbi. They had different experiences of Jesus: Peter had been with Jesus since the beginning of His ministry, Paul was a new convert. Each had experience to share with the other, and it is likely that Peter spoke mainly about the life and teaching of Jesus as he knew it in the past and Paul spoke chiefly of the presence of Jesus 'here and now'; that Peter spoke about the beginnings of the Church, and Paul spoke of the need for its development; that Peter spoke about the Christian community, and Paul spoke about his personal experience. Each had a different outlook which the other needed, just as Christians today need to hear the different outlooks of other Christians. For example, those who emphasize the traditions of the Church, and those others who look to the Holy Spirit to guide the Church into new ways, each need to listen to the other and learn from them.

Disciples. The word 'disciple' means 'learner', 'pupil', 'student', and Greek and Jewish teachers used the word to describe their followers.

1. John the Baptist had his 'disciples' (Mark 6.29).

2. Jesus had His 'disciples'. Some were the group of Twelve men he chose to be with him, and to whom He gave special training (Matt. 10.1). But there were many others, men and women, who followed Him and were also disciples (Mark 2.15).

3. In Acts Luke uses the word to describe all those who followed Jesus. Other words which he used in this way are 'brethren' (e.g. 1.15), Christians (11.25) and 'saints' (26.10).

4. Christian disciples today who understand the meaning of the

word will be learners and pupils throughout their lives (see also note on
9.36).

9.29: The Hellenists ... were seeking to kill him. See note on 6.1. Some
of the Hellenists were Christians, but those who wanted to kill Paul
were not. When Paul tried to debate with them, they realized that his
teaching (like Stephen's) was very different from their own traditional
ideas about God and about the Law. So they planned to kill him.
Christian friends helped him to escape to the port of Caesarea. For
Paul's note on this event see 22.17–21.

9.30: Sent him off to Tarsus: See also Gal. 1.21, 'into the regions of
Syria and Cilicia'. These two regions formed the Roman Province of
'Cilicia', of which Tarsus was the chief city. So it was in his own home
country that Paul now carried out his many years of evangelism. But he
faced many difficulties. Perhaps Paul's family and friends, who followed the Jewish Law strictly, could not accept his new ideas and
teaching, and some of the events to which he refers in 2 Cor. 11.23–27
may have occurred at this time. But it was also at this time that he
probably founded Christian congregations which, later on, he strengthened (Acts 15.41).

9.31: The church ... had peace. The word 'church' is a translation of
the Greek word *ecclesia*. When the Old Testament was translated into
Greek this was the word for the meeting together of the 'people of
God', e.g. Josh. 8.35,   'All the assembly of Israel'.

1. The first Christians knew that they were the true 'Israel of God'
(the new and reformed Israel, see Gal. 3.29; 6.16), so they used the same
word.

2. In the New Testament it usually means the whole body of
Christians wherever they lived. Even when Paul wrote 'the church of
God which is at Corinth' (1 Cor. 1.2) he meant the one universal
Church as the Christians at Corinth experienced it. He also called it the
'body' of Christ (Col. 1.24), i.e. the instrument through which He
works in the world. This is the meaning of the word 'church' in 9.31 and
20.28.

3. In Acts it usually means a congregation of Christians in a town or
village, (see 14.23; 15.41) and occasionally seems to refer to the leaders
of a congregation (11.22; 15.4).

4. There are two *un*helpful ways in which we use the word 'church'
today which make it very difficult to remember the true meaning: (a) a
building: there were no buildings called churches in the Roman Empire
until about AD 300; Christians met together in each other's homes, (b) a
denomination, e.g. 'The Baptist Church': New Testament writers
would probably have called it 'The Baptist Branch of Christ's Church';
there is only one Church.

STUDY SUGGESTIONS

REVIEW OF CONTENT

1. Where did Paul go after his first visit to Damascus?
2. When Paul preached in Damascus, what words and phrases did he use when speaking about Jesus?
3. Why did Paul have to escape from Jerusalem?
4. Why did the first Christians use the same word for their assembly (*ecclesia*) which the Israelites had used before the time of Jesus?
5. How did Paul travel from Jerusalem to Tarsus?
6. What does the word 'church' usually mean in 'Acts'?

BIBLE STUDY

7. The word 'disciple' means 'learner', 'pupil' ... (p. 97). Read the following verses and in each case say, if you can, who the disciples were, and what you think they were learning through that event.
   (a) Matt. 27.57   (b) Luke 9.51–55   (c) Luke 11.1
   (d) John 6.8–11   (e) Acts 9.10–16   (f) Acts 9.36
8. In each of the following verses does the word 'church' mean (i) the whole body of Christians everywhere, or (ii) a congregation of Christians in one place?
   (a) Matt 16.18   (b) Acts 13.1   (c) Acts 14.23   (d) Acts 20.28
   (e) 1 Cor. 4.17   (f) Phil. 3.6

DISCUSSION AND APPLICATION

9. (a) Why did Luke give one account in Acts of the events after Paul's conversion and Paul give rather a different account when he wrote to the Galatians?
   (b) If people say that they 'cannot trust the New Testament' because these two accounts are not the same, and because Gal. 1.19 does not agree with Acts 9.27, what reply can you give?
10. When Peter and Paul met in Jerusalem, 'each of them had a different outlook which the other needed' (p. 97).
    (a) Give an example of sincere Christians or Christian groups who find it difficult to agree with each other because each is emphasizing a different truth.
    (b) In what chief ways is it possible for Christians to gain by sharing their different outlooks at such a meeting?
11. 'Christian disciples today ... will be learners and pupils throughout their lives' (pp. 97, 98).
    (a) Why is it necessary to go on learning?

(b) In what ways can Church members be helped to be lifelong learners? Give examples in each case.

12. New Testament writers would probably have called the Baptist Church 'The Baptist Branch of Christ's Church', (p. 98).
(a) What reason was given for this statement?
(b) Should any change be made to the title of the denomination to which you belong? Give reasons.

9.32—11.18

Peter and Cornelius

OUTLINE

9.32–43: Peter, in Lydda and Joppa, heals Aeneas and restores Dorcas to life.

10.1–48: Peter and Cornelius the Gentile.
(a) Cornelius's vision (1–8).
(b) Peter's vision (9–16).
(c) Cornelius's messengers reach Peter (17–23).
(d) Cornelius and Peter meet (24–33).
(e) Peter's sermon (34–43).
(f) Cornelius and friends speak in tongues and later are baptized (44–48).

11.1–18: Jerusalem Christians criticize Peter, and Peter gives them an explanation.

INTERPRETATION

WHY WERE THESE EVENTS IMPORTANT?

After first showing Peter at work in Gentile territory (9.32–43), e.g. healing Dorcas, Luke tells how Peter, the Jew, took food with Cornelius, an uncircumcised Gentile and a Roman soldier. This was so new an event that he described it twice over, and ever since that time life has been different for all Christians. Thousands of years ago someone somewhere invented the wheel, and since that time the way human beings live has been different. Peter's eating a meal with Cornelius was like that. Before that meal most Christians believed that Jesus was for the Jews. After the meal they discovered that He was for all nations.

WHAT HAPPENED?

Cornelius, as a result of a vision, sent messengers to Peter, and Peter, in obedience to his own vision, invited them in (see note on v. 23). The next day they began the 42 kms walk to Caesarea, Peter bringing six witnesses with him. When they reached Caesarea, Cornelius with his family and friends made Peter his guest and invited him to speak. Peter spoke about Jesus, showing that He is 'Lord of all'. While he was speaking, his listeners began speaking in tongues, and Peter was certain that God had given them His Spirit. They were later baptized.

This event seemed sinful to some Christians in Jerusalem, but Peter was able to persuade them that it was God's doing. However, this and other similar events troubled these Jerusalem Christians so much that a conference had to be called (ch. 15). It was a long time before all Jewish Christians accepted Gentiles as fellow-Christians (see note on 15.7).

THE GENTILES

'Gentiles' is one of the words which translators use for non-Jews. Other words (mainly used in the Old Testament) are 'the nations', 'the peoples', 'the heathen'.

The Jews regarded Gentiles as dangerous, mainly because they did not worship the one true God and were not circumcised, see Ps. 135.15. They kept apart from Gentiles in order to keep their own religion pure. But from time to time there were Jews who believed that God loved the Gentiles and would one day include them among His 'chosen' (see Gen. 22.18; Luke 2.32).

In the first century AD most Jews regarded Gentiles as not only dangerous but evil, and unloved by God. A Jew was not allowed to have a Gentile as a guest or to be the guest of a Gentile (see 10.28). Some even taught that it was wrong to be a midwife to a Gentile, because that would help Gentiles to multiply. However, not all Gentiles were excluded from Jewish worship. 'Proselytes' and 'God-fearers' (see notes on 2.10; 10.1) took part in synagogue worship. It was mainly proselytes and God-fearers who accepted the gospel in the early years of the Church.

Luke wrote Acts partly to show how Jewish Christians, step by step, ceased to regard Gentiles as 'unholy', and accepted them as full members of the Church (see Introduction p. 1). And Paul in his letters explained how this was happening, e.g. in Eph. 2.11–22. Because many Gentiles but few Jews became Christians, he said, 'God is accepting the Gentiles, so that through them the Jews will be converted (Rom. 11.11–12, 25, 31).

Many of us Gentiles have forgotten that it is through us that Jews can come to faith in God through Christ. We have even persecuted them, and on many occasions.

THIS EVENT AND PRESENT-DAY CHRISTIANS

Many who study this event will ask questions about the Church today, e.g. (a) How can present-day Christians avoid the mistake which Peter made before he met Cornelius, i.e. seeing one part of God's creation as 'holy' and another part as 'un-holy'? (see note on 10.15), (b) When is it right for Christians to make a major change in their rules? Peter and others changed the rules by admitting an uncircumcised Gentile into the Church (see note on 10.25).

NOTES

9.32: Peter ... came down also to the saints that lived at Lydda. When present-day air-passengers arrive at Lod Airport, the airport for Tel Aviv, they are very near the 'Lydda' that Peter visited (called Lod in the Old Testament). He found Christians there (here called 'saints', see note on 26.10), because Philip had already been at work there (8.40).
9.34: Aeneas, Jesus Christ heals you; rise and make your bed. Luke's description of Peter healing the paralysed Aeneas is like his description of Jesus healing another paralysed man (Luke 5.18–26). He probably wanted to show that the Jesus who once healed is still healing. Note that Peter does not say 'I heal you in Jesus's name' but 'Jesus Christ heals you'.

The Greek words translated 'make your bed' could also be translated 'prepare the table' (i.e. for a meal).
9.36: At Joppa a disciple named Tabitha, which means Dorcas.
Joppa was then the sea-port for Jerusalem, and is now the suburb of Tel Aviv called Yafo.
A disciple. The Greek word should be translated 'a female disciple'. Luke was making clear that women were important in the Church.
Tabitha means a 'gazelle', and Dorcas is the Greek word for gazelle.
9.38: Since Lydda was near Joppa, the disciples ... sent two men to him. In the New Testament we read of many people working in pairs (see 10.7; Luke 10.1). It seems to be important for Christians to work in this way, as did the evangelists Moody (the preacher) with Sankey (the musician).

Lydda is 18 kms from Joppa.
9.40: 'Tabitha, rise.' And she opened her eyes. This account is like the account of Jesus bringing Jairus's daughter alive in Luke 8.40–56. He gives us another such account in Luke 7.11–17, (compare also 1 Kings

17.17–24; 2 Kings 4.32–37). On all these occasions it was not 'resurrection' that took place, because those who were brought to life died later. What did happen? Some Christians say that God was at work, doing miraculously what no human being could do. Luke probably believed that. Other Christians think that those patients appeared to be dead, but perhaps were only in a coma, like the Mexican who sat up in his coffin just before his funeral (see Additional Note, Miracles, p. 190).

9.43: He stayed . . . with one Simon, a tanner. Jews regarded tanning as an 'unclean' trade, so, by staying with Simon, Peter showed that he was no longer holding closely to Jewish traditions. Simon's house was probably beside the sea, because tanners needed water for their work, and owing to the bad smell of tanning they needed to be away from the main town. Perhaps it was for the same reason that Peter went up on the house-top to pray (v. 9). If you are the guest of a tanner that is the best place to be!

10.1: At Caesarea there was a man named Cornelius, a centurion.
Caesarea was an important port and the headquarters of the Roman Governor of Judea. It was, therefore, a mainly Gentile town, and had an enormous statue of the Roman Emperor in its centre.
Cornelius was probably a retired soldier (at that time the Italian cohort was not on active service in Caesarea). As a centurion his position was like that of a Sergeant Major.

Luke does not call Cornelius a 'God-fearer' (see note on 2.10), but v. 2 shows that he followed the Jewish religion very closely; he worshipped the one true God, he had a household of worshippers, he was generous to people in need, and he prayed regularly. But he was looking for a way of life that would satisfy him more fully.

10.3: He saw clearly in a vision an angel of God. See note on 16.9 for the words 'vision' and 'trance' (see note on 10.10–11 below). Luke was saying that Peter and Cornelius did not meet by chance but according to the will of God. It was God who was making Himself known to them, whether Luke uses the word 'angel' (here and in 10.22) or a 'voice' (10.13 and 15), or the Spirit (10.19; 11.12) or 'God' (10.28) or 'a man in bright apparel' (10.30) (see note on 5.19).

10.10–11: He fell into a trance and saw the heaven opened, and something descending, like a great sheet. Peter went up on to the flat roof to pray. It was time for the midday meal and he became hungry, and during this time he had this vision. Perhaps before he began to pray he had been watching sailors lowering a sail on a ship in Joppa harbour and the sail became the 'great sheet' in his trance. The 'sheet' contained creatures (v. 12), some of which were 'unclean' according to Leviticus chapter 11.

10.13–14: There came a voice to him 'Rise, Peter; kill and eat.' But Peter said, 'No, Lord; for I have never . . .' All his life Peter had been forbidden to eat some foods because according to Jewish Law they were 'unclean' or 'taboo'. Many peoples have taboos, e.g. in one part of East Africa women don't eat chicken and men don't eat animal kidneys; whistling is forbidden among the Lakalai of New Britain (as offensive to spirits who protect their food supply). For the Jews there were many taboos, such as not eating food with the blood in it (v. 20), which they believed were God's laws. But now God was telling Peter to disregard these 'laws'. What could he do? The first thing he did was to protest, 'No, Lord.' Many great people began a new stage of their lives by protesting at God's command, e.g. Moses (Exod. 3.10–11; 4.10–11); Jonah (1.1–3).

The reason why Peter protested was because God was telling him to do something he had not done before: 'Lord; . . . I have never . . .'. Over and over again Christians fail to obey God because they do not believe that He really wants them to do something for the first time. When the Roman Catholic bishops met in 1962 it was decided that the Mass should usually be said in people's everyday language instead of in Latin. They believed that this was God's will. But some complained, 'We have never done this before.' What special thing do Christians need to do today which they have never done before?

10.15: What God has cleansed, you must not call common. The Jews made a clear distinction between what is 'holy' or 'clean' and what is 'common' or 'unclean'; rabbits were clean, but pigs were unclean; women were clean most of the time, but menstruating women were unclean; living Jews were clean, but the corpse of a Jew was unclean.

Peter may have heard Jesus say, 'Nothing outside a man can made him unclean' (Mark 7.14)—to which Mark added the words 'thus He declared all foods clean' (7.19). But it seems that Peter had not taken it seriously, for until this vision he followed the Jewish tradition. He divided God's creation into two parts, the 'holy' or 'clean', and the 'unholy' or 'unclean'.

In spite of the teaching of this verse, very many Christians have made the same mistake of dividing God's creation, e.g. by treating the Bible as holy, but money as unholy; treating prayers as clean, but sexual intercourse as unclean; treating Sunday as holy, but Monday as unholy; treating one race as clean, but another race as unclean. Paul warned us against splitting God's creation in this way: 'For "the earth is the Lord's, and everything in it" . . . So, whether you eat or drink, or whatever you do, do all to the glory of God' (1 Cor. 10.26,31).

10.23: He called them in to be his guests. Peter, the Jew, invited Gentiles to eat with him, just as he later accepted an invitation to eat in the Gentiles' house (11.3). So Peter broke the Jewish Law.

10.24: Cornelius . . . called together his kinsmen and close friends. It was not Cornelius alone who met Peter. There were friends and family who joined with him. See also 'two servants and a soldier' (10.7 and 19); 'many persons' (10.27); 'we are *all* here' (10.33). Peter also was joined by 'some of the brethren' (10.23b), the 'six brethren' (11.12). It seems that God wants us to take important decisions as members of a group rather than as separate individuals, e.g. sometimes He calls a whole family or all the members of a village to offer themselves together for baptism.

10.25: Peter entered, Cornelius met him. In this house in the part of Caesarea reserved for retired soldiers, not far from the sea, the event took place that changed the Church. Peter went into the house of the uncircumcised Gentile and they took food together (11.3). This meal was more important than any of the things that happened afterwards (e.g. the speaking in tongues, or the baptism, 10.44-48). Would there ever have been a Church today if Peter had become afraid and refused to eat with Gentiles? By taking part Peter broke Jewish laws and changed the rules of the Church.

Peter made this great change in response to God (as he firmly believed) and without first consulting the other Apostles. Since that time Christians have on many occasions had to answer the question, 'When is it right for Christians in one part of God's Church to make an important change in their rules?' For example, at this present time many are asking whether it is right for Churches to change their rules in order to ordain women (some have already done so). Christians hold different opinions e.g.

(a) That the only major changes that Christians are free to make have already been made and are recorded in the New Testament. The Apostles were male and no change was then made to that rule. So it is wrong to ordain women today, or make them bishops.

(b) That it is right to make such changes only if all Christian Churches agree that they should be made. Because not all Churches can agree to ordain women, women should not be ordained.

(c) That we ought to make such changes when our members believe that the Holy Spirit is guiding them to do so, in order that we may do God's work more effectively. So we are free to ordain women if we believe it is a wise change to make.

10.33: We are all here present in the sight of God, to hear all that you have been commanded by the Lord. By coming to Peter in this way, Cornelius and his friends set an important example to Christian congregations, e.g. (1) They realized that they were 'in the sight of God' (i.e. in God's presence), not only in the presence of Peter; (2) They wanted to discover God's will, not only to hear Peter's thoughts. (3) They had come with a desire to learn. A recent visitor to the weekly Bible Readings at St Makarios Monastery in Egypt, given by the Coptic Pope Shenouda, noticed not only the skill of the speaker, but also the enthusiasm of the listeners who travel into the desert each week to learn how to interpret the Bible.

10.34: Peter opened his mouth and said ... This is the first recorded sermon which any Christian preached to Gentiles. We note that in it Peter omitted the references to the Old Testament which he had used in his sermons to Jews, e.g. in 2.14–36.

The main points which he made are:

1. God has no favourites. He accepts anyone who reverences Him and does what is right (vv. 34–35, see note on 4.12).

2. It was through Jesus that God gave us the good news about reconciliation between different peoples (v.36). Jesus is Lord of *all*.

3. The events of Jesus's life, from His baptism to His resurrection (vv. 37–41).

4. Jesus is judge, but He enables everyone who believes in Him, of every race, to receive forgiveness of their sins (vv. 42–43).

10.44: While Peter was still saying this, the Holy Spirit fell on all who heard the word. Cornelius and his friends interrupted Peter's sermon by 'speaking in tongues' (see note on 2.4b), and Peter regarded this as a sign that they had received the Holy Spirit (see vv. 46–47).

10.48: He commanded them to be baptized in the name of Jesus Christ. On this occasion the people received the Holy Spirit first, and were baptized afterwards. The Samaritans were baptized first and received the Spirit later (8.12–17) (see Additional Note, Baptism, p. 79).

They were baptized 'in the name of Jesus Christ', as were most candidates in the early days of the Church. It was later that baptism was 'in the name of the Father, the Son and the Holy Spirit'.

11.2: When Peter went up to Jerusalem, the circumcision party criticized him. Peter took six witnesses with him when he went to Jerusalem, so perhaps he expected to be criticized, as Jesus had been criticized for eating with 'sinners' (Luke 15.2). The 'party' means the group of Jewish Christians who kept strictly to tradition. Probably some of the priests (6.7) or Pharisees (15.5) who belonged to the Church opposed Peter.

11.12: Making no distinction. i.e. between Jews and Gentiles.

11.18: They glorified God, saying 'Then to the Gentiles also God has granted repentance unto life'. As the result of Peter's explanation even those who held traditional ideas were able to thank God for what had happened (but they did not fully realize how important it was).

repentance. See note on 2.38a.

unto life. so that we can live as fully as God intended us to live (John 10.10).

STUDY SUGGESTIONS

REVIEW OF CONTENT

1. What two coastal towns do we read about in these verses? How far is it from one town to the other?
2. In these verses Luke uses the word 'angel' to refer to God making known His will. What two other words or phrases does he use for the same purpose?
3. Give two reasons why Peter went to Caesarea.
4. Why did Luke regard the meeting of Peter and Cornelius as specially important?
5. What was the main difference between the experience of Cornelius (and his friends) and that of the Samaritans (ch. 8)?
6. (a) What was the 'circumcision party' in Jerusalem?
   (b) Which action of Peter did that party criticize?

BIBLE STUDY

7. What do we learn about the Gentiles, or about God's plan for them, in each of the following passages:
   (a) Gen. 22.18   (b) Isa. 49.6   (c) Luke 2.29–32   (d) Acts 13.47
   (e) Acts 14.5   (f) Acts 26.17–20   (g) Rom. 11.25–27
8. 'In the New Testament we read of many people working in pairs, and it seems to be important for Christians to work in this way' (p. 102).
   (i) Read the following passages and say, if possible, in each case who the pairs were and what they were doing.
   (a) Matt. 18.15–16   (b) Mark 11.1   (c) Luke 10.1–9
   (d) Acts 10.7   (e) Acts 11.29–30   (f) Acts 19.22
   (ii) What has your experience been of working as one of a pair? What advantages did you find in doing so?

DISCUSSION AND APPLICATION

9. Two opinions concerning Peter's bringing Tabitha to life are given in the note on 9.40. What is your opinion? Give reasons.
10. The note on 10.15 gives examples of the way in which some Christians have divided or still divide God's creation. What other examples can you give of Christians making this mistake in the past or in the present? What do you think are the reasons why they do so?
11. 'Sometimes God calls a whole family or all the members of a village to offer themselves together for baptism' (p. 105)

(a) In what circumstances do you think God does so? How can people recognize His call?

(b) Describe any event of this sort of which you know.

12. 'When is it right for Christians in one part of God's Church to make a major change in the rules?' Three different answers to this question are quoted in the note on 10.25. What is your answer? Give your reasons.

13. 'Cornelius and his friends have set an important example to Christian congregations' (note on 10.33). In what ways did they 'set an example'? In what ways which are not referred to in the note on 10.33 should a congregation respond to a sermon?

11.19–30

The Mission in Syrian Antioch

OUTLINE

11.19–21: Greeks in Antioch become Christians.

11.22–24: The Church in Jerusalem sends Barnabas to investigate the event.

11.25–26: Barnabas and Paul work together in Antioch.

11.27–30: Agabus predicts a famine, and Paul and Barnabas are sent with famine relief to the Christians in Jerusalem.

INTERPRETATION

The baptism of Cornelius was, as we have seen, a very important event, because through it the Church began a new stage in its life (p. 105). But the birth of the Church in Syrian Antioch, which Luke describes here, may have been even more important. In the past, Gentiles who became Christians were 'proselytes' or 'God-fearers', or were people like Cornelius who were closely connected with the Jewish religion. So there was a link between such people and the Jewish followers of Jesus. But now for the first time people received the gospel who had no such links. They were Greeks. This is why we call the birth of the Church in Antioch a 'new' event and a 'turning-point'.

This event was new for two other reasons: (1) The unnamed 'men of Cyprus and Cyrene' (v. 20) visited Antioch as part of their activity as

Christians, not because they had received authority from the Apostles; nor were they 'elders' or 'prophets'. (2) The group of Gentiles who became Christians in Antioch were a strong body; previously only one or two individual Gentiles had become Christian.

There are many questions concerning this event to which we do not know the answer, e.g. Were other Churches, e.g. Alexandria, founded during this time and in the same way in which the Antioch Church was founded? But we do know that those of us who are Gentile Christians today are members of the Church partly because unnamed Jewish Christians broke away from tradition and welcomed Greeks into the Church.

NOTES

11.19: Those who were scattered ... travelled as far as Phoenicia and Cyprus and Antioch, speaking the word. Those who 'spoke the word' in Phoenicia (the country now called Lebanon) and in Cyprus and Antioch did so because of persecution (see 8.1–4). Many suffered greatly during that persecution. But what seemed at first to be nothing but disaster became an opportunity for missionary work. Those who had to escape from their homes to distant places lived and preached the gospel in their new surroundings. But most of them preached only to Jews.

The city of Antioch (today called Antakya) was in the north of Syria, in what is now Turkey. At that time it was the third largest city in the Roman Empire, and had a population of half a million. It was a Greek city, but most of the people were Syrians, and there were a great many Jews. It was an important centre of trade, with a large port, Seleucia, 7 kms away. We can see why Antioch rather than Jerusalem became the headquarters of the Church.

11.20: Men of Cyprus and Cyrene ... spoke to the Greeks also, preaching the Lord Jesus. This verse describes one of the most important events in the whole history of the Church. These 'men', Greek-speaking Jews, preached not only to Jews in Antioch but 'to the Greeks also'. Although they did such an important thing we do not know their names. We only know that some came from Cyprus, the large island 100 kms from Antioch in the Mediterranean Sea, and others from Cyrene, a city on the north coast of Africa, 300 kms away. In both places there were many Greek-speaking Jews.

They did not speak of Jesus as the Messiah (Christ) because Greeks would not have been interested. They spoke of Jesus as 'Lord', the One to whom total loyalty is due. The Greeks knew that word well (the Greek is *kyrios*).

Why did the Greeks 'turn to the Lord' (v. 21)? Surely it was because they had ceased to take seriously their old religion, and were searching for the true God. People cannot live fully without giving loyalty to someone or something greater than themselves.

11.22: The church in Jerusalem ... sent Barnabas to Antioch. The events in Antioch were so unusual that the leaders of the Church in Jerusalem wanted to know exactly what was happening. So they sent Barnabas to investigate (see note on 4.36).

Barnabas was a Greek-speaking Jew from Cyprus who was in Jerusalem at the time of Pentecost. Luke says that he was 'a good man' and 'full of the Holy Spirit and of faith' (11.24). Probably they chose him because both the Aramaic-speaking traditionalists and the Greek-speaking Hellenists trusted him. He did his investigation, and realized that God Himself had been at work in Antioch. God had shown His 'grace' (v. 23), i.e. had done more than anyone had hoped or deserved.

11.25: Barnabas went to Tarsus to look. for Saul. In 9.30 we read of Paul going to his home town of Tarsus after his conversion. It seems from Gal. 1.21 that he then spent fourteen years travelling in Syria and Cilicia (the province in which Tarsus was situated), preaching and teaching. It may have been during this time that he endured some of the sufferings to which he refers in 2 Cor. 11.23–27, and at the same time grew and developed as a Christian. When Barnabas needed help in Antioch he made the 280 kms journey to Tarsus. Then he had to 'look for' Paul, probably because Paul was travelling round Cilicia preaching the gospel. Finally he found him, and so Paul ceased to be a lonely missionary, and for a whole year became the partner of Barnabas and others in leading the growing Church in Antioch. There is still a cave-church there which may be the very place where they worshipped.

11.26: In Antioch the disciples were for the first time called Christians. For Jewish followers of Jesus the name 'Christ' meant 'the anointed Messiah we have waited for' (see note on 2.31). But later, as more and more Gentiles joined the Church, they used the name 'Christ' as a personal name, as we do today. So when the people of Antioch used this word 'Christian' they meant 'the followers of Jesus Christ'. Luke only uses the word here and in 26.28, and usually uses the words 'brethren' or 'disciples' or 'saints'.

It is important that we only use the word 'Christians' for those who genuinely try to follow Jesus Christ. Many people use it wrongly, e.g. as a name for a political party such as Christian Democrats.

11.27–28: Prophets came down from Jerusalem ... Agabus stood up and foretold ... a great famine. These 'prophets' were travelling preachers, some of whom predicted the future (see note on 15.32). Agabus was one of those who made predictions (see also 21.10).

The Jewish historian Josephus writes that there was a famine in

Judea in AD 46. That year was, as Luke says, during the reign of the Emperor Claudius.

11.29: The disciples determined, every one according to his ability, to send relief to the brethren who lived in Judea.

The disciples means the Christians of Antioch, and the 'brethren' means their fellow-Christians in Judea.

relief. This word is a translation of the Greek word *diakonia* which we usually translate 'ministry'. For New Testament writers there is only one ministry, which Christians do in different ways, as Jesus did. Some do it by preaching, others by nursing, and in other ways. In Antioch they did it by sending corn and money. See note on 21.19.

They were newly-converted Christians, but they understood better than many experienced Christians how to follow Jesus. Just as He relieved suffering when there was an opportunity, so did they, because they were His followers. For them there was no separation between believing in Jesus and being active for Him in the world. They had never seen the Christians of distant Judea, but they sent them relief. Most of them were Greeks, but they gladly sent corn to Jewish Christians. There was no racism or tribalism among them.

For the rest of his life Paul called on his fellow-Christians to send relief to the poor in Jerusalem (see Rom. 15.25–27; 1 Cor. 16.1–3; 2 Cor. 8.2; 2 Cor. 9; Gal. 2.10). He did this partly because sending and receiving relief was a way of uniting the Christians.

The Church in Antioch was able to do it because the country round Antioch was far more fertile than the hills of Judea. It was irrigated by the great River Orontes, and corn was not difficult to obtain. But the amount of aid which they sent to Judea was, of course, small compared to the aid which Christian bodies and others are sending to the famine areas today. The number of sufferers was small compared to those who suffer from famine today (more than 40,000 people die every day as the result of hunger). But the same Spirit of Jesus which moved Christians in Antioch still moves Christians today.

according to his ability. Each member contributed money or corn in proportion to what they possessed. Those who had much gave much, those who had less, gave less. Paul, in his letters, says that this is the right way to give. Each member should put something aside 'as he may prosper' (1 Cor. 16.2), and 'according to what a man has' (2 Cor. 8.12). This is still the right way for members of a congregation to give, whether they are contributing to their own Church or to strangers who are in trouble.

11.30: Sending it to the elders by the hand of Barnabas and Saul. So Barnabas and Paul took the corn and money, probably travelling by sea to Joppa and then on mules up to Jerusalem.

Most scholars think that this is the same visit to which Paul refers in

'Paul called on his fellow-Christians to send relief to the poor in Jerusalem . . . the same Spirit of Jesus . . . still moves Christians today' (p. 111).

Gifts of food, clothing, and medicines are here being distributed to people in Bangladesh who were suffering shortages, or were made homeless, as a result of disastrous floods.

Gal. 2.1–10. If this is so, then (1) it took place in AD 46; (2) they took the young Greek Titus with them; and (3) after delivering the corn to the elders, they met James, the brother of Jesus, as well as Peter and John. This visit was very important, not only because of the sharing that took place between one group of Christians and another but because Paul was able to return to Jerusalem after a long absence. During this visit he met Apostles who at last accepted him as a leader in the Church.

STUDY SUGGESTIONS

REVIEW OF CONTENT

1. In what way was the birth of the Church in Antioch a 'new' event and a 'turning point'?
2. Who first preached to the Greeks in Antioch?
3. Give two reasons why Antioch rather than Jerusalem became the headquarters of the Church.
4. Why did the Church in Jerusalem send Barnabas to Antioch?
5. Give three words in your own conversational English which describe the character of Barnabas.
6. Why did Barnabas have to search for Paul (v. 25)?

BIBLE STUDY

7. 'In Antioch the disciples were for the first time called Christians' (11.26):
   (i) What words does Luke use for the followers of Jesus in each of the following verses in Acts?
   (a) 6.1 (b) 9.13 (c) 9.26 (d) 10.23 (e) 11.1 (f) 26.10 (g) 26.28.
   (ii) Make a list of the various words which Christians and others use for present-day Church members.
   (iii) Which of those words do you think are the most suitable? Give reasons.
8. 'Send relief to the brethren in Judea' (11.29).
   (i) Read the following passages and say in each case what Paul was asking the Corinthians to do.
   (a) 1 Cor. 16.1–3 (b) 2 Cor. 8.1–2, 12–14 (c) 2 Cor. 9.1–5
   (ii) What guidance, if any, is there in those passages for Christians today?

DISCUSSION AND RESEARCH

9. 'People cannot live fully without giving loyalty to someone or something greater than themselves' (p. 111).
What is your opinion? If you agree, give examples both of religious people and of those who say that they are not religious.

10. What do you yourself mean by the word 'Christian'? What do you think non-Christians mean by the word?

11. 'Aid which Christian bodies and others are sending to famine areas today.' (p. 111).
(a) Discover and describe the work of one such body at work in one area of the world today, and say how the money or goods are distributed.

12. 'Each member contributed ... in proportion to what they possessed' (p. 111).
(a) To what extent do the members of your Church make their contributions in proportion to their possessions or incomes?
(b) In what way are members encouraged to give proportionately?

13. (a) In your opinion what were Barnabas's main achievements during the time referred to in 11.23–30?
(b) Which of them was the most important? Give reasons.

12.1–25

Herod Agrippa I Persecutes the Church

OUTLINE

12.1–5: Herod kills James the brother of John and imprisons Peter.
12.6–17: Peter escapes.
12.18–19: The guards are killed.
12.20–23: The death of Herod.
12.24: The growth of the Church.
12.25: Barnabas and Paul return to Antioch.

INTERPRETATION

We have read about officials of the Jewish religion persecuting the Church (see Acts 4 and Additional Note, Opposition and Persecution, pp. 44–50), and we shall study other opposition to the Church more closely in Ch. 21. In chapter 12 Luke tells of persecution carried out by Herod Agrippa I.

At the time to which Luke refers in this chapter, two events were coming to an end:

First, Peter was about to give way to Paul as the leading missionary, and to James the brother of Jesus as the leader of the Christians in Jerusalem (see note on v. 17).

Secondly, the early period during which the Church was mainly Jewish was ending, and from ch. 13 onwards we read about the Church becoming mainly a Gentile Church.

The events which Luke describes in ch. 12 took place *before* the ministry of Barnabas and Paul described in 11.19–30. The order of events was:

1. Herod's persecution (AD 44); 12.1–24.
2. Barnabas and Paul in Antioch and then travelling to Jerusalem (AD 46); 11.19–30.
3. They return from Jerusalem to Antioch; 12.25.

NOTES

12.1: Herod the king laid violent hands upon some who belonged to the church. See note on 4.27 on the four Herods. The Herod mentioned in this verse was Herod Agrippa I, grandson of Herod the Great. At this time he ruled over Southern Syria, Perea, Galilee and Judea. The Roman Emperor Caligula had given him the title of 'King'. He made himself popular with the Jews by keeping Jewish laws and ritual and (in the end) by persecuting Christian leaders.

12.2: He killed James, the brother of John. This is the James who was one of the Apostles whom Jesus chose to be with Him on special occasions (see Luke 9.28). So far as we know he was the first of the Apostles to die (except for Judas), and the followers of Jesus must have been very distressed. We know of the deep distress felt by Sudanese Christians when their Bishop Malou was killed when the plane in which he was travelling was shot down. (We do not know why Luke mentions James's death so briefly and without comment.)

The other James to whom Luke refers was the brother of Jesus (see note on v. 17).

12.3: Herod proceeded to arrest Peter also. Herod arrested Peter in order to gain popularity among the Jews, and intended to kill him. But he kept Jewish ritual carefully, so he postponed the execution until the end of the Passover Festival (which Luke calls the Festival of Unleavened Bread).

12.5: Earnest prayer for him was made. Luke very often refers to the prayers of Jesus and of His followers (see note on 1.14). In this chapter he refers to the Christians' prayers twice, here and in v. 12. Note the word 'earnest' in v. 5 and compare Luke 22.44.

According to this passage the Christians prayed and Peter was set free. What do we learn here about prayers of asking, especially asking God to save us and others from great trouble? People have different beliefs about this:

(a) Some say that if Christians pray with enough faith God will always deliver them and those for whom they pray, as He delivered Peter.

(b) Others point out that Jesus prayed to be delivered from the 'cup of death' (Luke 22.42), but that God did not deliver Him. Indeed, God does not usually get Christians *out* of trouble however much faith they have. He gives them power to go *through* the trouble.

(c) All Christians agree that it is right to pray in all situations and that it is right to tell God of our needs (see Phil. 4.6).

But Jesus taught that prayer is chiefly getting in touch with God rather than getting something *from* God: 'Our Father . . . your will be done'.

12.6: Peter was sleeping between two soldiers. Peter was expecting to be killed the very next day, but he had such trust in God that he had peace of mind and so was able to sleep (see Rom. 14.8).

12.7: An angel of the Lord appeared, and a light shone. This is Luke's way of saying that God Himself was setting Peter free (see notes on 5.19 and 9.3). How should we interpret this event?

In a recent discussion about Peter's escape, three students interpreted it in three different ways:

1. That it was a miracle: 'It was done by God directly and without human co-operation. Luke and Peter believed this (see v. 11), and if we do not believe it, we do not believe in God.'

2. That God used a human being: 'A Roman soldier who was a friend of Christians or one whom Christians had paid to obtain the keys. It is not less God's work if He acts through a human being. God was not different then from what He is now, and in my experience God does not rescue Christians from their prisons, e.g. in S. America, except through human co-operation.'

3. That it is a mystery: 'We cannot ever know what happened, i.e. whether God acted "directly" or "indirectly". When a friend of mine recovered from a very severe illness after the doctors had said that she could never recover, I shared my joy with God, but could not tell what had caused her recovery.'

12.12: He went to the house of Mary, the mother of John whose other name was Mark. This house was perhaps the same house where Jesus celebrated the Last Supper, where His followers met at Pentecost, and which became a headquarters for Christians (see note on 1.13).

Luke mentions John Mark here for the first time. Later on he tells of his work (see note on 12.25).

12.13–14: Rhoda did not open the gate. Rhoda was the girl whom Mark's mother employed. Her feelings of joy and surprise were so great that she did not use her brains. She left Peter standing in the road and thus in great danger of being rearrested (the authorities knew that this house was a Christian headquarters).

12.15: It is his angel! The people in Mary's house assumed that Peter had been killed and that Rhoda was saying that she had 'seen his ghost'. Jews believed that each person has a 'guardian angel'; it was their way of saying that God has special concern for each person (see Matt 18.10 and note on 5.19).

12.17b: Tell this to James and to the brethren: This James was the brother of Jesus. Apart from Mary, the mother of Jesus, His family did not at first believe in Him (see John 7.5). But Paul said in 1 Cor. 15.7, that Jesus 'appeared' to James after He had risen, and after that James became a leader in the Church. Like other Aramaic-speaking Christian Jews he kept to Jewish traditions, with the result that the traditionalists put their confidence in him. But he was also open to new ideas (see note on 15.13).

12.17c: Peter departed and went to another place. Peter went into hiding, as many Christian leaders must do today when dictators become afraid of opposition and believe that the Church may be part of it. Luke does not tell us where Peter went, and only refers to him once again (15.7–11).

But Peter was not only ceasing to live in Jerusalem, he was also ceasing to be the leading missionary of the Church and the leader of Christians in Jerusalem. It was Paul who became the leader, because he worked among Gentiles (see Gal. 2.9). There even came a time when Paul rebuked Peter publicly (Gal. 2.11).

When we consider what Peter had done from Pentecost onwards, we can understand how painful it was for him to give up his old position, and to see others doing what he used to do (see note on 13.13). This is the reason why, when people retire from their life's work, or see others getting the promotion which they themselves had hoped for, they need much support.

Although Peter ceased to lead the Church in Jerusalem, there is a well-known tradition, supported by some second-century writers, that he became Bishop of Rome and died there as a martyr.

12.19: He examined the sentries and ordered that they should be put to death. Peter was saved but the sentries died. It was the custom for guards to be killed if they let a prisoner escape.

There are questions concerning this event that trouble some readers, e.g. (a) Four sentries died because Peter was saved; does this mean that Peter's life was more important in God's eyes than the lives of the sentries? (b) Are the lives of Christians more important to Him than the lives of others? (c) How can we judge whose life is the more important? (d) What did the wives of the sentries think? (e) What did Peter think?

12.20: Herod was angry with the people of Tyre and Sidon. He was probably angry because they were demanding that he should sell them food from Judea at a low cost. We know that from the time of Solomon the people of Tyre and Sidon needed food from Judea (1 Kings 5.9). In order to put their case before Herod they 'persuaded' (i.e. bribed) his treasurer Blastus to arrange a meeting in Caesarea. Josephus, the Jewish historian, also describes this meeting and Herod's death.

12.23: An angel of the Lord smote him. This is Luke's interpretation of Herod's death, i.e. that God killed him because he allowed the people to call him a 'god'. When Bishop David Jenkins was made a bishop in the great cathedral of York Minster in England in 1985, the cathedral was struck by lightning, and some Christians who disapproved of the bishop's teaching said that God had struck the building because He too disapproved of the bishop's teaching. The Jews certainly believed that God 'smote' sinners in this way (see e.g. Ezek. 7.9). But Jesus did not believe or teach that. See Luke 13.2–5: 'Do you think that ... those eighteen upon whom the tower of Siloam fell and killed them were worse offenders than all the others? ... I tell you, No.'

12.24: The word of God grew. In these words Luke was summing up what had happened up to that moment, and noting that the Church was making progress. He did the same in 6.7 and 9.31.

In the Bible, writers use the phrase 'the word of God' in four chief ways, to mean: (1) God's will or law, which He communicates to mankind (see Jer. 2.4); (2) God's Law as it has been written down. This is its meaning in Psalm 119 (see v. 16); (3) Jesus, God's visible communication to man (John 1.1); (4) The gospel message, the good news about Jesus (as in this verse).

12.25: Barnabas and Saul returned from Jerusalem ... bringing with them John whose other name was Mark. They went back to Antioch after giving the aid to the sufferers in Jerusalem. See the last paragraph in the Interpretation, p. 115.

STUDY SUGGESTIONS

REVIEW OF CONTENT

1. 'At the time to which Luke refers in this chapter two events were coming to an end' (p. 115). What were these two events?

2. Why did Herod kill James and imprison Peter?
3. Who prayed for Peter when he was in prison?
4. Who accompanied Barnabas and Paul on their journey to Antioch?

BIBLE STUDY

5. 'James, one of the apostles whom Jesus chose to be with Him on special occasions' (p. 115). What were these occasions according to the following passages?
   (a) Mark 1.29–31   (b) Luke 8.51   (c) Luke 9.28
   (d) Mark 13.3–4   (e) Mark 14.32–33?
6. In what way does Paul in Rom. 14.8 help to explain Acts 12.6?
7. Bible writers use the phrase 'the word of God' in four chief ways:
   (1) God's will; (2) God's will as it has been written down; (3) Jesus;
   (4) The gospel message (note on 12.24).
   (i) What does the phrase mean in each of the following verses?
   (a) 1 Sam. 9.27   (b) Ps. 119.42   (c) John 1.14
   (d) Acts 12.24   (e) Acts 13.44
   (ii) Which of those four meanings does the phrase 'word of God' have when Christians use it today?

DISCUSSION AND RESEARCH

8. The Christians prayed for Peter when he was in prison. What do we learn from this passage about asking God to save us from trouble? Read the different answers on p. 116 and give your own opinion.
9. Read again the comments of three students on Peter's escape, recorded in the note on 12.7.
   (a) With which of them (if any) do you agree?
   (b) What is your own opinion, and what are your reasons?
10. 'Four soldiers died because Peter was saved. Does this mean that Peter's life was more important in God's eyes than the lives of the sentries?' (p. 118). What is your answer to this question and to the other questions in that paragraph?
11. 'The angel of the Lord smote Herod. This is Luke's interpretation of Herod's death' (p. 118). After considering Luke 13.2–5, how do you interpret that event?

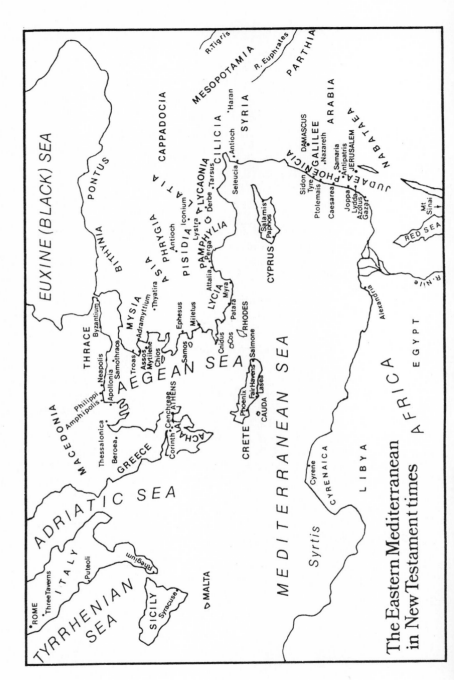

The Eastern Mediterranean in New Testament times

13.1–12

The Mission to Cyprus

OUTLINE

13.1–3: The Church in Syrian Antioch sends out Barnabas and Paul as evangelists.

13.4–12: Their work in Cyprus, first in Salamis, later in Paphos.

INTERPRETATION

Chapter 13 is of special interest because in it (and in the following chapters) Luke tells us of another new stage in the history of the Church. In what ways was this a new stage?

First, *the Church itself* became a missionary or 'sending' Church. Previously, outstanding leaders like Philip, and Peter and Paul had personally done evangelism. But now in Syrian Antioch it was the whole congregation who invited Barnabas and Paul to be their representatives, and who sent them out. The Church, as a body, had become missionary (13.3). So today a congregation as a whole is responsible for evangelism, and must not depend on an outstanding evangelist from its members or from outside to do the work. In the Moravian Church (one of whose members, Peter Böhler, greatly influenced John Wesley) every member is regarded as a missionary.

Secondly, they were sending their representatives *to Gentiles*. Some Christians had already, here and there, been leading Gentiles to faith in Jesus (Gentiles who had no connection with the synagogues, see 11.20). But now the Church in Antioch was giving authority to a mission to these Gentiles.

Thirdly, *Paul became the leader* of this work (13.13). *Note*: The journey described in chs 13 and 14 is usually called Paul's First Missionary Journey, but from Gal. 1.21–24 we see that he had already travelled in Cilicia and Syria and done missionary work there.

NOTES

13.1: There were prophets and teachers. See Additional Note, Leaders in the Church, p. 126.

The five people named in this verse shared in the work of ministry at Antioch. They were: Barnabas (a Jew from Cyprus), Simeon called 'Niger' (Niger means black, so perhaps he was an African), Lucius (who came from North Africa), Manaen (who had played with Herod Antipas when they were both children), and Paul. From them the Church chose two to go on the journey.

13.2a: Worshipping the Lord and fasting. According to the Old Testament the Jews fasted often and for various reasons (see 2 Sam. 12.16–23; Joel 2.12). But in this verse we are reminded that Jesus taught that it is good for us to fast if it helps us to pray (Luke 4.2). In the early days of the Church His followers probably fasted for this reason (see 14.23 and note on 17.9). But it seems that there was no rule about fasting (see note on 27.9).

13.2b: The Holy Spirit said, 'Set apart for me Barnabas and Saul'. There was no vision or dream. The words mean that after fasting and praying together the leaders of the congregation believed that God wanted Barnabas and Paul to be chosen (see also 20.28). The Holy Spirit gives guidance through human beings today, although even the best Christian leaders, being human, do not always interpret the Spirit correctly. It is not easy to tell the difference between being led by the Spirit on the one hand, and, on the other hand, being led by human advisers who may only be expressing opinions which are popular at that time.

13.3: They laid their hands on them. 'Laying on of hands' is an act of sharing something important in the name of God. Moses laid his hands on Joshua in order to pass on to him the leadership of the Israelites (Num. 27.18–23).

Christians laid their hands on people for two main reasons: (1) To give the other person the authority to serve in the name of God; that is the meaning here (see also 6.6; 1 Tim. 4.14; 2 Tim. 1.6); (2) To enable someone to receive God's power, e.g. to be blessed (Mark 10.16), to receive the Holy Spirit (Acts 8.17; 19.6), to be healed (9.12; 28.8).

In Antioch those who did the laying on of hands also prayed, showing that it was God who had given the gift. It had not been passed on mechanically (see 6.6; 8.15).

13.4: They went down to Seleucia ... to Cyprus. From Syrian Antioch, Barnabas and Paul went down the river by boat to the port of Seleucia. Then from Seleucia they sailed in another ship to Salamis, the chief commercial town of Cyprus.

13.5a: They proclaimed the word of God in the synagogues. There had been Jewish Christians in Cyprus since the time when they came as refugees from the persecution referred to in 11.19, 20, but Luke does not say that Barnabas and Paul visited them. Instead they went to the

Jewish synagogues, as Paul did throughout his journeys (see note on 13.46). There were a great many Jews in Cyprus, working in the copper mines.

Why did Paul go to the Jews? Partly because, being a Jew himself, he felt at home in the synagogues. Like many evangelists and missionaries, he began his work by meeting people with whom he had something in common. Similarly, preachers often begin a sermon by talking about an event which is familiar to the hearers.

13.5b: They had John to assist them. John Mark was the son of Mary, whose house was for a time the headquarters of Christians in Jerusalem (see notes on 1.13; 12.12). Now he joined Barnabas and Paul (perhaps it was Barnabas, his cousin, who invited him). He may have been the Mark who wrote the Gospel twenty years later, and who, according to one tradition, got his information from Peter. See also notes on 13.13 and 15.39.

13.7: The proconsul Sergius Paulus ... summoned Barnabas and Saul. They travelled across Cyprus and reached Paphos where the Roman Governor lived. His new title was 'Proconsul' (formerly it had been 'Procurator'). Luke uses the correct title, showing that he took trouble to get his facts accurate in writing Acts.

The proconsul invited them in and they taught him. But he had in his household a fortune-teller or astrologer, called Elymas Bar-Jesus, who tried to interrupt the conversation. Perhaps he thought that he would lose his job with the proconsul if his master became a Christian. He thought that a Christian would have nothing to do with fortune-telling. And he was right. Christians should entrust their future into the hands of God Himself instead of depending on human astrologers. See Acts 1.7 and notes on 8.9 and 19.11.

The proconsul 'believed' (v. 12), but Luke does not tell us if he became a Christian.

13.10: You son of the devil. Paul not only used these strong words, but caused Elymas to be blind for a time. People interpret this verse in different ways: (a) Some people think that Paul was right to do this, and that (as Luke says) he was inspired by the Spirit. They point to John 20.23: 'If you retain the sins of any they are retained', i.e. there are people whom a Christian leader must condemn in order to stand up for the truth. (b) Others point out that Paul, being human, was not free from error. They ask, 'Why did he not rebuke Elymas, but at the same time help him to a new way of living? They see harsh condemnation such as this as a sign of weakness in Paul, and point also to Acts 23.3–5. But we need not be surprised to find that Paul had weaknesses. All God's servants are sinners – but they know how to be forgiven. See note on 26.10.

'The Church was giving authority to a mission . . . authority to serve in the name of God' (p. 121).

This Italian bishop, on behalf of the Church, commissions and gives authority to four 'lay priests' to serve in God's name.

ADDITIONAL NOTE: LEADERS IN THE CHURCH

In the early days of the Church there were two sorts of leaders referred to in Acts: those who were officially appointed, and those who were not.

THOSE OFFICIALLY APPOINTED

1. *The Twelve Apostles* whom Jesus chose. There is no detailed information in the New Testament as to what He gave them authority to do, and this is a major reason why Christians are not united today.

All scholars agree that Jesus commissioned the Apostles to administer the Church (Acts 6.2–3) and to hand down the true gospel to others, (Acts 1.22). But on other matters scholars hold different opinions.

(a) Some (quoting Matt. 16.19) believe that Jesus commissioned the Apostles to pass on their authority to those who came afterwards and who were later called 'bishops', in order that those 'bishops' should pass on that authority to others, and so on.

(b) Others point out that there is no evidence in the Gospels that Jesus commissioned the Apostles in the way noted above and no evidence in Acts that the Apostles did pass on their authority in that way. It was Jesus's brother, James, not an Apostle, who presided at the Jerusalem meetings (15.13). It was Paul and Barnabas, not the Apostles, who appointed 'Elders' (14.23 and see notes on Elders below and on 15.2b).

It seems that in the early Church some congregations held one view, and other congregations held another view, and that there was no one official doctrine. Today we do not know enough to say what Jesus intended.

2. *The Seven* who were appointed by the Apostles to do social work that needed to be done at that time (see note on 6.2–6).

3. *Elders* (this word translates the Greek word *presbyteroi*) who were leaders of the Christians in one town or area. In Acts 20.28 Luke calls them *episcopoi*, which we translate as 'overseers' or 'guardians'. Some people believe that those who were later called 'bishops' were the successors of these 'Elders' rather than the successors of the Apostles (see note on 20.28).

THOSE NOT OFFICIALLY APPOINTED

These were leading Christians who believed that God had given them a gift to do special work. The Church gave them permission to work, but did not usually appoint them as leaders. In Acts Luke mentions two groups of 'unofficial leaders':

1. *Prophets* who travelled to any place where they were needed. When an important event took place they spoke in God's name to strengthen their fellow-Christians (see 15.32). Some, like Agabus (11.28; 21.10–11), predicted the future, often by speaking in tongues, but most prophets preached and gave counsel rather than predicting the future or speaking in tongues (1. Cor. 14.4–5). Paul taught that in public worship it was more helpful to preach than to speak 'in tongues' (1 Cor. 1).

2. *Teachers* who probably did work similar to that of the prophets, but mainly in their own local congregations (see Acts 13.1; Rom. 12.7).

3. *Paul and Barnabas* were prophets and teachers but they were more than prophets or teachers (13.1). They were such outstanding leaders that in two verses (Acts 14.4 and 14) Luke calls them 'Apostles'. But they did not belong to the Twelve, and there is no evidence in the New Testament that any of the Twelve gave them the same authority which they themselves had been given by Jesus. Paul also calls himself an Apostle in his letters (e.g. Rom. 1.1; 1 Cor. 1.1, etc.), partly because the word means 'someone who is sent' and partly because he believed that God had commissioned him just as truly as He had commissioned the Twelve. But, except in Acts 14.4 and 14, no New Testament writer calls him an Apostle.

STUDY SUGGESTIONS

REVIEW OF CONTENT

1. In what *two* ways did the Church move into a 'new stage' according to Ch. 13?
2. Who appointed Barnabas and Paul to go on the journey?
3. Where were (a) Seleucia, and (b) Salamis?
4. Whom did Barnabas and Paul visit first in Cyprus?
5. What three groups of Church leaders were officially appointed in the early days of the Church?
6. Why did Paul call himself an Apostle?

BIBLE STUDY

7. 'Worshipping the Lord and fasting' (v. 2).
(i) Why was fasting practised: (a) By David (2 Sam. 12.16–22)? (b) By Jesus (Luke 4.2)? (c) By the Christians of Antioch (Acts 13.2)? (d) By the 'hypocrites' (Matt 6.16)?
(ii) How important do you think it is for Christians to fast? Give reasons.

8. 'John to assist them' (v. 5).
   What do we discover about John from each of the following verses?
   (a) 13.5   (b) 13.13   (c) 15.38   (d) 2 Tim. 4.11
   (e) 1 Pet. 5.13?
9. What can we learn about the work of New Testament prophets in each of the following passages?
   (a) Acts 11.27–28   (b) Acts 15.32   (c) Rom. 12.6
   (d) 1 Cor. 12.28   (e) 1 Cor. 14.4–5   (f) Eph. 4.11–12

DISCUSSION AND RESEARCH

10. 'A congregation as a whole is responsible for evangelism, and must not depend on an outstanding evangelist from its members or from outside' (p. 121). To what extent is your own congregation responsible for, and engaged in, evangelism?
11. (a) On what occasions, if any, have you witnessed the laying on of hands?
    (b) Say in each case why it was done.
    (c) What difference do you think it would have made if words only had been used?
12. 'A Christian would have nothing to do with fortune-telling' (p. 125). (a) Why would the Christians of Paul's time have nothing to do with fortune-telling?
    (b) How far do you think this statement is true of Christians since that time? How far is it true of Christians today? How far *ought* it to be true, and why?
13. 'You son of the devil'. The note on 13.10 gives two different opinions concerning Paul's words to Elymas. What is your own opinion, and why?
14. Read again the Additional Note, Leaders, concerning the authority which Jesus gave to the Apostles. What is the official teaching of your Church on this subject?

13.13–52

The Mission to Antioch-near-Pisidia

OUTLINE

13.13: Paul and Barnabas in Perga.
13.14–15: Their long journey to Antioch-near-Pisidia.
13.16–43: Paul's sermon and the people's request for further teaching.
13.44–52: Jews oppose Paul and Barnabas, Gentiles accept their teaching.

INTERPRETATION

In 13.1–3, we saw how the Church in Syrian Antioch sent out Paul and Barnabas as their representatives to preach the gospel in new areas. At first they met members of the Jewish synagogues, Jews, and Gentile 'proselytes' and Gentile 'God-fearers' (see notes on 2.10; 10.2). But now in Antioch-near-Pisidia, Gentiles who had no connection with the synagogues (see vv. 44–52) came to listen to their message.

This Antioch was near the district called Pisidia but was not in it, and was, of course, not the same as Syrian Antioch. It was an important Roman military headquarters, probably built to keep order in that wild country, and important roads passed through it. Its people included retired Roman soldiers, many of whom regarded their Emperor as a god, Greek settlers, and the indigenous inhabitants, the Phrygians. Many Phrygians were slaves, and all of them did the unpopular manual work of the city.

The whole area referred to in these verses and in ch. 14 was in the Roman Province of Galatia. When Paul later wrote his letter to the Galatians he was probably writing to those who became Christians as a result of the evangelism of which we read here and in ch. 14.

NOTES

13.13: Paul and his company ... came to Perga. They went by boat from Paphos to the mainland of Pamphylia in Asia Minor, stopping at Attalia before going on to Perga. It was there that John Mark left them, and Paul and Barnabas went on to Antioch without him.

It seems from this verse that Paul now led the expedition, and that Barnabas (who had been the leader) accepted second place. Many people who have held positions of leadership find it difficult to accept second place afterwards.

13.14: They ... came to Antioch of Pisidia. No one knows why they did not stay in Perga, but instead made the long journey to Antioch across the Tarsus mountains.

The Romans made their roads straight, and many of them went over mountains (as this one did) and were so steep that carriages and waggons were of no use. Travellers had to walk by day and sleep under rocks by night. The Romans were able to keep order in most of the Empire, but this part of it was full of terrorists, and the journey was extremely dangerous (this may be the reason why John Mark went home). Paul seems to have been ill when he was in Antioch (Gal. 4.13), perhaps as the result of this journey. He may be referring to the journey in 2 Cor. 11.26 ('dangers from robbers') and in Phil. 4.12 ('I have learnt the secret of facing plenty and hunger').

13.15: After the reading of the Law. The order of the synagogue service was (a) the recital of the 'Shema' (Deut. 6.4 and 5); (b) a prayer by the leader; (c) readings from the Law (the first five books of the Old Testament) and from the Prophets; (d) an address; (e) the blessing.

The synagogue leader perhaps saw from Paul's clothes that he was a Rabbi, and so asked him to give the address.

13.16: Men of Israel, and you that fear God. In his sermon Paul was addressing the God-fearers (see note on 2.10) just as much as the Jews (see also v. 26).

The sermon is in three parts:

1. Paul tells the history of the Jews from the time they were slaves in Egypt to the coming of John the Baptist and of Jesus Himself, showing that everything had happened according to God's plan (vv. 16–25).

2. He explains that Jesus's death was followed by His resurrection, thus showing that God's plan was not defeated (vv. 26–37).

3. He calls upon his hearers to accept God's gifts of 'forgiveness' and 'freedom' (vv. 38–39), and solemnly warns them not to miss this opportunity (vv. 40–41).

13.25: John ... said ... I am not he. See note on 19.2–5.

13.26: Brethren. See also v. 38. The 'God-fearers' had probably never before heard themselves called 'brothers' by a Jew.

13.27–28: Those who live in Jerusalem ... asked Pilate to have Him killed. We have already noticed (note on 2.23b) that, according to Luke, the first Christians blamed Jews of Judea rather than the Romans for the death of Jesus, perhaps in order not to give offence to the Roman authorities. But here Paul mentions the Roman governor Pilate as well as the Jews 'in Jerusalem' as being responsible.

13.30: God raised Him. Paul, like Peter, emphasized in his sermon the fact that Jesus rose from the dead (see also vv. 31–35).

13.33: Thou art my Son. This is the first of three references to the Old Testament and comes from Psalm 2.7. The second (v. 34) is from Isaiah 55.3, and the third (v. 35) from Psalm 16.10. Paul, who interpreted the Old Testament in the same way in which Peter did (2.14–36), explains that in each case the words refer to the Messiah, not to David. Psalm 2.7 is a difficult verse for Muslims who are making enquiries about Jesus. The Qur'an forbids Muslims to say that God has a 'son'.

13.38–39a: Forgiveness of sins is proclaimed . . . every one that believes is freed. Here Paul was declaring a truth which, for him, was specially important, as we see from his letters to Galatians and to Romans. He was saying, 'As the result of the death and rising again of Jesus, you can have a new and right relationship with God.' In order to explain this, he used two words, 'forgiveness' and 'freedom'.

By *'forgiving'* God restores us to full fellowship with Himself in spite of our wrong-doing (see note on 26.18). We may compare His action to the action of friends who forgive us although we have injured them, or to the father in Jesus's parable who welcomed home the son who had wasted much of his life (Luke 15.20–24).

By *'freeing'* us, God releases us from the pain of being separated from Him. The Greek word here translated 'freed' is usually translated 'justified' or 'acquitted', e.g. in Paul's letters, and is a word used in the law courts. Paul means, 'God wipes away the accusation and treats you as one treats an innocent person.'

Paul could not avoid using picture-language (e.g. the language of families or of the law courts) when talking about our relationship with God, nor can any Christian avoid such language. But it is important to see what is behind the language. To interpret it literally would lead to misunderstanding.

We should note that: (1) We *cannot buy* God's forgiveness. It is always His gift (Rom. 3.23, 24); (2) When God forgives us He is *not pretending* that we are innocent; He knows our sinfulness and accepts us in spite of it; (3) When we are forgiven *we do not escape the results* of our sins; e.g. those who steal can be forgiven by God, but they must give what they stole back to the owners.

Paul emphasizes that this good news is for *'everyone'* (v. 39a).

13.39b: You could not be freed by the law of Moses. The only way in which we can have a right relation with God is by trusting Jesus and what He has done. Keeping the Jewish Law is not an effective way (see Rom. 3.28; 9.30–31; 10.4).

13.40: Beware. Alongside the good news that God is ready to accept us into a right relationship with Himself, Paul gives a severe warning. 'Do not miss the opportunity of receiving God's forgiveness. To miss it is to be lost.' Christian preaching includes both giving the good news and giving a warning or even a condemnation.

13.43: Many Jews and devout converts to Judaism followed. This happened at the end of the first Sabbath which Paul spent in Antioch. The 'devout converts' were the 'proselytes' (see note on 2.10). These were Gentiles who had the opportunity in Antioch of meeting many different religions (e.g. Persian, Egyptian, Roman), but who had chosen to associate with the Jews because they admired the Jewish way of living, their cleanliness, their family life.

13.44: The next sabbath almost the whole city gathered. Until this time it was Jews and their proselytes and God-fearers who had met Paul, but now the rest of the people came: Romans, Greeks and Phrygian slaves. So at last Paul and Barnabas were meeting Gentiles ('the multitudes' v. 45) who had no connection with the Jews. In this verse and in vv. 46–50 we are reading of a 'new stage' in the life of the Christian Church.

But the result was that the Jews who had listened to Paul a week before began to attack him (v. 45). They did so believing that it was wicked to say that 'everyone' (even uncircumcised people) could have full fellowship with God.

13.46: It was necessary that the word of God should be spoken first to you. Since you thrust it from you ... we turn to the Gentiles. They were brave to say this (see the word 'boldly') because the Jews could have had them beaten. It was an important statement because: (1) as in Syrian Antioch Christians gladly welcomed into the Church Gentiles who had no connection with the synagogues; (2) Paul did not say it in anger or in order to hit back at the Jews, but in the belief that 'turning to the Gentiles' was God's will (see v. 47 and 9.15); (3) And in spite of these words Paul continued to visit the Jews first in whatever place he was (see 14.1); he believed that this also was God's plan (see Rom. 1.16); (4) to the end of his life Paul was concerned that both Jews and Gentiles should be saved (Rom. 2.10,11).

13.48: As many as were ordained to eternal life believed. Some scholars think that 'ordained' here means 'predestined', i.e. that Luke believed that when people are born God chooses some for eternal life and marks others for eternal separation from Him (see note on 4.28). But others point out that the Greek word here translated 'ordained' was used to describe soldiers being lined up for battle, and explain the verse as 'Those whom God had prepared and who were at that time ready for eternal life believed.'

13.50: The Jews drove them out. See Additional Note, Opposition and Persecution, p. 50. We may note that whenever Paul preached in Jewish synagogues after this he was rejected (see e.g. 14.2; 17.1–5). On this occasion influential women God-fearers and 'leading men' (perhaps magistrates) helped the synagogue leaders to expel Paul and Barnabas.

The God-fearers were probably angry that people were welcomed into the Church and into full fellowship with God without having to perform any of the duties which God-fearers undertook in the synagogue.

13.51: They shook off the dust from their feet. This was not a curse. It was a sign that for a period of time they were not concerned with the people who were rejecting them, and were entering on a new piece of work (see Luke 9.5).

13.52: The disciples were filled with joy and with the Holy Spirit. After Paul and Barnabas had left Antioch the new Christians in the town met together, in each other's houses. They were more and more filled with joy and the Holy Spirit, they 'kept on being filled' (this is the real meaning of the Greek word here translated 'were filled'). They were *growing* as Christians.

STUDY SUGGESTIONS

REVIEW OF CONTENT

1. Where are the two towns which are both called Antioch in this chapter?
2. What do we call the letter which Paul afterwards wrote to the Christians of whom we read in these verses?
3. What different groups of people were there in the city referred to in 13.43?
4. Why were Paul and Barnabas expelled?
5. What is known about the Christians who remained in Antioch after Paul and Barnabas had left?

BIBLE STUDY

6. RSV translates the Greek word *dikaio* in v. 39 as 'being freed'. Other translations are 'being justified', 'being absolved'. How is the word translated (i) in RSV; (ii) in another language or other English version in each of the following verses?
   (a) Luke 18.14   (b) Rom. 3.24   (c) Rom. 6.7   (d) 1 Cor. 4.4
   (e) Gal. 2.16
7. 'Paul was concerned that both Jews and Gentiles should be saved' (p. 131). What does Paul say about Jews and Gentiles in each of the following?
   (a) Rom. 2.9–11   (b) Rom. 9.3–5   (c) Rom. 10.1
   (d) Rom. 11.11–14   (e) 1 Cor. 9.20–21

DISCUSSION AND RESEARCH

8. 'John left them' (v. 13). Suggest two reasons why John Mark may have gone home.

9. (a) Which of Paul's sufferings (that he refers to in 2 Cor. 11.23–27) do you think he endured on the journey from Perga to Antioch?
(b) What enables Christians to endure sufferings of that kind?

10. Read again the order of service for synagogue worship in the note on 13.15.
(a) What are the greatest differences between that service and the main Sunday Church service to which you are accustomed?
(b) What has caused the changes?

11. 'Christian preaching includes both giving the good news and giving a warning' (note on 13.40).
(a) Is this true of the present-day sermons you hear? If not, should it be? Give your reasons.
(b) A reader said 'Warnings are necessary in sermons but condemnation is un-Christian'. What is your opinion? Give an example to support it.

12. 'The Qur'an forbids Muslims to say that God has a "son"' (p. 130). If you were talking with a Muslim about Jesus, what words would you use when speaking about His relationship to God?

13. Two interpretations of the words 'as many as were ordained to eternal life' are given in the note on 13.48. Which of them do you accept, and why?

14.1–28

The Mission to Iconium and Lystra

OUTLINE

14.1–7: Paul and Barnabas preach in Iconium, but have to escape.
14.8–18: In Lystra:
   (a) they heal a cripple,
   (b) they are treated as gods by the inhabitants,
   (c) Paul addresses the crowds.
14.19–20: Paul is stoned but travels to Derbe, and returns to Lystra.
14.21–28: Paul and Barnabas revisit the newly-founded Churches, and return to Syrian Antioch.

INTERPRETATION

Paul and Barnabas continued their work in Galatia, visiting towns and villages, and doing so with success. Again it is useful to remember that it was to the Christians of these places that Paul wrote his letter to the Galatians.

Ch. 14 is of special interest, and important to modern pastors and evangelists, for three reasons:

1. Paul and Barnabas were ready to do work that was new to them. In chs. 11 and 13 we saw that there were some Gentiles who became Christians, although they had not been connected with the synagogues. But in Lystra (vv. 8–18) the mission was entirely to Gentiles, and Paul preached to Gentiles who had no connection with the synagogues, perhaps for the first time.

2. In almost every place there was opposition, but Paul and Barnabas refused to give up the work (see note on v. 22).

3. They took care to follow up their work, e.g. to revisit the groups of new Christians, and to appoint leaders who could continue the care of the congregations (see note on v. 23).

NOTES

14.1: At Iconium. From Antioch-near-Pisidia to Iconium (the modern name is Konya), was 150 kms, and again the long road went over high mountains. At first Paul and Barnabas were welcomed by the synagogue ('a great company believed'), but then there was opposition (v. 2). (There is opposition to the gospel in the modern city, where 99.9 per cent of the people are Muslims.) The 'Greeks' were God-fearers. If they had not been God-fearers, they would not have been in the synagogue.

14.3a: Speaking boldly for the Lord, who bore witness to the word of his grace. I.e. they preached in spite of the opposition. Grace was the subject of their preaching or 'word'. God showed His 'grace' by enabling them to heal the sick (see note on 4.13 for the word 'boldly').

In his letter to these Galatians Paul later reminded them of God's 'grace', that is His generosity in accepting us although we have done nothing to deserve it (see Gal. 5.4 and note on 18.27).

14.3b: Signs and wonders. See note on 3.12.

14.4: Some sided with the Jews, and some with the apostles. Luke here calls Paul and Barnabas 'Apostles' (as he also does in v. 14). But in these verses he is surely using the word to mean 'those who are sent' (which is its meaning in Greek). See Additional Note, Leaders in the Church, pp. 125, 126.

14.5–6a: When an attempt was made . . . to molest them . . . they learnt of

it and fled. The Jews referred to in v. 2 had persuaded some of the Gentile God-fearers not to listen to Paul and Barnabas, and now they made a plan together to expel them violently. So Paul had to run out of the town and take the road to Lystra. Jesus had taught, 'when they persecute you in one town, flee to the next' (Matt. 10.23). But it is not easy for Christian workers to know when it is right to stay and face opposition and when it is better to move away. When a youth centre in Nairobi was being attacked and damaged continually (often by those who had been expelled from membership) the leaders decided to move the club to a different area. But some members called this decision 'faithless' and 'cowardly'.

14.6b–7: To the surrounding country, and there they preached the gospel. Luke reminds us that they did not only work in the towns. The towns were a base from which they (and those whom they were training) also visited the villages round about.

14.8a: At Lystra. They went to Lystra because it was in the district of Lycaonia, not in Phrygia, and, therefore, no longer under the authority of the officials in Antioch. It was a Roman colony, and so few Jews lived there that there was no synagogue. Three languages were spoken: Latin (by Roman officials), Greek (which Paul used), and Lycaonian (by the indigenous inhabitants).

It was the home of Timothy (see 16.1), who probably gave Luke information about these events.

14.8b: There was a man ... a cripple from birth. One of the chief buildings in Lystra was the temple of Zeus. Some people, having read v. 13, think that the cripple was begging outside that temple, like the cripple at the gate of the Temple in Jerusalem (3.2).

14.9: Paul ... seeing that he had faith to be made well. See note on 'faith' in 20.21. This is the only passage in Acts where we read that someone who needed healing had 'faith'. See note on 3.16. How did Paul know that the man had faith?

14.10: He sprang up and walked. Compare 3.8 and see Additional Note on Healing, pp. 40–42. It was this healing that made the Lycaonians call Paul and Barnabas 'gods'.

14.11: The gods have come down to us in the likeness of men. When the Lycaonians said this, they were remembering two stories in their tribal tradition. The first was about Lycaon, who was visited by two gods disguised as human beings and who entertained them. But he gave them human flesh to eat and they turned him into a wolf. In the other story the two gods Zeus and Hermes (called Jupiter and Mercury by the Romans) visited an old man and his wife, named Philemon and Baucis. These gods also were disguised as human beings. Philemon and Baucis gave them such a warm welcome that they were rewarded, while everyone else in the village was destroyed.

It is not at all surprising that the Lycaonians did their best to honour Paul and Barnabas, considering what they believed about 'gods'.

14.12: Barnabas they called Zeus, and Paul ... they called Hermes. Greeks regarded Zeus as the supreme god, and Hermes as his messenger (the Lycaonians had 'borrowed' these gods from the Greeks).

14.13: The priest of Zeus ... brought oxen and garlands. Suddenly Paul and Barnabas saw that the priest was bringing oxen, with garlands of red wool tied round their necks, to sacrifice them in their honour, as if they were gods. So they tore their clothes (v. 14), which was a Jewish way of showing horror at blasphemy against God (see Mark 14.63; Acts 18.6), and stopped the sacrifice.

14.15: Men, why are you doing this? We also are men, of like nature. When there was an opportunity Paul gave his address to the people, saying:

1. We are human beings, not gods. 'Of like nature' really means 'we have the same feelings that you have'. The peace of the world depends on members of different nations, races and cultures believing this and saying it to each other. After the earthquake in Armenia in 1988 people from many nations joined in giving help to the sufferers. One of the helpers said, 'We put aside national differences and saw ourselves as human beings helping other human beings.' See note on 17.26.

2. We bring the good news that there is only one God and He created everything that exists—'a living God'.

3. Turn away from your many gods—'vain things'.

4. God allowed you to worship such gods in the past, but now He calls upon you to worship Him (v. 16).

5. You have already seen the signs of God's continuing creation (v. 17).

14.17: He did not leave himself without witness.

(a) Paul did not mention Jesus at this time, but preached only about God the creator of nature, (vv. 15 and 17). Because Jesus is God-in-human-flesh, it was no use talking about Jesus until his hearers understood what he meant by 'God'. Paul was an expert, when preaching or writing a letter, in taking into account the beliefs of those whom he was addressing. When he spoke to Jews his message was based on what they already believed (see 1 Cor. 9.20–23).

In this address Paul was speaking about the way in which God shows Himself in 'Nature', but later, like every Christian preacher, he had also to speak of God's revelation of Himself in Jesus. And Paul did have an opportunity to follow up his address, as we see from v. 21, 'they returned to Lystra'.

(b) All preachers—and indeed all Christians, need to hold together these two truths about God: First, the natural material world is God's creation ('the earth is the Lord's', Ps. 24), and He reveals Himself through it. So Christians must both value it and also take care of it (if they do not look after it there will be no earth on which to live as Christians!). Secondly, God has also shown Himself in a special way, namely in the life of Jesus, through whom we can have a right relationship to God.

Both these ways in which God shows Himself to us are of great importance.

14.19: They stoned Paul and dragged him out of the city, supposing that he was dead. 'They' were Jews from Antioch (perhaps they had come to Lystra for the big corn market there) and some of the Lycaonians who had heard Paul. They stoned him, and when they thought he was dead, they pushed the body outside the city where the city authorities could not see it and where the dogs and vultures could get at it.

14.20a: The disciples gathered about him, i.e. they formed a ring round Paul to save him from the dogs and to give him a proper burial. The 'disciples' were either Lycaonians who had accepted Paul's teaching or other Christians who were accompanying Paul and Barnabas on their journey.

14.20b: He rose up and entered the city. This was not a miraculous resurrection, but an action of extraordinary courage, such as the courage of Jesus when he 'set His face to go to Jerusalem' (Luke 9.51–53). When Paul recovered he not only went back to Lystra, but returned there a second time after visiting Derbe (v. 21).

What gave Paul such courage? (We may find part of the answer in passages such as Phil. 4.10–13.)

There are many sorts of courage: the courage to face dying or physical pain, to face failure or rejection by friends, to face disappointment and loss. We are mistaken if we think that one sort of courage is more costly or more to be praised than another. To illustrate this we turn to the Church in Myanmar. Not long ago a pastor spent ten years translating the Bible into the vernacular. He did this in addition to his duties as a pastor and trainer of his many congregations. But before it could be printed, it was destroyed by fire. He was almost overwhelmed by the loss. But eventually he began translating all over again. He is still engaged in the work, and says he hopes it will be better than his first translation. That is one sort of courage.

14.20c: He went on with Barnabas to Derbe. The people of Derbe were Lycaonians like those in Lystra, and from v. 21 it seems that many of them accepted the gospel.

Derbe is south-east of Lystra. Why did Paul and Barnabas not continue eastwards and so return to Syrian Antioch through Tarsus? The answer is that they wanted to revisit and strengthen the new congregations (see v. 22), which was Paul's plan in all his journeys; so they 'returned to Lystra and Iconium and to Antioch-near-Pisidia'

(v. 21), and from there back to Perga and the sea-port of Attalia (v. 25, and see note on 15.36).

14.22a: Exhorting them to continue in the faith. From what Paul wrote to the Galatians we see that 'continuing in the faith' was very difficult for the Christians of this area, e.g. 'I am astonished that you are so quickly deserting him who called you in the grace of Christ' (Gal. 1.6). After Paul's visits some of the Jewish Christians and others there persuaded them to rely more on the keeping of Church rules (and some Jewish ones) than on Jesus Himself.

Luke only uses the phrase '*the* faith' twice in Acts. it seems to mean 'everything that Christians think about God'. See also 6.7. In later times it was often used to describe the creeds. But 'faith' (as Luke uses it in 14.9 and 27) is different, and refers to the whole attitude of Christians towards God, i.e. trusting Him whole-heartedly and what He has done in Jesus (see note on 20.21).

14.22b: Through many tribulations we must enter the kingdom of God, i.e. 'we have to pass through many troubles before we can enter the kingdom of God' (Compare 1 Thess. 3.3).

Paul and Barnabas were wise to prepare the people for 'tribulations', just as it is necessary to prepare any new Christians for unpopularity or persecution. We have to pass 'through' such tribulations and not try to walk round them or over them.

'Entering the kingdom of God' probably meant 'entering the life which we can have with Christ in the new age'.

14.23: They appointed elders for them in every church. This was an important way in which they followed up their preaching, so that when they had left there would be people who had the authority to be leaders. It did not mean that these elders would be without faults, but that they were not self-appointed. They had to be given formal authority, because then (as now) members of their congregations would from time to time disagree with them or oppose them (see 1 Cor. 16.16 and 1 Thess. 5.12, 13). See also Additional Note, Leaders in the Church, (p. 125), and note on 20.28.

14.26a: They sailed to Antioch [in Syria]. In 2 Cor. 11.25, Paul said that he had been shipwrecked three times, and this sea-journey from Attalia to Syrian Antioch may have been one of these times.

14.26b: Where they had been commended to the grace of God, i.e. where they had been entrusted by the Christians into the hands of the gracious God who gives us more than we deserve (see 15.40 and note on 18.27).

14.27a: They gathered the church together and declared all that God had done with them. The Church in Syrian Antioch was the first Church to send out its representatives to evangelize the Gentiles, and now it welcomed its representatives home again. Paul and Barnabas drew attention to what God had done rather than to what they themselves had achieved, which is the truly Christian way in which to rejoice at the conclusion of a piece of work. Yet God had not done it without them. God did it 'with them', i.e. together with them. God is the creator of new life, but He uses human agents. See Phil. 2.12–13: 'Work . . . for God is at work in you'.

14.27b: How he had opened a door of faith to the Gentiles, i.e. 'how he had opened the way for Gentiles to believe' (GNB). God opens doors so that those who decide to follow Jesus, may do so. The evangelist's job is to clear away the obstacles which prevent people from going through the door, e.g. fears, prejudices, false ideas. Paul often used this picture-language about open doors, e.g. 1 Cor. 16.9.

14.28: They remained no little time. They probably spent a year in Antioch, because it was that Church which was welcoming Gentiles into the Church. But, as we see in ch. 15, not all the Churches agreed with the Church in Antioch.

STUDY SUGGESTIONS

REVIEW OF CONTENT

1. What names did the Romans give to the Greek gods 'Zeus' and 'Hermes'?
2. Why was it important that Paul and Barnabas should appoint leaders in each Church?
3. Why did Paul and Barnabas, when they were in Derbe, not continue travelling eastwards towards Syrian Antioch?
4. What did they do when they met the Christians in Syrian Antioch?

BIBLE STUDY

5. Compare the teaching given by Paul in his address (14.15–17) with:
   (a) the teaching in the sermon of 13.16–41, and (b) his teaching in Rom. 1.19–25.
   Say in each case what the main differences are.
6. 'Through many tribulations' (14.22).
   (i) What tribulations did Paul himself endure according to chapters 9 and 14?
   (ii) What does he say about tribulations in each of the following passages?
   (a) Rom. 8.17–21   (b) 1 Thess. 3.3   (c) 2 Tim. 3.12

DISCUSSION AND RESEARCH

7. 'They took care to follow up their work' (p. 134).

With what groups of people and in what ways does a lively congregation today 'follow up' work that it has begun?

8. Compare the events in 14.6 with those in 14.19–20.

(a) When is it right for Christian evangelists to face opposition, and when is it better to go away and avoid it?

(b) How can Christians decide which is right?

9. In your opinion, why did Paul not speak about Jesus to the Lycaonians?

10. During a discussion on 14.17 a girl disagreed with what is said in note (b); she said, 'Nothing matters except the salvation of each individual human being. Trees and rivers don't matter because they have no souls.' What would you have replied to her?

11. Paul's return to Lystra was 'an action of extraordinary courage' (p. 137).

(a) If you agree that 'there are many sorts of courage', what sort of courage had Paul?

(b) Why do you think he was brave?

(c) Quote one brave thing you have done in your life, and say why you were able to do it.

15.1–35

The Jerusalem Meetings

OUTLINE

15.1–2: Aramaic-speaking Christians from Jerusalem visit Paul and Barnabas in Antioch, and criticize them for baptizing uncircumcised Gentiles.

15.3–5: Paul and Barnabas travel to Jerusalem to consult with Peter and others. Christians who had been Pharisees repeat that Gentiles must be circumcised.

15.6–7a: The meetings begin.

15.7b–11: Peter supports what Paul and Barnabas had done.

15.12: Paul and Barnabas give their report.

15.13–21: James, Jesus's brother, acts as chairman and gives a decision.

15.22–35: Members accept the decision and send a delegation to inform the Gentile Christians about it.

INTERPRETATION

WHY WERE THE MEETINGS HELD?

They were held chiefly because some Christians (e.g. Hellenists in Antioch) had baptized uncircumcised Gentiles, and because other Christians (mainly Aramaic-speaking Jews in Jerusalem) believed that that was wrong (see paragraph headed 'The Gentiles, p. 101). But the disagreement was not only about circumcision. They were debating whether Gentiles had to adopt Jewish customs before being baptized. Jewish Christians believed it was right to impose their own customs and culture as well as their religion on the Gentile Christians. This is the mistake which missionaries of all nations have made and are still making.

But, in addition, several things had been happening which made it necessary for leading Christians to consult together:

(a) Peter baptized Cornelius, but the 'circumcision party' criticized him (11.2).

(b) Christians from Cyprus and Cyrene travelled to Syrian Antioch and baptized Greeks. Church leaders in Jerusalem then sent Barnabas to investigate. He approved of what had been done (11.20–24), and he and Paul gave support to the Church in Antioch for a year (11.26).

(c) The Jerusalem Church leaders did not accept Barnabas's report (15.1). Paul refers to this in Gal. 2.4.

(d) Peter and Barnabas both changed their minds, and at one time refused to take meals with uncircumcised Gentiles (Gal. 2.11–14).

(e) Paul travelled in Galatia, Pamphylia and Lycaonia, and welcomed into the Church Gentiles who had no connection with the Jewish religion (chs. 13 and 14).

HOW MANY MEETINGS?

There may have been only one meeting of which we have two different accounts, Paul's account in Gal. 2.1–14, and Luke's, written much later, in this chapter. But many scholars think that there were several meetings. If so, the first one may have been a large gathering (reported by Luke) after which some of the leaders had discussions (to which Paul refers).

WHAT DID THE MEMBERS DISCUSS?

According to Luke there were two questions which the Apostles and elders had to answer: (1) Must Gentiles be circumcised before baptism? (2) Can Gentile Christians be allowed to eat with Jewish Christians, either at the 'breaking of bread' or socially?

'Christians sometimes need to engage in controversy in order to discover the truth' (p. 143).

In this group of Christians meeting in London there was strong difference of opinion as well as agreement and good humour.

According to Paul (Gal. 2.9–10), the chief question was 'In what parts of the country shall Peter and Paul each work?' But he also says that they discussed the problem of circumcision (see Gal. 2.1–8).

WHAT WAS THE RESULT?

By the end of the meeting Christians had agreed that: (1) Gentiles need not be circumcised, but that, (2) when they eat with Jewish Christians they must keep some of the traditional Jewish regulations (see note on v. 20).

Although this agreement was reached, it was a long time before all Jewish Christians accepted it (see 21.18–22).

WHY WERE THE MEETINGS IMPORTANT?

If these meetings had not taken place the Church would have become nothing more than a small Jewish sect, and it would probably have died out. The Gentiles would not have agreed to be circumcised.

HOW RELIABLE IS LUKE'S ACCOUNT?

Some scholars think that, because Luke wrote thirty years after the events, his account is less reliable than what Paul wrote in Galatians. But it is not useful to try to judge between Luke and Paul in that way because each of them wrote for different reasons. Luke was making a report to show how it happened that non-circumcised Gentiles were admitted to the Church. But Paul in Galatians was writing a letter, not a report, and his chief aim was to show that he was a real apostle and preached the real gospel. See Special Note A, Luke as Historian, p. 56.

NOTES

15.2a: No small dissension and debate, i.e. there was serious disagreement and controversy.

Although Christians need to 'live in harmony' (Rom. 12.16), they sometimes need to engage in serious controversy with each other in order to maintain or discover the truth (see note on 6.1a).

In this controversy Peter and Paul were facing the question: 'What is basic and essential in our religion, and what is of secondary importance?' They said that circumcision was good but not essential, whereas being 'saved through the grace of Jesus' was basic and essential (15.11). Those who opposed them said that circumcision was essential.

Christians often disagree today because they give different answers to the question 'What is essential?'. E.g. 'Is it essential for American

Indians, or African Church leaders, to receive a European-style training?' 'Is it essential for all Christians to be monogamous?'

15.2b: To the apostles and elders. In some books these meetings are called the 'Apostolic Council', as if the Twelve arranged it and led it. But this is not what Luke says. In the earliest days of the Church the Twelve Apostles were the only leaders, but gradually they shared their leadership. In this chapter Luke writes about 'the apostles *and the elders'* five times (vv. 2,4,6,22,23), and it was James, Jesus's brother, not an Apostle, who was the chairman of the conference. The Apostles took full part in it, but did not organize or lead it.

It is true that in later times there were 'overseers' or 'bishops' (see Titus 1.7–9), who acted as heads of the Church in each area and who, as time went on, were called 'successors of the Apostles'. But there is no information in the New Testament as a whole to show who appointed them as 'heads'.

15.3: They passed through Phoenicia and Samaria . . . and gave great joy to all the brethren. This shows that a Christian congregation ('the brethren') had grown up in Phoenicia (Lebanon), where some of the refugees had gone during the persecution (11.19).

15.7: Peter rose and said . . . Here Luke has put into four verses what was surely a far longer speech. In the same way, James's speech as recorded in vv. 14–21 is only a summary.

Peter spoke about his experience of meeting Cornelius. Through this meeting Gentiles had 'believed' (v. 7), and God had shown that He accepted them by giving them His Holy Spirit (v. 8). Therefore, Peter said, people are not saved by keeping the Jewish traditions (such as circumcision), which he called a 'yoke' (v. 10). We are saved, he said, by believing, i.e. by trusting in Jesus and in what He has done for us (v. 11). This is like the teaching of Paul, e.g. Eph. 2.7–8.

It was difficult for Peter to make this speech, because he had many friends among the Aramaic-speaking traditionalists (see Gal. 2.11–12). But because he spoke as the result of an experience of his own he was in a strong position. He was not repeating what others had said. Christian preachers speak most effectively when they speak as the result of their own experience. (They sometimes go further than this and describe the experience itself, as Peter did.)

This is the last time that we read of Peter in Acts (see note on 12.17).

15.12: They listened to Barnabas and Paul. The only part of the speeches of Barnabas and Paul which Luke records is their speaking of 'signs and wonders'. They said that their doing miracles among Gentiles showed that God approved of their welcoming Gentiles into the Church.

We should notice that later on Paul had to warn the Thessalonians and others that not all signs and wonders prove that God is at work (see 2 Thess. 2.9, 1 John 4.1).

15.13: James replied, 'Brethren, listen to me'. This James, Jesus's brother, seems to have been the chairman of the meeting. Before this he had been a leader of the Aramaic-speaking traditionalists, but in this speech he supported the views of Peter (whom he called 'Symeon') and of Paul and Barnabas. He may have changed his previous opinions, but it is more likely that, as chairman, he was summing up the general wish of members.

In his speech he said:

(a) It was a fulfilment of prophecy that Gentiles were now being welcomed into the 'people of God' (vv. 14–18; see Amos 9.11–12).

(b) Because God was welcoming the Gentiles in, they should be welcomed without conditions (v. 19), e.g. without being circumcised. Luke does not record that James mentioned circumcision in his speech, but James surely did speak of it because it was one of the two main subjects at the meetings.

(c) However, in order not to give offence to Jewish Christians, they should keep *some* of the Jewish regulations (v. 20).

15.20: To abstain from the pollutions of idols and from unchastity and from what is strangled and from blood. *The rules* which Gentiles must keep (and which are like the laws in Leviticus 17.8–13) were: (a) No 'pollutions of idols': i.e. not eating meat which has been offered to idols and later sold in the market. (b) No 'unchastity': this may mean keeping the law by which Jews could marry some relatives but not others; but it may refer to those forms of sexual intercourse which were usually forbidden. (c) Nothing strangled: when they killed an animal they must draw off its blood. (d) No blood: food with blood in it was forbidden.

The decision which James announced was one which the members were able to agree on because it was a 'Christian compromise', that is to say, each group accepted less than it had hoped for in order that the work of Christ's Church should go forward. The Aramaic-speaking Jerusalem group failed to persuade the conference that all Gentiles must be circumcised before baptism, and the Greek-speaking group from Antioch were disappointed that Gentiles were forced to keep some of the Jewish ritual laws.

There are people who make compromises because they are weak or dishonest. But real Christian compromise is possible. In one part of Tanzania, Pentecostals accused Anglicans of being 'second class Christians' because (they said) they 'did not have the Holy Spirit and did not heal and did not baptize in deep water'. Anglicans called the Pentecostalists 'heretics', e.g. because they did not have bishops. For one whole day the councils of both Churches met for silent prayer and discussion. By the end of the day they had agreed on a statement which contained the following: (1) Every baptized person has the Holy Spirit; (2) Every Church should heal in Christ's name; (3) The amount of water used at baptism is less important than the reconciling of the candidate with God; (4) Pentecostals are real Christians.

Because of this 'compromise' the two bodies have since that time been able to work in harmony.

15.22: It seemed good . . . to choose men from among them and send them to Antioch. After the council members had agreed on a decision they had to make it known to the Churches, especially to Syrian Antioch.

They chose four men to carry the news, Paul, Barnabas, Judas and Silas. Nothing is known about this Judas except what we read here and in v. 32, but Silas was an important leader (see note on 15.40).

They gave them a letter to take and sent it to the Gentiles in Antioch, Syria and Cilicia (v. 23).

In the letter they: (a) explained that those who 'troubled the Gentiles' (i.e. insisted that they must be circumcised) had no authority to do so (v. 24); (b) commended Paul and Barnabas as men who had risked their lives for the sake of Jesus (vv. 25–26); (c) said that it was the Holy Spirit who had led them to make the decision (v. 28, and see note on 16.6); (d) listed the regulations which Gentiles must keep (v. 29).

15.30: They went down to Antioch. When the four messengers reached Syrian Antioch the congregation there welcomed them warmly. Judas and Silas then worked for a time in Antioch before they returned to Jerusalem. Paul and Barnabas continued working there in co-operation with many others (v. 35). They knew how to share their ministry with others.

This was the last occasion on which Paul and Barnabas worked together (see note on 15.39).

15.32: Judas and Silas, who were themselves prophets, exhorted the brethren with many words and strengthened them. This verse shows that Judas and Silas, like most prophets, were preachers and counsellors. They used 'many words' in their preaching. Fortunately not all preachers follow their example!

STUDY SUGGESTIONS

REVIEW OF CONTENT

1. What was the chief reason for holding the Jerusalem meetings?
2. What experience did Peter refer to in his speech?
3. To what extent did the Twelve Apostles lead the meetings?

4. We have called the decision a 'Christian compromise' (see note on v. 20). What does that phrase mean?

5. Why did the Christians in Antioch receive the decision gladly?

BIBLE STUDY

6. There are five passages in this section in which Luke draws attention to what 'God has done'. Which are they?

7. Read Romans 14.15–21 and 1 Cor. 9.19–21, and from those chapters list the examples which Paul gives of 'Christian compromise' (see note on v. 20).

DISCUSSION AND RESEARCH

8. (a) Describe any disagreement and controversy among Christians in which you took part, or about which you have some knowledge.
   (b) What decision was reached?
   (c) To what extent was that decision a 'Christian compromise'?
   (d) What was the attitude of the groups to each other as the decision was reached?

9. 'Christians often disagree today because they give different answers to the question, 'What is essential?' (p. 143).
   (a) What is your own answer to the two questions which follow that comment?
   (b) Name two other matters on which Christians do not agree whether they are essential or not.

10. (a) 'Peter spoke as the result of an experience of his own' (p. 144). Why are preachers more effective if they do this?
    (b) 'Preachers sometimes go further than this and describe the experience itself' (p. 144). What are the advantages and disadvantages of doing this?

11. If a Jewish reader pointed to 15.20 and said to you, 'If you Christians base your behaviour on the Bible, you should not eat meat which has blood in it', what would you reply?

12. Imagine that you are a traditionalist Jewish Christian in Paul's time, and that you sincerely believe it is God's will that Gentiles must be circumcised before being baptized. Write a short speech, showing how you would try to convince your hearers.

Christians take the Gospel Westwards

OUTLINE

15.36–41: Paul and Barnabas have a disagreement in Antioch, and Paul travels north alone.

16.1–5: At Lystra, Paul circumcises Timothy, and together they visit congregations in that area.

16.6–10: Paul and his fellow-workers are guided to travel westwards to Greece.

INTERPRETATION

THE NEW EVENT

Paul and his team took the gospel into Macedonia, i.e. into a part of the Roman Empire which Christians had not visited. During this journey they were learning what Christians everywhere have to learn, namely, that God sometimes wants them to do what they had not expected. When Luke wrote these words he knew that by turning westwards into Macedonia (16.10) they had taken an important step towards bringing the gospel to Rome (see Introduction, pp. 1–2).

THE JOURNEY

They travelled from Syrian Antioch to Macedonia by stages:

(a) They went north to the Roman province called Syria-with-Cilicia (v. 41), where Paul had been born;

(b) Then northwards again through the valley called the 'Cilician Gates' (p. 94) into Galatia, to Derbe and Lystra, which Paul had visited before (chs. 13 and 14);

(c) Then, after being uncertain for some time as to which way to go, they made the journey across mountainous country to Troas, a port on the Aegean Sea. This was a dangerous journey because of wolves and bands of robbers and sudden storms;

(d) And from there they went on to Macedonia (v. 10). Luke describes the rest of this journey in 16.11—18.23. This is often called Paul's 'Second Missionary Journey', but as we have seen (p. 121), it was his third or fourth.

TWO PROBLEMS

The travellers had to face two problems which all Christian workers face: (a) how to work harmoniously with a partner (vv. 36–39); and (b) how to receive God's guidance for the work (see p. 150).

NOTES

15.36: Let us return and visit the brethren. Why did Paul and Barnabas want to revisit the congregations they had founded? They may have heard that members were being persecuted or were being persuaded to return to the old Jewish religion (see Gal. 3.2); but the chief reason was to follow up work which they had begun. A farmer follows up the sowing of seeds by returning later to hoe and water the soil; and a good pastor keeps in touch with those whom he has guided at times of renewal, e.g. baptism, conversion, marriage (see 14.20; 15.41; 18.18–23).

15.39: There arose a sharp contention (the Greek word means 'violent disagreement'). See note on 15.2a.

Why did Paul and Barnabas quarrel? Chiefly because Paul refused to take John Mark with them. Mark had left them in the middle of a journey earlier on (13.13). But Paul may also have been angry because Barnabas had followed the Jerusalem 'traditionalists' in refusing to eat meals with Gentiles (Gal. 2.11–13).

Who was to blame? Most people blame Paul, because Barnabas had given him strong support when he most needed help (9.27; 11.25), and because in refusing to take Mark, he was not considering the effect this would have on him. We can imagine the conversation:

Barnabas: For the sake of Mark, our fellow-worker, give him a second chance, just as Jesus gave Peter a second chance.

Paul: For the sake of the work of the gospel, I cannot take the risk of having Mark in the team.

Christians who are making plans often have to answer the same difficult question which Paul and Barnabas faced: 'Which is more important, the work or the worker?'

Others blame Barnabas, thinking that he was showing special favour to Mark because he was his cousin (Col. 4.10).

What was the result? Barnabas set off on a separate journey with John Mark, and so gave him another chance, while Paul travelled on with Silas. In the end Paul accepted both Barnabas and Mark as fellow-workers (1 Cor. 9.6; Philemon 24).

Luke's message. By reporting what took place here Luke showed that these early Christian leaders shared our human weakness and imperfection. He wanted to show that God can use the weak as well as the strong (compare 1 Cor. 1.27).

16.1: He came also to Derbe and to Lystra. A disciple was there, named Timothy. Paul had been in Lystra five years before this time (14.6), and Timothy may have become a Christian and been baptized by Paul then (see 1 Cor. 4.17, where Paul calls him 'my beloved child in the Lord'). Timothy's grandmother and mother were Jewish Christians (2 Tim. 1.5). His father was Greek and was not a Christian. Later Timothy became a faithful fellow-worker with Paul.

16.3: Paul wanted Timothy to accompany him; and he circumcised him. At first sight it seems that Paul, by circumcising Timothy, was acting against the decision of the Jerusalem conference, and was contradicting what he had written to the Galatians: 'If you receive circumcision, Christ will be of no advantage to you' (Gal. 5.2–6).

But Paul did it for two reasons. First, because the Jerusalem conference decision applied only to Gentiles, and Timothy was partly Jewish and partly Gentile. Secondly, Paul wanted Timothy to work with him among Jews, and many Jews regarded an uncircumcised child of a Jew-Gentile marriage as illegitimate (v. 3). As Paul explained later, in writing to the Church at Corinth, he had to consider the feelings of Jews in order to work effectively among them. 'To the Jews I became as a Jew, in order to win Jews' (1 Cor. 9.20). If Timothy had asked to be circumcised in order to be fully Christian, Paul would have refused.

After this event, Paul and the elders probably commissioned Timothy (1 Tim. 4.14; 2 Tim. 1.6). Then he and Paul 'went on their way', telling congregations the decision of the Jerusalem conference (16.4).

16.6: They went through the region of Phrygia and Galatia, having been forbidden by the Holy Spirit to speak the word in Asia. They planned to go into 'Asia', the Roman province of which Ephesus was the major city, but because of 'the Holy Spirit' they realized that they must cancel that plan. In the same way, they did not go into Bithynia (north-west Asia Minor) because of 'the Spirit of Jesus'. Luke uses these two phrases 'the Holy Spirit' and 'the Spirit of Jesus' in order to refer to God Himself actively making His will known. Both phrases have the same meaning.

But how did they receive God's guidance, i.e. what happened which caused them to cancel their plans? Did some event occur, e.g. was Paul ill, or did the Jews prevent them, or was there a local war? Or did a Church leader interpret God's will, e.g. did Silas, who was a 'prophet', predict disaster if they proceeded? Or did one of them have a vision? Or did they pray together and then take a decision? Luke does not tell us. But in some way they received guidance as to what they must not do (and later what they should do).

God has not changed, and Christians still receive guidance from Him, and they do so in very many different ways.

16.7: When they had come opposite Mysia. This shows that they had come on a very long and dangerous route, over very high mountains in which robbers and bandits were active. Very probably Paul was ill during this part of the journey, and perhaps it was one of the journeys to which he refers in 2 Cor. 11.26–27.

16.9: A vision appeared to Paul in the night: a man of Macedonia was standing ...

A vision. Paul had a vision, and because of it he was sure that God was guiding him to go across the sea into Macedonia.

What are 'visions'?

(a) They are experiences in which people believe that God is sending them a message which is in the form of something 'seen' or something 'heard'. Here a Macedonian man was 'seen'; Paul at his conversion 'heard' a voice.

(b) Those who have visions have usually been searching for guidance for some time before, as Paul had (vv. 6–7).

(c) God guides people through visions, but they are free to make their own choice.

(d) People do not have visions in order to enjoy them or to boast about them, but in order to follow them up by action (see v. 10: 'immediately we sought to go', and 26.19).

(e) People need to test their visions by *seeking God's guidance in other ways also*. Testing is necessary because often it is not clear if a vision really carries God's message. A senior girl in a school in Zambia who had a vision in which she saw herself dressed in a white robe believed that God was calling her to be a minister. Her teacher told her to 'test' her vision, e.g. by consulting friends and senior people, especially Christians, and by studying other ways in which people received guidance in the New Testament.

(f) The two words 'trance' (10.10) and 'vision' mean the same, and the word 'dream' has a similar meaning, although in the New Testament only Matthew uses the word.

A man of Macedonia. Perhaps Luke was a Macedonian and had visited Paul some time before his vision and had invited him to visit Macedonia (see note on v. 10). If this is so, we can see why Paul saw 'a man of Macedonia' in his vision.

16.10: We sought to go on into Macedonia. Luke uses the word 'we' in this verse to show that he had now joined Paul's team. After this he was often with Paul (e.g. 16.11–18), especially during the events which he describes in chs 20—28. Luke tells us almost nothing about himself except in Acts 1.1. But we know that he was Greek from his name, and he may be the same Luke whom Paul calls 'the beloved physician' in Col. 4.14.

STUDY SUGGESTIONS
REVIEW OF CONTENT

1. What was the 'new event' of which Luke tells us in these verses?
2. What was the most dangerous part of Paul's journey, and what made it dangerous?
3. Why did Paul and Barnabas quarrel?
4. Why did Paul circumcise Timothy?
5. What three workers were with Paul at Troas?
6. How do we know that Luke was one of them?

BIBLE STUDY

7. In what way does Gal. 3.1–2 help us to understand why Paul wanted to visit the Christians in Lystra, Derbe and Iconium?
8. Read the following passages and then write a brief description of Timothy's character: 1 Thess. 3.1–3; Phil 2.19–22; 1 Tim. 1.2; 2 Tim. 1.5.
9. 'A vision appeared to Paul' (16.9). Read the following passages in Acts and say in each case: (i) Who had a vision, (ii) What did they see or hear, and (iii) What action, if any, did they take to follow up the vision?
   (a) 9.10   (b) 9.12   (c) 10.3   (d) 10.10   (e) 22.17   (f) 26.19

DISCUSSION AND RESEARCH

10. 'A good pastor keeps in touch with those whom he has guided' (p. 149). Give an example from your experience to show why this 'keeping in touch' is important.
11. In your opinion who was chiefly responsible for the quarrel between Paul and Barnabas (15.39)? Give reasons for your answer.
12. In the note on Paul's circumcising of Timothy (p. 150), 1 Cor. 9.20 was quoted. In your opinion are Paul's words in that verse: (a) helpful, (b) harmful, or (c) dangerous, for a Christian today? Give reasons.
13. 'How did they receive God's guidance, i.e. what happened which caused them to cancel their plans?' (p. 150).
    (a) Through which of the various ways of receiving guidance listed on p. 150 do you most often seek or receive guidance?
    (b) What suggestions would you have made to the Zambian girl described in note (e) on pa. 151?
14. 'The words 'trance' and 'vision' mean the same, and the word 'dream' has a similar meaning' (p. 151). To what extent can a Christian receive God's guidance through dreams? Give examples.

16.11—17.15
Paul in Macedonia

OUTLINE

INTERPRETATION

Paul, with Luke, Silas and Timothy set out from Troas, believing that God's Holy Spirit had guided them to make this journey (16.10). They went by boat which called in at the island of Samothrace, and the next day arrived at Neapolis. This was, and still is, a fishing port at the north of the Aegean Sea (16.11).

From there they travelled 45 kms to Philippi (16.12) along the great Roman road, the Via Egnatia, which went from Byzantium (Istanbul) to Rome. After working at Philippi for some time they continued westwards along the same road, 150 kms to Thessalonica. Eventually they travelled south-west and came to Beroea.

In two of the three towns they began by speaking in the Jewish synagogues and a Christian congregation was born. In each town there was severe opposition and they had to escape.

Luke reports these events very briefly, but we can discover more by reading Paul's letters to the Christians of Philippi and of Thessalonica (see notes on 16.12 and 17.1).

NOTES

16.11: We made a direct voyage. Because of this word 'we' most scholars think that the author Luke was one of Paul's companions (see also 20.7). In earlier chapters he had written 'they'.

16.12: To Philippi which is ... a Roman colony.

The town of Philippi was one of those towns which the Romans had chosen to be 'colonies'. They were military headquarters where retired Roman soldiers also lived, and their inhabitants were Roman citizens. Philippi was called 'little Rome'. As we know, Paul greatly hoped to reach Rome itself, and hoped that it would become the centre from which Christians could go out all over the Empire.

The Church in Philippi. Paul usually began his visits by going to a synagogue (see 13.14), but there were so few male Jews in Philippi that there was no synagogue. However, a mile outside the town he found some Jewish women praying beside the gently flowing River Gangites. Jews needed water for some of their religious rituals. There Paul 'sat down' and talked with them. This is how the Church in Philippi was born. There is a Chinese saying: 'A 1,000-mile journey begins with one step.' From the letter which Paul later wrote to this Church, we learn of the very close fellowship which they had together, and also of the opposition which he and they experienced (see Phil. 1.5–7; 1.28–30; 4.15–18).

16.14: A woman named Lydia ... The Lord opened her heart.

A woman. In this section Luke refers four times to Christians who were women: here and in 16.40; 17.4; 17.12. He, more than any other New Testament writer, shows the service which women gave during Jesus's ministry and in the early Church, for example, it is only in his Gospel that we read about Mary and Elizabeth. Throughout Acts also, Luke draws special attention to what women did, e.g. 'All these with one accord devoted themselves to prayer, together with the women and Mary the mother of Jesus' (1.14).

Why did Luke do this? Partly because in order to give an accurate report of events he could not omit what the women did. Partly, perhaps, because there were traditionalists in the Church who believed that women should be kept in the background.

We cannot find an answer in Luke's writings to the question whether women should be ordained as 'priests' or 'ministers'. But we do see that women gave great and special service in the Church, and that they should do so today. One Nigerian woman said, 'We are only allowed to clean the Church building.' But every part of the Church (including Nigeria) has its outstanding women. For example, Arab Christians in Jerusalem have Helen Shehadeh, the blind leader of the school for blind children. The Church in Bangladesh has Sister Sushila, who was born in South India but has for 40 years been of great influence among the Christians in Bangladesh by her life of witness, prayer and leadership. **Lydia** was a Gentile, a business-woman who travelled round the country selling purple cloth. This cloth was made in her birthplace, Thyatira, where the dye was made. She was a 'God-fearer'. Luke points to the three parts of her conversion (and of most conversions): (1) God's part, 'the Lord opened her heart'; (2) the evangelist's part, 'what was said by Paul'; and (3) the hearer's part (her response), 'she gave heed'.

16.15: She was baptized, with her household. Cornelius (11.14), the jailer (16.33), and Crispus (18.8) were also baptized 'with their households'. This is not surprising, because Jewish families, like most families in the world today, were very closely united. What the senior member did, other members also did.

Some Christians ask, 'Does this mean that infants were baptized?' Luke does not provide an answer. It may be right to baptize infants, but we cannot prove this by quoting these passages. 'Household' may mean the servants rather than the children.

Others ask if Paul always gave candidates teaching before baptizing them, but again Luke does not give us an answer.

16.16: A slave girl who had a spirit of divination. This girl told fortunes for a fee, speaking in a strained voice as if she was in a trance. Some people think that she was a fraud, others that she was mentally ill, others that an evil spirit possessed her. She kept shouting out that Paul had a message about 'salvation'. But Paul did not want people to confuse his preaching with fortune-telling, so he 'exorcised' the spirit: 'In the name of Jesus Christ ... come out'. After that she could no longer work for her employers.

Today there are Christians who exorcise patients in the name of Jesus. But they need to do it in consultation with ministers or doctors, because it is possible to harm patients in this way. A minister in South Africa told a sick woman that she had an evil spirit and that he would cast it out. He tried to do so twice but without any result. When she became more seriously ill her doctor found that she had had diabetes for some time, and should have been receiving insulin.

The men who employed the slave girl in Philippi made money from her work, and were furious with Paul because he had healed her (v. 19). Paul had done something good, but they called it evil. They were like a politician who votes against changing the laws concerning agriculture, because he owns farms and would lose money if the laws were changed.

16.22: The magistrates gave orders to beat them with rods. The crowd took Paul and Silas to the market-place where the Roman magistrates settled disputes. It was a wide paved area, which we can still see today. The people did not accuse Paul and Silas of being Christians. Nor did

'Paul did not want people to confuse his preaching with fortune-telling' (p. 155).

But this famous American fortune-teller, Jeane Dixon, does seem to be confusing her fortune-telling with the gospel, as we see from the cross she is wearing (visible through the crystal ball she uses to aid her 'clairvoyance'). Why is it necessary *not* to confuse the two?

156

they explain the true reason for their accusations (19a). They accused Paul and Silas of belonging to the Jewish race and of attempting to spread Jewish ideas and customs. Roman law allowed Jews to practise their religion, but not to try and win converts. The magistrates did not give Paul and Silas a trial but simply ordered that they should be flogged. They were stripped naked, tied to posts, beaten till blood ran down their backs, thrown (still naked) into the darkest part of the prison, tied by their feet to wooden bars (v. 24) and left to sit on the stone floor that was already deep in urine. This is what Paul refers to in 2 Cor. 11.25. This is what Christian evangelists are experiencing today in very many parts of the world.

16.25: Paul and Silas were praying and singing hymns. The hymns which they sang were 'psalms', probably such a psalm as 130: 'Out of the depths I cry to Thee' (v. 1) . . . 'In his word I hope' (v. 5). By praying and singing they showed what 'believing' means. It is not chiefly having the right ideas, it is keeping in touch with God and trusting Him when things are going wrong (see note on 20.21).

16.30–31: 'What must I do to be saved?' . . . 'Believe in the Lord Jesus'. After the earthquake the jailer was terrified, because he thought that the prisoners would escape and that he would be killed by the authorities. When Paul spoke to him, he asked how he could be 'saved'. What did he mean? *Either* 'You are in prison because you have supernatural powers, so do a miracle for me and help me to escape punishment', *or* 'You have shown that you have confidence in your God. Save me from my fear.'

Paul told him to 'believe in the Lord Jesus':

Believe. Paul was saying 'Trust Jesus to look after you, and accept that His teaching is true' (see note on 20.21, Faith).

In the Lord Jesus. 'I believe that Jesus is Lord' was the earliest Christian Creed, and means, 'Jesus has a claim over my whole life' (Rom. 10.9).

16.33: He . . . washed their wounds, and he was baptized at once, with all his family. Washing their wounds and believing in Jesus were parts of the same event. According to New Testament writers, service and belief go hand in hand. They belong together. We cannot do either well unless we also do the other.

Two sisters went regularly to Church services for many years. After Billy Graham had visited their town, they were renewed in their faith, and since that time have visited patients in the local hospital every Sunday afternoon (see 1 John 4.20).

All his family. See note on 16.15.

16.37: They have beaten us publicly, uncondemned. When the magistrates discovered that Paul and Silas were Roman citizens they apologized for the flogging and asked them to leave. Magistrates were not allowed to flog a Roman citizen without first holding a proper trial.

17.1: They came to Thessalonica, where there was a synagogue.

The town of Thessalonica was, and still is, an important centre for commerce. Part of it is on a level with the sea-port, and part on a high hill where, according to tradition, the synagogue was.

The Church in Thessalonica. Paul and Silas, very weak after their flogging, somehow travelled the 150 kms from Philippi. On the first three sabbaths they met Jews in the synagogue, and were able to form a small group of believers. They stayed for a further period, but were eventually expelled. We learn from Paul's letters what happened during this time: the new Church members, and perhaps Paul, took the gospel to other areas. Paul worked for his living, Gentiles as well as Jews persecuted them, leaders were appointed for the Church in order to carry on what Paul began. And there was deep fellowship between Paul and the members (see 1 Thess. 1.7–9; 2.7–14; 5.12–13).

17.2: He argued with them from the scriptures.

Argued. See note on 17.17. Paul had to give his message both to Jews and to Gentiles.

1. According to this passage, Paul explained that Jesus was the Messiah for whom the Jews had been waiting, and that they should not be surprised that He had had to suffer. Jesus's suffering fulfilled the prophecies in the Old Testament. (Whenever the word 'scriptures' appears in the New Testament it means the Old Testament.)

2. According to Paul (1 Thess. 1.10 and 5.2–4) he was also teaching Gentiles about the future coming of Jesus, and telling them to be ready.

Probably he gave the first message to the Jews, and the second message to the Gentiles. Good preachers make their sermons fit their hearers.

17.6: They dragged Jason . . . before the city authorities. The Jews were afraid that Gentiles would follow Paul instead of becoming proselytes of the Synagogue. So they paid unemployed men to attack the house where he was staying (v. 5). Because he was not there, they attacked the owner, Jason. It was, and in many parts of the world still is, dangerous to be a supporter of a religious leader who seemed to be 'turning the world upside down', i.e. calling on people to change their way of living.

The Greek word here translated 'city authorities' is *'politarchs'*. Recently a stone has been found which was once part of a first century AD archway in Thessalonica. According to the inscription on it, city authorities in Macedonia were called politarchs at the time when Paul was there. Luke had taken the trouble to get his facts correct.

17.7: Saying that there is another king, Jesus. Paul did not call Jesus 'king'. But as we saw, he very often called Him 'Lord', the same title which they commonly used for the Roman Emperor. In a great many countries today Christians are accused of being disloyal to the State and its President because they have to repeat Peter's words 'We must obey God rather than men' (5.29), or the words of Revelation 19.6, that Jesus is the 'King of kings and Lord of lords'.

17.9: When they had taken security from Jason. They made Jason promise to see that Paul did not return.

17.10: The brethren immediately sent Paul and Silas away by night to Beroea. They took them to an unimportant town, 90 kms away, hoping that they would be free of trouble there. At first the Jews received them well, and accepted their teaching, 'examining the scriptures daily', e.g. passages such as Isa. 53 in which the prophet spoke about a 'servant' who would have to suffer. (Paul was explaining what sort of Messiah Jesus was.)

But Jews from Thessalonica came, and once again Paul had to escape. From Thess. 3.1–6 we learn that Timothy courageously returned to Thessalonica. Both Timothy and Silas joined Paul later in Corinth.

Although Paul had again met opposition, the Church had been born in Beroea, of which Sopater was one member (20.4).

STUDY SUGGESTIONS

REVIEW OF CONTENT

1. How did Paul travel from Troas to Philippi?
2. Why was there no synagogue in Philippi?
3. What two people, of whom we read here, were baptized along with their households?
4. Why were the owners of the girl who had a spirit of divination angry with Paul?
5. What did Paul and Silas do in prison in Philippi?
6. Why did the Jews persecute Paul and Silas in each town which they visited?
7. In what modern country is Thessalonica?

BIBLE STUDY

8 What do we discover about Paul's time in Philippi from each of the following?

    (a) Phil. 1.5–7   (b) Phil. 1.28–30   (c) Phil. 4.15–18

9. 'Luke, more than any other New Testament writer, shows the service which women gave during Jesus's ministry and in the early Church' (p. 154). In each of the following passages say (i) who were the women; (ii) what they did.

(a) Luke 1.39–56   (b) Luke 23.27–29   (c) Luke 24.10
(d) Acts 1.14   (e) Acts 12.12   (f) Acts 18.2–3.

10. 'We learn from Paul's letters what happened during this time'
(p. 158). Read the following passages from 1 Thessalonians and say
in each case what it is that we learn about what happened in
Thessalonica.
(a) 1.6–7   (b) 1.9   (c) 2.9, also 2 Thess. 3.7–8   (d) 2.7–8 and
3.9–10   (e) 2.14

DISCUSSION AND RESEARCH

11. 'Women gave great and special service in the Church' (p. 154).
(a) In what ways do women give service in your congregation?
(b) In what ways could they give greater service?
12. 'Paul "exorcised" the spirit' (p. 155). Find out: (a) Which Christians (if any) practise exorcism in your part of the world, and (b)
Who gives them authority to do it. (c) What sorts of people have
been healed in this way?
13. '"I believe that Jesus is Lord." This was the earliest Christian
creed' (p. 157). Should this be the only creed which the Church
requires candidates to say before they are baptized? Or is a fuller
creed needed? Give reasons for your answers.
14. 'According to New Testament writers, service and belief go hand in
hand' (p. 157).
(a) Read Matt. 25.34–40; Luke 6.46 and Luke 7.44–50, and show
how each of these passages supports that statement.
(b) Give another example from your own experience.

17.16–34
Paul in Athens

OUTLINE

17.16: Paul sees Athens.
17.17–18: He has discussions with Jews and 'God-fearers' and Greek
philosophers in the city centre.
17.19–31: He makes a speech to the Council of the Areopagus.
17.32–34: The result of his work.

INTERPRETATION

THE CITY OF ATHENS

Five hundred years before Paul came to Athens it was the centre of commerce for all Greece, was very powerful politically, and was governed democratically. It also had the most beautiful buildings and sculptures and some of the best literature the world has ever known. We can see many of these buildings and statues today, and the writings of its poets and philosophers are still studied. When Paul saw Athens, it was part of the Roman Empire, and was no longer powerful, politically or commercially. But it still had its buildings and statues, its famous university and its philosophers.

PAUL'S WORK IN ATHENS

Paul had not intended to visit Athens, and he came to it alone. But having arrived there he made use of the opportunity. (He shows in his letters that he could face such unexpected problems, relying on God's Spirit to guide him.) He also met leading thinkers of that time, the philosophers to whom he made his speech.

PAUL'S METHOD

Paul began by agreeing with his hearers, e.g. that 'God is our creator' (vv. 22–29), and then turned to a message that was different and new to them, i.e. that God had revealed His will through Jesus (vv. 30–31).

THE RESULT

Many rejected his message, but some believed it, including a member of the Council of Areopagus (vv. 32–34).

NOTES

17.16: His spirit was provoked within him as he saw that the city was full of idols. The Greek word here translated 'provoked' means 'enraged'. Why was Paul so angry when he saw the idols, those beautiful statues of Greek gods and goddesses? He was angry because, for many hundreds of years, the people had by seeing them obtained a false idea of God, and had given total loyalty to something less than God Himself. For Paul what people believed about God mattered far more than their admiration for what is beautiful to look at.

17.17: He argued in the synagogue ... and in the market place. In some passages in the New Testament the Greek word here translated 'argue' means 'dispute', but in this verse and in most places it means 'hold discussion' or 'have dialogue' or 'teach by question and answer' (see 20.9). If Paul had 'disputed' with the people he would not have made converts.

The 'market place' was not simply a place for shops and stalls. It was the city centre, a square containing great public buildings, a place where people met each other and listened to public speakers.

17.18a: Some also of the Epicurean and Stoic philosophers met him. These were highly educated Greeks who followed the philosophers of ancient times, asking and answering the question, 'What is the object of living?' We can see how different their beliefs were from Paul's:

Epicureans believed: (1) that the gods are so far removed from us that they are not interested in human beings; (2) that everything happens by chance; (3) that the chief aim in life is to have happiness which is not followed by pain.

Stoics believed: (1) that God lives in everything, and in human beings, and cannot exist apart from us; (2) that everything which happens has been fated; (3) that we should above all live by reason and without depending on other people.

Many educated Christians today follow some of those beliefs without realizing that they are doing so.

17.18b: What would this babbler say? The philosophers thought that Paul was doing nothing except picking up odd pieces of information like a bird pecking up seeds, and chattering on about them. (That is the meaning of the Greek word here translated 'babbler'.)

17.18c: He seems to be a preacher of foreign divinities. Greeks honoured so many gods and goddesses that when Paul spoke about Jesus and the resurrection, they thought he was referring to two more, namely Jesus (a god) and Anastasis (a goddess). *Anastasis* is the Greek word for 'resurrection'.

17.19: They brought him to the Areopagus. Areopagus was a hill to the south of the city centre. It had once been the place where the City Council met to pass laws and judge cases. But at the time when Paul was in Athens the Council met in a building in the city centre. So *either* they took him to a meeting of the Areopagus Council in the city centre *or* to an open-air discussion on the Areopagus hill. (On this hill every year on 19 June, leaders of Church and State in Athens still join in giving thanks for Paul and Peter.)

17.22: Paul . . . said, Men of Athens, I perceive that in every way you are very religious. This is the beginning of Paul's speech, which Luke gives in a very shortened form. Paul began (vv. 22–29) by making statements with which many of his listeners agreed. He had used the same method when talking to Jews in the synagogue at Antioch-near-Pisidia (13.16–

17) and to the tribes in Lystra (14.15–17). Whether we are preaching the gospel or selling drinks, Paul's method is a good method. A Pepsi-Cola Manager in Kenya gave the following instructions to his agents: 'One, Have conversation with the shop-keeper. Two, Agree before you disagree. Three, Ask him to stock Pepsi.'

Paul began by saying: 'Since you are religious people, let me tell you about the God whom you say is "unknown": (a) He created everything (v. 24a); (b) He does not live in buildings (v. 24b and see 7.48); (c) He does not depend on human beings (v. 25a); (d) Human beings depend on God (v. 25b); (e) He is for all nations' (v. 26, see note below). Most of the philosophers, unlike many of the people of Athens, probably agreed with this part of his speech.

17.26: He made from one every nation of men ... having determined allotted periods and the boundaries. Paul not only said that God is for all nations, but that He made them all 'from one', i.e. 'of one stock' (NEB), 'from one forefather' (GNB). So no race is superior to another race. All human beings are one family even though most people forget this when there is suspicion between them, or in time of war (see note 5 on 14.15).

having determined allotted periods means 'having taken care of mankind by arranging for food to grow at different seasons'.

boundaries does not refer to national frontiers, but to the natural 'boundaries' between sun and earth, sea and landscape (see Psalm 104.5–9).

17.27: In the hope that they might feel after him and find him. Yet he is not far from each one of us. People 'feel after' God as a blind girl feels for the door of her home. Jesus taught that God searches for us (Luke 15.3–10), but it is equally true that we need to 'feel after' Him (Isa 55.6).

Then Paul said 'Finding Him is not impossible because He is already very near you' (see also v. 28).

17.28: In him we live and move and have our being. In this verse Paul was quoting non-Christian Greek poets, thus showing that, although Greek philosophers and poets did not accept Jesus as Lord, they possessed some truth about God, and His Spirit was in some way in them. Many Christians who knew Mahatma Gandhi, and knew that he was a Hindu, also knew that he had unusual awareness of God. After his death an Indian Christian was visiting Australia, and was asked, 'Do you think Gandhi is in heaven or hell?' The Indian said, 'The Almighty has not given me the responsibility of making that decision. But wherever he is, I would like to be' (see Additional Note, Christians and Other Religions, pp. 166, 167).

But Paul did not only quote other people's writings. He also spoke from his own experience of being '*in* Christ' (2 Cor. 5.17), and of Christ 'living in him' (Gal. 2.20).

17.29: We ought not to think that the Deity is like gold. Paul was referring here to the popular ideas about God, not to the philosophers' ideas. The philosophers well knew that a statue of gold or stone could not be a god. There was as much difference between the popular ideas and the philosophers' ideas as there is between popular Hindu ideas and those of the scholarly Vedantist Hindus.

17.30: The times of ignorance God has overlooked, but now he commands all men everywhere to repent. Having agreed with his hearers on many matters concerning God, Paul then gave the new part of his message, the part which was different from their philosophy. This was the part in which he referred to what God *does* and *reveals*, and not only to what He *is*.

This new message is in vv. 30 and 31:

1. God is actively concerned about us. He commands people to repent. In the past people did not know what He was saying and so they could not be blamed (See Rom. 3.25). But those who now hear the truth about Him and yet take no notice, they do need to repent.

2. He will one day judge us all (v. 31a).

3. He will judge us through 'a man' (v. 31b).

4. He has raised this 'man' from the dead (v. 31c).

This part of Paul's speech occupies only two verses here, but it surely occupied an hour, or perhaps much more. Paul had to explain the words he used, especially that the 'man' was Jesus. Also, it was the custom in Athens for listeners to ask questions and to make speeches.

17.31: A man whom he has appointed, and of this he has given assurance ... by raising him from the dead.

A 'man'. This is one of the many words which New Testament writers use for Jesus, showing that He was really human (see also 2.22 and 1 Tim. 2.5). Many Christians find it easier to believe that Jesus was divine than to believe that He was human. But He is not our Saviour, our mediator, unless He was both fully human and fully divine.

Raising him from the dead. This was the part of Paul's speech which his hearers found it most difficult to accept. They believed that a person's soul could continue after death, but not that a dead man (Jesus) could come alive again. They also knew that 'rising again' takes place in nature. The Greeks had stories of the 'rising' of Adonis, and the Egyptians had stories of the 'rising' of Osiris. These 'gods' were examples of what happens continually, like the annual rising of the River Nile. But Paul was speaking of Jesus's resurrection as one special event in history.

When Paul spoke about Jesus's resurrection he may have found it helpful that his listeners had 'resurrection' stories in their traditions. On the other hand he may have found it a hindrance, because some of his

'They brought him to the Areopagus' (17.19).

The rocky hill called the Areopagus, or 'Mars Hill', as it is today. In the background is the Acropolis on which were many of the 'idols' (17.16) which troubled Paul so deeply.

listeners might think that he and they meant the same thing when they used the word 'resurrection'.

17.32–34: Some mocked ... but some men joined him. Did Paul fail or succeed in Athens?

In the past many scholars thought that Paul failed. They said that when he left Athens and went to Corinth, he knew he had made a mistake in agreeing so fully with the philosophers. They quoted 1 Cor. 2.2, 'I decided to know nothing among you except Jesus Christ and him crucified.' This shows, they said, that Paul knew that he should have preached about the cross in Athens. But most scholars today hold a different opinion, and say that: (1) no one can tell the story of the resurrection without referring to the cross; (2) when Paul wrote 1 Cor. 2.2 he was not referring to his time in Athens; (3) the conversion of Dionysius, a member of the Areopagus 'Council', and of Damaris and others, is a sign of success, not of failure (v. 34).

ADDITIONAL NOTE: CHRISTIANS AND PEOPLE OF OTHER RELIGIONS

Luke's description of Paul meeting the Greek philosophers and using their poets as part of his own speech (v. 28) raises such questions as: 'What was Paul's attitude to other religions?' 'What should be the attitude of Christians to people of other religions today?' Different Christians give different answers, e.g.:

1. That all religions are equally true. No group should claim that it has more of the truth than others have. All of us are partly right. See 1 Tim. 4.10a, 'God ... is the Saviour of all'.

2. That only Christians have truth. We are accepted by God only because we have Jesus. Others have no truth that is important. Those who give this answer believe that John 14.6 and Acts 4.12 support their view. (Some add that members of other religions are agents of the devil.)

3. That Christians have truth and are accepted by God through Jesus, but that others also have some truth, and are not totally rejected by God. Those who give this third answer quote v. 28 of this chapter. Paul, by quoting Greek poets, showed that he believed that they had some knowledge of the truth about God. People who give this answer also point to:

(a) Acts 14.17: 'God did not leave himself without witness', i.e. without some way of showing them (the non-Christians) His nature.

(b) Acts 10.2–35: Luke says that the non-Christian Cornelius is 'devout' (v. 2) 'upright and God-fearing' (v. 22), and Peter said that 'In every nation anyone who fears God and does what is right is acceptable to him' (v. 35, and see note p. 106).

(c) John 14.6 and Acts 4.12: These verses may mean that the way to God is indeed through Jesus, but Jesus is at work in the hearts of all who 'feel after' God, even when they do not know His Name. An elderly Hindu in India, after hearing a talk about Jesus given by a Christian evangelist, said 'I have known Him all my life, but now you have told me His name.'

It is clear from the above that we do not discover the truth from one or two verses of the New Testament, but from a careful study of the New Testament as a whole, and from our own experience of the working of God in His world.

STUDY SUGGESTIONS

REVIEW OF CONTENT

1. Why did Paul come to Athens?
2. Why was he angry when he saw the idols?
3. What three groups of people did he meet?
4. With which part of his speech did most of his listeners disagree?
5. Why did they disagree with it?
6. What Athenian man became a Christian as the result of Paul's visit?

BIBLE STUDY

7. 'In some passages in the New Testament the Greek word here translated "argue" means "dispute", but ... in most places it means "hold discussion"' (pp. 161, 162). Read the following verses and say in each case whether the word means 'dispute' or 'discuss':
   (a) Mark 9.34   (b) Acts 19.8   (c) Acts 20.7   (d) Acts 20.9
   (e) Acts 24.12   (f) Jude 9
8. For each of the following verses, find a verse in Acts 17.24–31 which contains a similar truth.
   (a) Gen. 1.1   (b) Ps. 104.9   (c) Isa. 55.6   (d) Acts 7.48
   (e) Acts 13.30   (f) Rom. 3.25

DISCUSSION AND RESEARCH

9. 'The people had ... given total loyalty to something less than God Himself ...' (p. 161).
   (a) Suggest *two* things or people or 'gods' to which people today give total loyalty instead of giving it to God.

(b) In what ways do they show that they are giving such loyalty?
10. 'All human beings are one family' (p. 163).
   (a) On which verse was the above sentence a comment?
   (b) What are some ways in which Christians can (1) show that this is true, and (2) fail to show that it is true?
11. 'Paul was quoting non-Christian Greek poets' (p. 163). Should Christians use the sacred writings of other religions in corporate worship or for personal reading? What would be the purpose of doing so? What would be the dangers?
12. 'Many Christians find it easier to believe that Jesus was divine than to believe that He was human' (p. 164).
   (a) What is your opinion, and what is the opinion of other Christians whom you consult?
   (b) Quote one piece of evidence to show that Jesus was really human. Why is this an important truth?
13. Do you think that Paul's visit to Athens was a success or a failure? Give reasons for your answer.
14. 'What should be the attitude of Christians today (to people of other religions)? Different Christians give different answers' (p. 166).
   (a) Comment on *each* of the three answers, giving your reasons for agreeing or disagreeing with it.
   (b) What is your opinion of the saying about Mahatma Gandhi on p. 163?

18.1–28

Paul in Corinth

OUTLINE

18.1—4: Paul meets Aquila and Priscilla and begins his preaching in the synagogue.

18.5–8: The Jews reject him, but he continues his work in the house of Titius.

18.9–11: Paul's vision.

18.12–17: The Jews try to persuade Gallio to arrest Paul, but are not successful.

18.18–23: He travels to Syria.

18.24–28: A note about Apollos.

INTERPRETATION

THE CITY OF CORINTH

Corinth was famous throughout Greece for four reasons:

1. Unlike Athens, it was very important commercially. The city stood on a narrow strip of land, with one sea-port on the west which faced the Adriatic Sea and a second port on the east (Cenchreae) facing the Aegean Sea. Thus traders came by ship from east and west, and naturally Corinth became rich.

2. It contained people of many different nationalities. It was the capital of the Roman province of Achaia (see v. 12) and a Roman colony, with many retired Roman soldiers living there. But in addition there were large numbers of Greeks, Egyptians, Phoenicians and Jews, and as a result the people followed many different religions.

3. Many Greeks came there for the Isthmian Games, which were almost as important as the Olympic Games.

4. It was famous for the evil habits of its people. When an actor in a Greek play took the part of a Corinthian he had to act as if he was drunk. The Greeks had a verb in their language 'to corinth', which meant to be sexually immoral. This immorality was partly due to the practices of the one thousand prostitute-priestesses at the temple of Aphrodite. This huge temple was on the top of the mountain above Corinth. Paul, in the letter which he wrote after he left the city, describes the people of Corinth before they became Christians as 'immoral, idolaters, adulterers, sexual perverts, thieves' (1 Cor. 6.9–10).

PAUL'S WORK IN CORINTH

That was the city into which Paul walked alone in the spring of AD 50. It is not surprising that his task sometimes seemed impossible: 'I was with you in weakness and in much fear and trembling' (1 Cor. 2.3). He urgently needed the encouragement which he received from God through a vision (v. 9). A Church leader's life is often a lonely life, as it was, for example, for a priest from the Philippines when he was chosen to cross the world to be Bishop of the Gambia in West Africa.

Although Paul spent eighteen months in Corinth, Luke does not tell us much about his work as an evangelist. He says that Paul worked at first among Jews and that they rejected him. But from Paul's own letters we learn more, e.g.: (a) He travelled outside Corinth, in the province of Achaia (Rom. 16.1; 1 Cor. 16.15; 2 Cor. 1.1); (b) Most of the congregation that grew up under his guidance were Gentiles; we see this from the names of the 'brethren' whom he mentions, e.g. in 1 Cor. 16.15–19; (c) During this visit to Corinth he wrote at least two letters to

169

the Church in Thessalonica. Timothy had been in Thessalonica and now came to Corinth bringing with him good news about the Thessalonian Christians (1 Thess. 3.6). Paul wrote to them with affection, 'We were gentle among you, like a nurse taking care of her children' (1 Thess. 2.7).

Paul continued to keep in touch with the Church in Corinth by writing to them and by paying them another visit (see note on 20.2).

NOTES

18.2: He found a Jew named Aquila ... with his wife Priscilla. Paul knew no one in Corinth, but by making inquiries he discovered these two Christians who had come from Rome. They seem to have become Christians in Rome, but no one knows who first took the gospel to Rome. They worked with Paul in Corinth, and then moved with him to Ephesus (v. 19), where they led a house-group (1 Cor. 16.19). They were some of the best fellow-workers that Paul ever had (see note on v. 24).

They had been expelled from their home because they were Jews, as have millions of Jews since that time. (In the 13th century the English expelled all Jews and for 400 years no Jew could live in England.) Aquila and Priscilla returned to Rome when the persecution was ended (Rom. 16.3–5).

18.3: Because he was of the same trade, he stayed with them ... they were tent-makers. Priscilla and Aquila may have made cloth for tents (Paul came from Tarsus near the Taurus mountains where the goats' hair grew longer than anywhere else and so made the best cloth), or they may have been leather-workers.

Some Christians today ask, should ministers have a trade? Paul was a Jewish Rabbi, and there was a rule that all Rabbis must learn a trade, so that they should be in touch with the ordinary life of the people they taught. In very many parts of the world ordained ministers have a trade, perhaps in farming or taking private pupils, as well as leading a congregation. The question is often asked, 'Should all ministers follow this practice, or should they undertake it only until their congregations can pay them or provide for them in other ways?'

Paul carried out a trade as well as his ministry. Although he said that he had a right to be paid for his preaching, he earned his living as far as possible by his trade. He did this partly because many Christians were too poor to pay him, and partly to prevent people saying that he made a profit out of the gospel (20.33–34). Perhaps he also spread the gospel by the way in which he conducted his trade, and by his conversation as he did so.

But some Christians sent him money, and then he devoted himself fully to preaching and teaching (2 Cor. 11.7–9).

18.6: Your blood be upon your heads! ... From now on I will go to the Gentiles. See note on 13.46.

18.7: He ... went to the house of a man named Titius Justus. When Paul was rejected by the Jews he made his headquarters at the house of this God-fearer. As the house was next to the synagogue, other God-fearers called at this house rather than attend the synagogue, and so the Christian congregation was born. Even the ruler of the synagogue, Crispus, joined the congregation (v. 8a).

18.8: Many of the Corinthians, hearing Paul, believed and were baptized. These 'many Corinthians' were the first Christian community in Corinth, who met in each other's houses for fellowship and worship. From this chapter and from Paul's letters we can tell what sort of people they were. They were mostly Gentiles. Some were rich and well-educated, others were poor (see 1 Cor. 1.26; 11.18–19), with the result that they found it difficult to live in fellowship. We also know the names of twelve of them. Luke mentions five in this chapter (six if we count Sosthenes as a Christian, see v. 17), and Paul refers to seven more in Rom. 16.23; 1 Cor. 1.11–16; 16.15–17; 2 Cor. 1.19.

18.9–10: The Lord said to Paul one night in a vision, 'Do not be afraid ... I am with you'. See note on 16.9. Paul needed this encouragement from God partly because he had been rejected by the Jews, but chiefly because it was such an enormous task to spread the gospel in a city like Corinth.

18.12: When Gallio was proconsul of Achaia, the Jews made a united attack upon Paul and brought him before the tribunal. The Jews hoped that because Gallio was newly appointed he might try to gain favour with them by arresting Paul. But he refused to do this (vv. 14–15). He declared that the case was between Jews and Christians and did not concern Roman law. By saying this Gallio probably saved Christians from being arrested under Roman law for the next ten years or so.

The 'tribunal' was the blue and white marble platform in the middle of the huge city centre, on which judges sat to try cases. Part of it can still be seen today.

An inscription has been found on a stone in another part of Greece from which we know that Gallio became proconsul in the middle of AD 51. From such inscriptions we can (a) give dates for many of the events in Paul's life, and (b) see that Luke gives accurate reports in Acts.

18.17: They all seized Sosthenes, the ruler of the synagogue ... But Gallio paid no attention to this. 'They' may mean the non-Jewish crowd who were showing their anti-Jewish feelings by attacking Sosthenes, or it may refer to the Jews, who were angry because they saw that

Sosthenes was becoming a Christian. (He may be the same Sosthenes whom Paul mentioned in 1 Cor. 1.1.) Gallio paid no attention, i.e. he refused to take sides.

18.18: Paul ... sailed for Syria, and with him Priscilla and Aquila. At Cenchreae he cut his hair, for he had a vow. He left Corinth and sailed from Cenchreae, the sea-port on the east side of the city, and travelled through Ephesus, where Priscilla and Aquila stayed behind (v. 19). Paul went on to Caesarea and Jerusalem (see note on v. 22). This was a very long journey indeed. It may have taken a whole year, and was perhaps one of the journeys Paul refers to in 2 Cor. 11.25 (or 11.26).

Because Paul was going to Jerusalem he wanted to show the 'traditionalists' (see note on 15.7) that he had not cut himself off from the Jewish traditions. So he kept the custom referred to in Numbers 6.1, 5, 18. After a time of trouble, Jews let their hair grow for thirty days. They then cut it off and offered it up as an act of thanksgiving to God for deliverance. Paul seems to have made this thanksgiving at Cenchreae, where, either then or later, there was a Christian congregation of which Phoebe the deacon was the leader (see Rom. 16.1).

18.22: When he had landed at Caesarea, he went up and greeted the church, and then went down to Antioch. In vv. 22 and 23 Luke describes the end of one journey and the beginning of another.

The very long journey during which Paul visited Athens, Corinth and Ephesus came to an end when he returned to his headquarters at Syrian Antioch. He sailed from Ephesus to Caesarea, went 'up' to the Church in Jerusalem, and from there returned to Syrian Antioch.

Paul's next journey (which is often called the 'Third Missionary Journey') began when he left Antioch and revisited Christians in Galatia and Phrygia (v. 23b, and see 16.6).

18.24: A Jew named Apollos. Apollos later became a leader of the Church in Corinth, so Luke has written a note (vv. 24–28) to explain how he began his ministry.

Apollos came to Ephesus from Alexandria, which was famous for its schools and its university, and he was an excellent speaker. He knew the Old Testament well ('the scriptures', v. 24), had received the Holy Spirit ('fervent in spirit', v. 25), and was expert at talking about the life and teaching of Jesus. But he had never received Christian baptism and so had never fully acknowledged Jesus as his 'Lord'.

When Priscilla and Aquila heard him speak in the synagogue they noticed that something was missing in his preaching. No one appointed or authorized them to speak to him about this; they did so as members of the Christian community. Those who hear sermons can be a great help to those who preach them, e.g. they can ask a preacher to explain some point that has puzzled them, or they can persuade preachers to use ordinary language instead of 'technical' theological terms they learnt at college.

Because these two tent-makers were brave enough to share their experience with the highly-educated Apollos, and because he was humble enough to listen to them, he became an outstanding leader in Corinth. His ministry there began after he had crossed from Ephesus to Achaia, i.e. to Corinth (vv. 27–28; see also 1 Cor. 3.4–6; 4.1–6).

18.27: Those who through grace had believed, i.e. those who believed because God in His 'grace' had led them to believe.

Grace. 1. In the New Testament 'grace' sometimes means the generosity which people show to others. 'Grace was upon them' (Acts. 4.33) probably means that 'a wonderful spirit of generosity pervaded the whole fellowship' (Phillips).

2. But 'grace' usually refers to the generosity of God Himself, i.e. the way in which He treated human beings (especially by becoming man in Jesus), and by the way in which He still treats us. No one deserves to be accepted by God; He offers his love and acceptance as a free gift. We cannot earn it. As Peter said, 'We shall be saved through the grace of the Lord Jesus' (Acts. 15.11).

3. Paul saw the 'grace' of God as the central part of preaching: 'the gospel (good news) of the grace of God' (Acts 20.24). He explained that, although God offers it to everyone, it is received by those who trust God, i.e. have 'faith': 'By grace you have been saved through faith' (Eph. 2.8).

4. In saying this Paul was closely following the teaching of Jesus Himself, e.g. the parables in Luke 15. It is not true that Paul and Jesus preached different gospels.

STUDY SUGGESTIONS

REVIEW OF CONTENT

1. Why did Corinth become a rich city?
2. What, in your opinion, made Paul feel weak and fearful (1 Cor. 2.3) when he was in Corinth?
3. In what two ways was he supported and strengthened while he was in Corinth?
4. What letters did Paul write from Corinth which we can read today?
5. Who was in charge of the congregation at Cenchreae?

BIBLE STUDY

6. What do we learn about the life and character of Aquila and Priscilla from each of the following passages?
   (a) Acts 18.2–3   (b) Acts 18.26   (c) Rom. 16.3–5
   (d) 1 Cor. 16.19.
7. What does each of the following passages tell us about the way Paul obtained money to live by (see note on 18.3)?
   (a) Acts 20.33–34   (b) 1 Cor. 9.11–15   (c) Phil. 4.15–16
   (d) 1 Thess. 2.9.
8. 'A Jew named Apollos' (v. 24). What do we learn about Apollos's ministry from 1 Cor. 3.4–6 and Acts 18.26–28?
9. 'Grace' (v. 27).
   (i) How is this word translated in other languages known to you? To what extent do those translations give the real meaning of the word?
   (ii) What was the result of receiving God's grace according to each of the following passages?
   (a) Acts 15.11   (b) 1 Cor. 15.10   (c) Gal. 1.15
   (d) 2 Thess. 2.16.

DISCUSSION AND RESEARCH

10. (a) 'Paul carried out a trade' (p. 170). What are some of the advantages and disadvantages of a modern ordained Church leader's carrying out a trade?
    (b) 'Perhaps he also spread the gospel by the way in which he conducted his trade, and by his conversation as he did so' (p. 170). In what ways is it possible for a Christian to do that? Give examples if possible.
11. Read again the note on 18.8 about the 'first Christian community in Corinth'. In what ways is your own Christian community (a) like, and (b) *un*like, the one which Paul knew in Corinth?
12. 'Those who hear sermons can be a great help to those who preach them' (p. 172). From your own experience, suggest two special ways in which those who hear sermons can help the preacher.

Paul in Ephesus

OUTLINE

19.1–7: Paul baptizes a group of John the Baptist's disciples.

19.8: He teaches in a synagogue for three months.

19.9–10: For two years he teaches in a public lecture-room and sends evangelists into other parts of the province.

19.11–20: He performs healing miracles and brings to an end the work of some exorcists.

19.21–22: He sends helpers to collect aid for the poor of Jerusalem.

19.23–41: He is accused of preventing the sale of images of Greek gods and goddesses, and there is a riot.

INTERPRETATION

After visiting the Christians in Galatia and Phrygia (18.23), Paul arrived in the great and important city of Ephesus. He spent three years there, and built up Christian congregations, not only in the city but in many areas round about. And in addition to the events which Luke records in Acts, many other events took place there, as we see from Paul's letters:

1. Paul endured great persecution and suffering. The letters which he wrote from Ephesus to the Church in Corinth show that during these three years he was ill, unhappy, puzzled, hungry, deprived of his possessions, imprisoned, flogged, and almost killed (see 2 Cor. 11.23 and Acts 20.19).

2. Paul sent evangelists into even more areas than Luke mentions, and people from those places came to Ephesus to meet him, e.g. he sent Epaphras to Colossae, Laodicea and Hierapolis (Col. 4.12–16), and probably to the other 'seven churches' in the Roman Province of Asia (Rev. 1.4).

3. Paul kept in touch with the Christians in Corinth. He wrote them two letters, one of which is lost. The other we call '1 Corinthians'. Then he paid them a visit, but they rejected him (2 Cor. 2.1). As a result he wrote an angry letter (probably this is found in chapters 10—13 of what we call 2 Corinthians). Then, after Titus had visited Corinth and brought him good news, he wrote a joyful and friendly letter (2 Cor. 1–

9). Many scholars believe that it was especially while he was in Ephesus that Paul grew and matured as a Christian. They say that in his early ministry he was sometimes discourteous (Gal. 2.6) and boastful (2 Cor. 11.17), but that after his painful experiences he wanted reconciliation with those who opposed him (2 Cor. 2.4), realized his own weaknesses (Phil. 3.12–15), and accepted his suffering (2 Cor. 4.16).

NOTES

19.1: Paul ... came to Ephesus. Ephesus was the most important city in the Roman Province called Asia, and had a population of 250,000. Ships came to its sea-port from the east (Egypt and Phoenicia) and from the west (Spain, Italy, Greece), and many thousands of people of all races came to the shrine of the goddess Artemis and to her huge temple (see note on v. 24). As Paul landed from his ship, he walked into the city up a wide road (along which travellers can still walk today). On each side of the road were pillars and statues of gods and goddesses, and in front of him were temples of white marble and other great buildings, shining in the sun, and on the hill the huge theatre. Here, even more than in Athens or Corinth, Paul surely felt, 'How can I achieve anything in this great city, whose people's beliefs are so different from mine?'

19.2: Did you receive the Holy Spirit when you believed? Paul probably asked this question because, in his opinion, when people received Christian baptism they received the Holy Spirit at the same time (see Additional Note, Baptism, pp. 78, 79). So here he was asking them, 'Did you have a real Christian baptism when you believed?'

But it is not clear what these 'disciples' (v. 1) had experienced, and it would be wrong to base present-day Church practice on this passage alone. Here, for example, are two different interpretations: (1) Some people point to the word 'disciples' and say that they had already received real Christian baptism. If they had, then in v. 5 Luke is reporting that Christians received a 'second baptism' (the only verse in the New Testament where any writer mentions it). (2) But most scholars point out that Paul in his letter to the Romans wrote about baptism as an event which could not be repeated (see Rom. 6.3–4). So 'disciples' in v. 1 *either* means 'John's disciples' *or* people whom Paul mistakenly thought were Christian disciples.

These people had probably been taught by John the Baptist to wait for Jesus the Messiah. But their belief was lacking in two ways: (1) they accepted John's severe warning to repent, but did not know about Jesus's good news that God forgives; (2) they were still waiting for the Messiah and did not know that He had come (v. 4, see note on 18.24).

These were the people who, when they had been made full members of the Church, became the Ephesian congregation through whom and with whom Paul was able to do his important work.

19.6: When Paul had laid his hands upon them, the Holy Spirit came on them; and they spoke with tongues and prophesied.

Laid his hands. This verse and 8.17 are the only places in the New Testament where the writer says that people received the Spirit because hands had been laid on them (see note on 13.3).

Spoke with tongues. See note on 2.4b. Luke often states in Acts that believers showed that they had received the Spirit by speaking in tongues (e.g. 2.4; 10.44–46). And indeed great numbers of present-day believers show in the same way that they have received the Spirit. But Paul emphasized that there were many other signs that a believer had received the Spirit (see Gal. 5.22; 1 Cor. 12.8–11 and 1 Cor. 13). There is sometimes division between Christians who follow Luke in this matter and those who follow Paul. There would be greater fellowship in the Church if members took into account the ideas of both Luke and Paul.

Prophesied. Here the word means the same as 'speaking in tongues' (see Additional Note, pp. 18, 19).

19.8–9a: He entered the synagogue ... but when some were stubborn ... speaking evil of the Way ... As in all other cities, Paul began his work by speaking to members of the synagogue who later rejected him (see 13.13–52; 18.1–7).

Twice in this chapter (vv. 9,23) Luke calls the Christian gospel 'the Way' (see note on 22.4).

19.9b: He ... argued daily in the hall of Tyrannus. For the next two years Paul did his teaching in a public lecture-hall, because the synagogue members had rejected him. For the word 'argue' see note on 17.17. People came from all parts of the Province called Asia ('all the residents of Asia' v. 10).

In some manuscripts of Acts, there is an extra phrase in this verse: 'from the fifth hour to the tenth', i.e. from 11 a.m. to 4 p.m. If this is correct, then Paul worked in the hottest time of the day. Anyone who has worked in Turkey knows that this is the time when most people rest rather than work. But Paul was so keen to teach that he was willing to work in the heat. Some of his hearers probably came because it was cooler in the hall than outside, and by doing so heard the gospel for the first time. See Special Note, Manuscripts of Acts, (pp. 182, 183).

19.11: God did extraordinary miracles by the hands of Paul, so that handkerchiefs ... were carried away from his body to the sick. We have to distinguish between Paul's actions and the way in which the people interpreted them. Paul, with God's power, certainly healed people who were ill (2 Cor. 12.12). But people in Ephesus thought that he healed people by using magic. They thought that his handkerchiefs and aprons were magical, i.e. that they had supernatural power in them because the cloth had touched Paul's skin. When they were healed they said it was because they had obtained these bits of cloth, not because of the love of God Himself.

There were many 'magicians', 'shamans', 'sorcerers' who were regarded as doing magic, and there are many today. They make people believe that something marvellous has happened, either by using their special knowledge, e.g. of plants, or by hypnotism or by trickery. They do their magic by using special words or objects, and they say that secret powers of nature or of departed spirits live in such words or objects. They do this in order to make a living for themselves and to have power over people. (Magicians are of course not the same as herbalists and 'nature healers' who can cure the sick because of their knowledge of the medicinal value of plants.)

What is the main difference between magic and the miracles of which we read in Acts? First, those through whom God did miracles depended upon Him, rather than on words or objects; and secondly, they gave Him the glory rather than themselves (see 3.12). In the same way a magical object is different from a Christian sacrament such as the bread at Holy Communion; Christians use the bread as a means through which they open themselves to God Himself, not as an object containing power.

But unfortunately Christians have sometimes depended on magic, e.g. when they have treated the bones of a saint as if the bones had the power to heal, or when they have bowed to the moon in order to have 'good luck'. See notes on 8.9; 13.7.

19.13: Jewish exorcists undertook to pronounce the name of the Lord Jesus. 'Exorcists' means people who cast out evil spirits. In those days, when anyone was ill, everyone said that the illness was caused by an evil spirit (see note on 16.16). No one knew about germs and infection.

These Jewish exorcists practised magic. They uttered special words and special names for God, and sick people believed that healing power came from that uttering of the word of the name. When these exorcists heard of Jesus, they added His name to their list of 'powerful names'. They did not want to follow Jesus, they only wanted to make use of His name. (There are many people today who do this.)

When seven of these exorcists used the names of Jesus and Paul in this way, the person they were trying to cure became violent, and attacked them and tore off their clothes (v. 16). Luke says that as a result more people began to respect the name of Jesus (v. 17), and some of those who practised magic burnt their books which contained magical words and names (v. 19).

We have seen here that people often use the name of Jesus wrongly, but see note on 3.6.

19.21: Paul resolved in the Spirit to ... go to Jerusalem, saying 'After I have been there, I must also see Rome'. Paul himself said this in his letter to the Church in Rome (Rom. 15.22–25). As we know, he had special reasons for reaching Rome. He hoped that from Rome, the capital city, the gospel would be taken all over the Empire.

19.22: Having sent into Macedonia two of his helpers. Why did Paul send them to Macedonia? From Paul's letters we learn that there was a danger of serious division in the Church, between Jewish and Gentile believers (e.g. Gal. 2.11–14)) So Paul did what he could to heal the division by encouraging the Gentiles to give aid to the poor Jewish Christians in Judea (see note on 11.29). This is why he sent Timothy and Erastus to the Gentile Christians of Macedonia.

See 16.1 for a note on Timothy. Erastus was perhaps the person whose name appears on a first-century inscription and who was director of the public works department in Corinth.

19.24: A man named Demetrius, a silversmith, who made silver shrines of Artemis. In vv. 23–41 Luke records one of the many times when the people of Ephesus opposed Paul. This probably took place at the end of his three years in the city.

The people who opposed Paul were those who worshipped the goddess Artemis (called 'Diana' by the Romans). The metal-workers who made images of the goddess (or of her temple) to sell to pilgrims also opposed him. For a thousand years the people of that district had made sacrifices and gifts to Artemis, and it was said that pilgrims came from every country in the world to her temple. They worshipped her as the spirit of nature, the 'great mother' who, they believed, gave power to women to have children and to the fields to produce crops. Her temple was enormous, and was one of the 'eight wonders of the world', with 1,000 female slaves assisting the priests.

Of course there were many Ephesians who wanted to stop Paul from preaching against this Artemis-worship. But we see from Demetrius's speech (vv. 25.27) that he and other members of his trade were thinking more about their profits than about their goddess. They pretended that they objected to Paul because they loved their nation and their religion, but that was not the chief reason. 'If people begin to follow Jesus instead of Artemis,' they said, 'there will be unemployment.'

What can Christians learn from this story concerning the preaching of the gospel? First, that the gospel will not usually be popular, because it calls on those who hear it to change their way of living (see Luke 6.22, 23, 26). Secondly, that as a result of Christian preaching people must sometimes lose money. When, in many countries, parents see that it is

179

their duty as Christians to send their children to school, they know that by doing so they will not be able to grow as much food in their farms as in the past, and that they will have to raise extra money to pay for school fees and uniforms.

19.29: They rushed together into the theatre. After Demetrius's speech the crowd ran into the huge open-air theatre, where there were seats for 34,000 people. We may note the following:

(a) Most of them did not know why they were there, as is often the case when crowds collect (vv. 29.32).

(b) They seized two of Paul's supporters from Macedonia, but could not find Paul (v. 29).

(c) Paul, with great courage, tried to go to the theatre to speak to the crowd, but his friends held him back. Paul gave way and accepted their advice (v. 30).

(d) Some of the leading politicians of the Province of Asia ('Asiarchs') also advised him not to go. This shows that he had made friends with such people, as part of his work in Ephesus (v. 31).

(e) A Jewish leader, Alexander, tried to calm the crowd, but without success. As often happened at that time (see 18.2; 18.17) the meeting became an anti-Jewish riot (vv. 33–34).

(f) The secretary of the town council had to come and remind the people that the government would punish them unless they went home peacefully (vv. 35–41).

STUDY SUGGESTIONS

REVIEW OF CONTENT

1. For how long did Paul work in Ephesus?
2. What do we know about Paul's activities in Ephesus from reading his letters?
3. Where did he do his teaching after members of the synagogue had rejected him?
4. Why did he send two workers to Macedonia?
5. Why did the people of Ephesus worship Artemis?
6. Why did Paul not speak to the crowd in the theatre?

BIBLE STUDY

7. From the letters which Paul wrote from Ephesus to the Church in Corinth it seems that while he was in Ephesus he was: ill, unhappy, puzzled, hungry, deprived of his possessions, imprisoned, flogged, almost killed. Which of these experiences does he mention in each of the following passages?

'The crowd rushed into the theatre, seized two of Paul's supporters, and the meeting became an anti-Jewish riot' (p. 180).

Archaeologists have uncovered much of the ancient theatre at Ephesus. These columns are some of those still standing along the road to the huge arena with its tiers of seats like a modern football stadium, where the angry crowd gathered.

(a) 1 Cor. 15.29–32   (b) 2 Cor. 1.8   (c) 2 Cor. 4.8–12
(d) 2 Cor. 6.4   (e) 2 Cor. 6.8–10   (f) 2 Cor. 11.23

8. 'The Holy Spirit came on them; and they spoke with tongues' (v. 6).
What are the signs that someone has received the Spirit, according
to each of the following passages?
(a) Acts 2.4   (b) Acts 10.44–46   (c) 1 Cor. 12.9–10
(d) Gal. 5.22

DISCUSSION AND RESEARCH

9. 'People in Ephesus thought that Paul healed people by using
magic' (pp. 187, 188).
(a) What do you yourself mean by the word 'magic'? Give an
example.
(b) Why should Christians not use magic?
(c) Why *do* Christians sometimes use it?
(d) Give examples of the sorts of magic which people use in your
area.
10. 'They did not want to follow Jesus, they only wanted to make use
of His name' (p. 178).
(a) In what ways do people misuse the name of Jesus?
(b) Why do those who misuse it use it at all?
11. 'They worshipped Artemis as the spirit of nature, the "great
mother" who, they believed, gave power to women to have
children . . .' (p. 179).
(a) Give an example of people today who worship the spirit of
nature rather than the God and Father of Jesus Christ.
(b) Why do they do so?
12. 'As a result of Christian preaching people must sometimes lose
money (p. 179). Give an example of this happening.

Special Note C
The Manuscripts of Acts

When Luke wrote Acts he or his secretary wrote it on strips of papyrus,
paper that was made from a sort of grass. This papyrus wore out from
being used, and copies had to be made. Later more copies were made
from the first copies, and so on. We refer to these as 'the manuscripts'
or 'MSS'. This is the way in which the whole of the Greek New
Testament was handed down.

But those who made the copies did not and could not always make
completely accurate copies. Sometimes, being human, they made a
mistake, *or* they could not read a word and had to guess what it had

originally been, *or* they corrected what they thought was someone else's mistake, *or* they had extra information and added it.

Most copyists did not travel long distances, and they used the copy which was nearest to them. This is the reason why the MSS from the eastern part of the Church, e.g. Egypt and Syrian Antioch, are alike and form one group. MSS from the western part, e.g. from Italy and France, also form a group, which today we call the 'Western Text'. It is in Acts that the Western Text is most different from other MSS, being longer and fuller. The following are a few examples of the many words and phrases which we find in the Western Text but not in other MSS:

12.10: 'down the seven steps';

15.20: 'and not to do to others what they would not like to be done to themselves';

17.31: 'Jesus' (thus explaining who the 'man' was);

19.9: 'from the fifth hour to the tenth'.

Because no one possesses any of the original writings, scholars try to discover what the author probably wrote: (a) by comparing the many different MSS which have been found; (b) by treating the earliest MSS as likely to be the more reliable. There are so many of these that it is possible to discover fairly accurately what the author wrote. We can also compare these MSS with the translations of the Greek into other languages, and with quotations in the writings of theologians.

Some Christians say that God did not allow copyists to make mistakes or add to what others had written. But according to the New Testament God does not prevent His servants from making mistakes in this way or in other ways.

STUDY SUGGESTIONS

1. What sort of material did Luke (or his secretary) write his books on?
2. Give an example of a phrase or word which we find in the 'Western Text' of Acts, but not in other manuscripts.
3. In what ways do scholars try to discover what New Testament writers originally wrote?
4. 'Those who made the copies (of early manuscripts) did not and could not make completely accurate copies' (p. 182).
   (a) Why could they not do so?
   (b) What is your opinion of the statement (p. 183) that 'God did not allow copyists to make mistakes'?

20.1–38

Paul's Journey to Jerusalem

OUTLINE

20.1–6: Before making his journey, Paul revisits Macedonia and Greece.

20.7–12: He goes south to Troas and 'breaks bread' with the Christians there.

20.13–16: The journey from Troas to Miletus.

20.17–38: At Miletus, Paul says farewell to the elders from Ephesus.

INTERPRETATION

Luke's chief aim here was to show that Paul was at last going to Jerusalem (see 19.21). This is the reason why he wrote fully about the journey itself (vv. 7–38), but only a short note (vv. 1–6) on the year's work that Paul did in Macedonia and Greece before making the journey.

Luke also describes *Paul as a pastor* who looked after those who had become Christian, and not only a travelling missionary. Paul did spend much of his time travelling, but he stayed three years in Ephesus, and more than a year and half in Corinth. Moreover he: (1) trained leaders to look after congregations after he himself had left; (2) kept in touch with those congregations by letter; and (3) whenever possible revisited congregations which he had founded.

Verses 18–35 especially show that Paul, (a) was able both to preach and to teach (v. 20), (b) taught in small house groups as well as to large crowds in public (v. 20), and (c) accepted suffering as part of his life as pastor (v. 19).

Luke also names *Paul's fellow-workers*, those who shared this ministry with Paul (Luke himself was one of them, v. 5), and describes Paul's attitude to them (vv. 4; 17; 28; 37).

NOTES

20.1–2: Paul ... departed for Macedonia ... and came to Greece. From Paul's letters as well as these verses we discover what he was doing at this time, i.e.:

1. He sailed from Ephesus, and on his way to Macedonia stopped for a short time in Troas (2 Cor. 2.12–13), where he left his travelling cloak behind, 2 Tim. 4.13.

2. In Macedonia his chief work was arranging for people to collect aid for the poor in Jerusalem (see note on 11.29–30). He did this partly in order to relieve suffering, and partly to show those who were against him in Jerusalem that he wanted to heal the division between them.

There Paul also met Titus, who brought him good news from Corinth (2 Cor. 7.5–8). And he may have travelled to the district of Illyricum at this time (Rom. 15.19).

3. He spent three months in Greece (in Corinth), where he visited the Christians and went on with his work of collecting aid (Rom. 15.26). He also wrote his letter to the Christians in Rome (Rom. 15.23–33).

4. He then wanted to sail straight to Syria (and so to Jerusalem), but he heard that some Jews had a plan to push him overboard if he took a boat, and so returned overland to Macedonia (v. 3). He remained there for some time with Luke while his other fellow-workers sailed to Troas (v. 5).

5. Paul and Luke met the others in Troas later (v. 6).

We can see from these verses that Paul was keen to revisit Churches which he had founded.

20.4: Sopater of Beroea ... accompanied him ... and Timothy. Paul's fellow-workers, Sopater and the six others mentioned here, were those who had collected the 'aid' from the Churches to which they belonged and brought it to Troas.

Paul was their leader, but did not work on his own. He trusted those who worked with him, and they supported him and later on suffered with him.

Timothy. See note on 16.1.

20.6: We sailed away from Philippi after the days of Unleavened Bread. Luke's use of 'we' here and 'us' in v. 5 shows that he was with Paul again. Probably he had stayed in Philippi (Macedonia) since the events he recorded in ch. 16.

Days of 'Unleavened Bread'. These are the days of the Jewish Passover Festival in March or April. Paul probably celebrated both the Jewish Passover and the Christian Easter.

20.7: On the first day of the week, when we were gathered together to break bread, Paul talked with them.

First day. This verse and 1 Cor. 16.2 are the only places in the New Testament where we learn on which day Christians met for worship. They met on the 'first day' because that was the day on which Jesus rose again and on which He broke bread (Luke 24.1,13,30). Some members of the Society of Friends call the day on which they meet 'First Day', but most Churches use other names e.g. 'Lord's Day' (following Rev. 1.10).

In KiSwahili it is called the 'second' day (i.e. the second day after the Muslim holy day, Friday) because of Arab influence. It is usually called 'Sunday' in English and other north European languages, but this is not a good name because it is the name which Sun-worshippers used. Some call it the 'Sabbath', but that is incorrect, because the Jewish Sabbath is the seventh day (Exod. 20.10).

Break bread. See note on 2.42c. This meant prayer and a meal together, during which bread was broken. This 'breaking of bread' was the event later called 'Eucharist' or 'Holy Communion' or 'Lord's Supper'.

Talked with them. The Greek word used here and in v. 9 means 'discussed with them', not 'preached to them' (see note on 17.17). Luke says that it went on till 'midnight', but does not say if it was the midnight at the start of the First Day or at the end of that day.

20.9: A young man ... fell down from the third story and was taken up dead. Those who came for the meeting had brought oil lamps to light the upstairs room (v. 8). The young man Eutychus fell asleep (Luke calls him a 'lad' in v. 12), not because Paul was preaching a long sermon, but probably because of the fumes from the lamps.

Did Eutychus die when he fell? Some readers believe that he did and that in v. 10 Luke is describing a miracle (see Additional Note, Miracles, p. 190). Others believe that the boy was so relaxed in his sleep that, when he fell, he was unharmed. Doctors say that this happens from time to time.

20.13: We set sail for Assos. When they left Troas, Luke and the others travelled south by boat to the sea-port of Assos, but Paul walked the 30 kms along the road. They all met in Assos and sailed together to Miletus, stopping at the islands of Mitylene and Samos on the way. Luke explains that they did not stop at Ephesus because Paul wanted to celebrate Pentecost in Jerusalem (v. 16).

20.17: From Miletus he sent to Ephesus and called to him the elders of the church. Paul did not want to delay, but for some reason he was forced to spend a few days in Miletus (perhaps the ship needed repairs). So he sent a messenger to Ephesus, asking the elders to come to Miletus (see note on 14.23). Although Ephesus was 80 kms away, the messenger found the elders at home and the elders were able to travel to Miletus.

20.18: When they came to him, he said to them, 'You yourselves know how I lived among you'. This is the beginning of the address which Paul made to the elders, as he remembered the three years he had spent with them in Ephesus and in the Province of Asia.

In these verses Luke shows us Paul as a pastor, and also gives a guide to missionaries and pastors of today as to the way they need to work.

What Luke has written in vv. 18–35 is a summary of Paul's address, and because Luke was present, it is likely to be an accurate summary. Also, what Luke reports here agrees with what Paul wrote in his letters, e.g. compare v. 34 with 1 Cor. 4.12. It is the only address recorded in Acts which Paul gave to Christians.

20.19: Serving the Lord with all humility and with tears.

Serving the Lord, i.e. being aware that it was God Himself whom he was serving and not only the people. Pastors are often tempted to do what the congregation wants rather than what God wants.

With all humility, i.e. sharing ministry with others, so that when things go well everyone shares in receiving the praise and credit. A 'humble' person is not one who says 'I am of no use', but one who says 'I am part of a team'.

With tears. See p. 175, numbered para. 1, about the sufferings which Paul endured in Ephesus (2 Cor. 11.23–29). Faithful pastors, like faithful parents, cannot escape suffering.

20.20: I did not shrink from declaring ... and teaching you in public and from house to house. 'Declaring' and 'teaching' are not the same.

Paul was *'declaring'*, i.e. preaching the gospel concerning Jesus and doing so out of his own experience. But he also *'taught'*, i.e. he talked with people, asking them questions, listening to their questions, explaining the ways in which they could find guidance in the gospel.

He spoke both to large crowds, and to small groups of people in private houses ('house to house').

20.21: Of repentance to God and of faith in our Lord Jesus.

Repentance. See note on 2.38a. Paul had the courage to call people to change the way they lived. Most pastors find it difficult to do what Paul was doing.

Faith. The Greek word is also translated 'belief', 'trust', 'confidence'. Paul used this word very often in his letters.

1. 'Having faith' means 'trusting'. People show that they have 'faith' in a bus-driver by treating him as trustworthy and travelling in his bus. So believers in God show that they have 'faith' when they treat Him as trustworthy. Paul treated God in this way during the shipwreck (Acts 27.25).

2. In the New Testament 'having faith' means the same as 'believing' or 'trusting'. There is only one Greek word which is translated in these different ways.

3. 'Having faith' means having faith in God or in His Son Jesus (Acts 16.31). It is not the same as having a cheerful outlook or 'hoping for the best'. 'Believing in God' is not the same as holding the right ideas about God. A 'believer' is a truster in God, not just a member of the Church.

4. If we have faith in God we no longer think that we can earn His love. By 'having faith' we trust Him to give us His love as a gift. Paul emphasized this truth (e.g. Eph. 2.8).

5. When our faith in God is real, we show it by our behaviour, e.g.

'having faith' and caring for other people go together (James 2. 15–17). (In Acts 14.22 and in 1 Timothy (e.g. 4.1) the phrase '*the* faith' has a different meaning. See note on 14.22a.)

20.22: Bound in the Spirit, not knowing what shall befall me. I.e. 'I know that God's Spirit is leading me to Jerusalem, but not what will happen there.' So Paul left the future in God's hands, willing to live one day at a time.

20.24a: I do not account my life of any value. Paul was willing to die if that was necessary in order to complete the ministry which Jesus had given him (see note on 21.13).

20.24b: Testify to the gospel of the grace of God. See also v. 32: 'I commend you to God and to the word of His grace.'

Grace was a word which Paul often used (see note on 18.27).

20.27: I did not shrink from declaring to you the whole counsel of God. Paul did not mean that he had fully understood God's will or that he had preached it perfectly. He had written to the Corinthians, 'Our knowledge is imperfect and our prophecy is imperfect' (1 Cor. 13.9). He meant that he had never held back any truth in order to gain popularity.

20.28a: Take heed to yourselves and to all the flock, in which the Holy Spirit has made you overseers.

Take heed, i.e. be aware of the temptations which come especially to ministers of the gospel, e.g. to get promotion rather than to give service, or to maintain the congregation rather than to develop it.

All the flock. By calling the congregation a 'flock' Paul was urging the elders to be like faithful shepherds. He was not telling them to treat the members of their congregations as if they were sheep who cannot think for themselves, or infants who could not defend themselves against danger.

Holy Spirit. Paul was saying that it was God's Holy Spirit and not Paul himself who had appointed them. We may ask: (a) How did he know that they had been chosen by God's Spirit? (b) How can we discover whether present-day Church leaders have really been appointed by God?

Overseers. The Greek word *episcopoi* which is here translated 'overseers' can also be translated 'guardians', 'shepherds', 'bishops'. Those whom Luke here calls 'overseers' (*episcopoi*) were the same people whom he called 'elders' (*presbyteroi*) in v. 17. At that time different congregations had different customs. In some the leader was called 'elder', in others he was called 'overseer'.

It was only later that throughout the Church one person was appointed to be the head over all other Church leaders in each area, and was given the rank and name '*episcopos*' or 'bishop'.

Much later still, at the time of the Reformation, many Christians believed that it was right to follow the custom which we find in Acts and to do without area heads who had the rank and name of 'bishop'.

20.28b: Care for the church of God which he obtained with the blood of his own Son. The Greek word here translated 'obtained' means 'bought'. Paul gave this teaching in his letters, i.e. that Christ brought us into fellowship with God at the cost of His own life, i.e. that He 'bought' us (1 Cor. 6.20).

20.29: Fierce wolves will come. As a wise pastor Paul was preparing the elders for the time when he would no longer be present and they would meet opposition. By 'wolves' he probably meant Church teachers who gave false teaching (see 1 Tim. 1.3–7; Rev. 2.2,6; John 10.12).

20.34: These hands ministered to my necessities. It seems that people in Ephesus had been accusing Paul of making a profit from his work as a missionary and a pastor. So here he reminds them that he worked with his own hands in order to feed himself (see note on 18.3).

20.35a: Help the weak. Paul had worked with his hands not only to feed himself but also in order to give help to those in need. People often forget the 'weak', e.g. those who are too old or too ill to work. It is the special task of Christians to care for them.

20.35b: It is more blessed to give than to receive. Paul says that he helped the weak because Jesus had said this. It seems surprising that Luke reports these words of Jesus here, but does not include them in his Gospel.

20.36: He knelt down and prayed with them all. In those days people did not usually kneel down to pray. Christians used to stand for prayer (Mark 11.25).

20.37: They all wept and embraced Paul and kissed him. Paul was not an easy person to work with. He was sometimes too certain that he was right and that everyone else was wrong (see note on 15.39). But we see from this verse how much he loved his fellow-workers, and how much they loved him. Congregations need a minister who is hard-working and honest, but they also greatly need one who is affectionate and loving.

ADDITIONAL NOTE: MIRACLES

1. Most Christians use the word 'miracle' when they are interpreting unusual events as a special sign of God's loving activity. When Luke reported miracles in Acts he was saying, 'This is God's doing', rather than saying 'This is extraordinary'. (The word 'miracle' is only used in 8.13 and 19.11 in the RSV translation of Acts. The words 'signs', 'wonders' and 'powers' are used instead. See note on 3.12.)

2. Since New Testament times, and especially during the last 500 years, scientists have been discovering more and more what the laws of nature are. But only God Himself knows fully what these 'laws' are. When God, through Paul, cured a man who had been lame all his life (14.8–10), He did so according to His laws of nature. God was not breaking His laws.

3. Because God has given people intelligence to make discoveries through science, we know why some events have occurred which previously were called 'miracles'. But this does not mean that our belief in God's power is weakened. He is the author of the discoveries and of all life.

4. We cannot know whether some of the events described in the Bible should be called miracles or not. God may have enabled Paul to perform a miracle for Eutychus (20.9–10). But Eutychus may not have died. Luke does not tell us. God does indeed do miracles, but it is possible that He did not need to do a miracle for Eutychus. We do not believe in God any less if we think that this event was not a miracle.

5. We need to distinguish carefully between miracles and magic. See note on 19.11.

6. We should not call all strange events miracles. If a cow is born with two heads, it is an 'oddity' not a 'miracle'. We interpret an unusual event as a miracle when we believe that God did it because of His love for us.

7. Many people, including some Christians, think that God does miracles in order to prove that He exists and that He is a loving God. But Jesus did not do miracles to make people believe in Him. He refused to give a 'sign' (Mark 8.11–12), and taught His disciples to believe in Him in 'faith', not because they saw His miracles ('Only believe', Luke 8.50).

8. God does miracles of many different sorts. We could call the courageous speech of Peter, who had been cowardly and afraid, just as miraculous and just as much·God's act as His healing of the lame man (see 2.14–36 and 3.6).

STUDY SUGGESTIONS

REVIEW OF CONTENT

1. For what two reasons did Paul go to Macedonia and Greece before travelling to Jerusalem?

2. Why did Christians meet on the first day of the week?

3. How do we know that Luke was with Paul during the journey to Jerusalem?

4. From what city did the elders come to meet Paul?

5. Why did Paul remind the elders that he had been earning his living by tent-making?

BIBLE STUDY

6. In v. 4 we read of seven of Paul's fellow-workers.

(a) In what way did they assist him?

(b) What else do we know of each of the following: Sopater (or 'Sosipater', see Rom. 16.21), Aristarchus (see Acts 19.29 and 27.2 and Col. 4.10), Trophimus (see 2 Tim. 4.20).

7. (i) What do we learn about the meaning of the word 'faith' (v. 21) from each of the following passages?

(a) Luke 5.19–20   (b) John 14.10   (c) Rom. 3.28

(d) Heb. 11.1   (e) Jas. 2.26

(ii) Give an example from everyday life to show the difference between 'faith' and 'optimism'.

DISCUSSION AND RESEARCH

8. Choose *four* passages from 20.18–35 which especially show Paul as a pastor. In what ways can these verses provide guidance to ministers and missionaries today?

9. 'On the first day of the week' (v. 7).

(a) What different names do Christians use (in English and in any other languages known to you) for the day on which they meet for worship?

(b) Which is the best name to use? Give your reasons.

10. 'Eutychus ... was taken up dead' (20.9).

Do you think that Eutychus died and that Paul raised him from the dead miraculously, or that there is another explanation of the event? Does it matter? Give your reasons.

11. 'The temptations which come especially to ministers of the gospel' (p. 188).

What are the *two* most serious temptations which ministers have to face in your Church?

12. 'Many Christians ... believed that it was right to return to the custom which we find in Acts, so they did not appoint "area heads" who had the name and rank of "bishop"' (pp. 188, 189). (a) Why did they take that step? (b) What is the custom of your Church? (c) Should all Churches do the same in this matter or is each Church free to make its own rules? Give your reasons. (d) Which is the best method in your opinion?

13. How would you answer someone who asked you, 'What is a miracle?'?

21.1–36
Paul's Arrival in Jerusalem

OUTLINE

21.1–16: Paul and his companions travel from Miletus to Jerusalem.
21.17–26: Paul meets the Jerusalem Church leaders and agrees to take part in a Temple ritual.
21.27–36: Jews (probably from Ephesus) attack Paul, but the Roman officer rescues him and arrests him.

INTERPRETATION

Chapters 21—28 contain the account of Paul's journey to Jerusalem and from Jerusalem to Rome, and occupy one quarter of the book of Acts. Luke had several reasons for giving so much space to this one journey. He wished to show: (a) That Paul was still determined to heal the separation between Jewish and Gentile Christians by bringing the Gentiles' gift to Jerusalem (see note on 11.29); (b) That Paul reached Rome, from which centre he believed that great missionary work would spring; (c) That Paul was never disloyal to the Roman Empire, and; (d) Perhaps the chief reason—to show that Paul in making this journey was following Jesus who 'went up to Jerusalem' (Luke 19.28).

JESUS AND PAUL

Like Jesus, Paul spoke of his future sufferings (21.13), was arrested (21.33), was condemned by the Jewish crowd (21.36), was tried by the Jewish religious leaders (22.30—23.10), was tried by a Roman Governor (24.10—26.32), was found innocent (26.31), not yet set free (28.16). And, according to a tradition, like Jesus he was condemned to death.

NOTES

21.1: When we had parted from them and set sail. The Greek word here translated 'parted from them' really means 'painfully torn ourselves away from them', and we can understand this in view of 20.36–38.
  Their journey was in seven stages:
  1. From Miletus to the island of Cos, in a small boat (v. 1);
  2. To the city of Rhodes, on the north of the island of Rhodes;

3. To the mainland port of Patara, in Lycia, where they could board a large ship to sail the 650 kms across the Mediterranean Sea (v. 2);

4. To Tyre, where they spent a week (v. 4), then on by sea

5. To Ptolemais (called Akko today) for one day (v. 7), and then, probably by sea

6. To Caesarea, the sea-port from which after some days they finally made the 100 kms journey, southward through the hills

7. To Jerusalem (v. 15).

21.4: Through the Spirit they told Paul not to go on to Jerusalem. When Paul and his friends landed at Tyre they 'sought out' the Christians in the town. Probably these were refugees who had escaped to Tyre at the time of the persecution in Jerusalem (11.19).

These Christians said that God had told them ('through the Spirit') that Paul should not go to Jerusalem. But Paul had said that he was 'bound in the Spirit' to go (20.22). Each was certain that God had sent a message, but the messages did not agree (see notes on 6.1a; 15.2a). This happens very often among Christians, e.g. some Church leaders in South America are sure that God is telling them to take part in politics for the sake of the very poor, others are equally sure that God is calling them to avoid politics in order to concentrate on personal evangelism. How should we explain this?

(a) As human beings who make mistakes we can never be completely certain that we have interpreted God's guidance rightly.

(b) Because of our own very strong feelings we may sincerely think that what we want is what God is saying. This seems to have happened in Tyre. These Christians wanted to have Paul with them more than they wanted Paul to do his work for Jesus Christ. They probably felt afraid that they would be unprotected if Paul was arrested in Jerusalem, so they honestly believed that God did not want him to go there.

(c) Although it is difficult to interpret God's will rightly, it is not impossible. God does offer guidance.

21.5–6: They all, with wives and children, brought us on our way ... and ... we prayed and bade one another farewell. In vv. 4–6 we read of Paul and his group finding out where the Christians of Tyre lived and having warm fellowship with them. Because the followers of Jesus are a world-wide family, its members need to meet each other and to 'search out' other Christians, especially when they are a minority in their country. Pilgrims to the Holy Land need to meet the Christians there, and not only to visit the ancient places. Some years ago a Scandinavian businessman went to the Gambia on behalf of his firm, and while he was there went up country to visit Christian congregations. As a result there has been a link for the last ten years between his home congregation and a Christian training college in Gambia (see also v. 7 and 20.36–38).

21.8: We ... came to Caesarea; and we entered the house of Philip the evangelist. Luke here explains that this Philip was not the Philip who was one of the Twelve (Luke 6.14), but one of the helpers whom the Twelve appointed to care for the poor (Acts 6.3–6). We read in 8.40 that he came to Caesarea.

He may have been officially appointed by the Church as an 'evangelist' (see Eph. 4.11), or perhaps he was a Christian who was able to evangelize freely.

21.10–11: A prophet named Agabus ... took Paul's girdle and bound his own feet and hands. We read in 11.28 that Agabus predicted a famine (which did indeed take place). According to v. 10 he predicted that if Paul went to Jerusalem he would be arrested, and that the Jews would hand him over to the Gentiles. This prediction was fulfilled, but not exactly. Paul was seized by the Jewish crowd, but they did not 'hand him over' to the Romans. The Romans arrested him themselves.

Agabus acted his message, just as some Old Testament prophets acted theirs, e.g. at a time when the people were in despair, expecting to be invaded, Jeremiah bought a field and went about showing them the receipt. This was his way of saying 'If we trust God and live in the way He wants, we shall survive any invasion and shall build houses on our land' (Jer. 32.6–15).

21.13: I am ready not only to be imprisoned but even to die at Jerusalem for the name of the Lord Jesus. We might think from this that Paul actually wanted to suffer and to die (see also 20.22 and 25). There have been many Christians who mistakenly believed that they were not being real Christians unless they were in trouble or being made to suffer. (Perhaps they wanted to follow Matt. 5.11 exactly, or to atone for their sins.) They really *wanted* to be martyrs. Shortly after Luke wrote Acts, Ignatius was bishop of Syrian Antioch. When he was accused of treason by the Roman authorities and was being arrested and taken to Rome, he wrote to the Church there. He begged them 'not to rescue him from the wild animals but to let them devour him'. He was killed in that way in AD 107.

But Paul was not like that. He went up to Jerusalem because he had work to do there (see Interpretation above) 'for the name of the Lord Jesus', not in order to suffer or to be a martyr. Paul knew, as most Christians know, that if you are faithful to Christ, you find enough suffering in life and do not need to search for it.

21.17: When we had come to Jerusalem, the brethren received us gladly. They made the journey from Caesarea up to Jerusalem. Probably they rode on horses or mules, having heavy baggage full of the money which they had collected from Gentile congregations 'for the poor in Jerusalem'. As they travelled they met the other pilgrims going up for the Festival of the First Fruits ('Pentecost'). When they arrived they were warmly welcomed by Mnason (v. 16) and by the Hellenistic Jewish Christians ('brethren'), those who supported Paul in his attitude to the Gentiles. On the next day they met James (see note on v. 23).

21.19: He related one by one the things that God had done among the Gentiles through his ministry. Paul described his 'ministry' among Gentiles to James.

The Greek word here translated 'ministry' is *diakonia*. This word, together with *diakonos* (minister) and *diakonein* (to minister), is an important New Testament word. Writers use it in five ways: (1) Being useful (like Martha, Luke 10.40); (2) Christ's giving Himself for mankind (Mark 10.45); (3) Christians' behaviour following Christ (Mark 10.43); (4) The service which Church leadersgive (as in this verse); (5) The work done by the leaders called 'deacons' (1 Tim. 3.10).

In the RSV several words are used to translate it: 'ministry', 'service', 'help', 'mission'. But the basic meaning in most of the passages is 'giving service of the sort which Jesus Himself gave'. That is what a Christian 'minister' is commissioned to do.

21.23–24: We have four men who are under a vow; take these men and purify yourself along with them. Paul and his group, who had been welcomed by the Hellenists, were now welcomed by James. This was James the brother of Jesus, who was the head of the Church in Jerusalem. Luke makes no mention of any of the Apostles being present.

James's problem. James praised God for what Paul had done for Gentiles (v. 19), but he and the elders in the Jerusalem Church had a problem to solve. On the one hand they admitted that the Church was growing through Paul's work. On the other hand they knew that they were respected by the Jewish community only if, in return, they respected the Jewish Law. Also they themselves were anxious to keep the ancient Law. It was in this way that they differed from the Hellenists (see note on 6.1). But they were very doubtful as to whether Paul did respect the Law.

James's problem became more serious when people began to say that Paul had told Jews to abandon the ancient custom of circumcision. This was not entirely true. Although he had written 'We Jews are not justified by works of the law' (Gal. 2.15–16), he had never told Jewish Christians to stop circumcising children. It was *Gentiles* to whom he had clearly said, 'Circumcision is unnecessary'.

So in order to solve this problem James told Paul to take part in a Jewish ritual publicly. This was a purification ritual (see 18.18). Four Jerusalem Christians had taken the vows, and Paul was told to share in the ritual and to pay all the expenses. By doing so he would show that he still kept the Law.

Paul's problem. Should he obey James or refuse? Paul decided to obey him.

Some people say that by doing this, Paul was acting a lie and was guilty of dishonesty and hypocrisy. He had written to the Galatians and to the Romans that Christ had put an end to the Law (Rom. 10.4). He was pretending to be a fully loyal Jew, but was not. Such pretence, they say, cannot be successful. Paul achieved nothing by taking part in the ritual. He had himself said that Christians must not do evil in order that good may result (Rom. 3.8).

Other people see Paul as courageously taking part in a compromise for the sake of unity among Christians (see also 1 Cor. 9.20–23). He took part in this ritual so that Hellenists and traditionalists should live together in fellowship. He put this hope before his own conviction. Those who hold this opinion explain that Christians cannot avoid 'compromise', because they often have to face two truths, not one. For Paul it was true that Christ had made sacrifices unnecessary, but it was also true that Christ needed a united Church. So today some Christians may object to some statements which are made in the Church services because 'they are not true', but they remain in that congregation for the sake of another truth, i.e. that we are one body in Christ (1 Cor. 12.12–13, see note on Acts 15.20, 'The decision').

21.27: The Jews from Asia . . . stirred up all the crowd, and laid hands on him. Some Jews from the province of Asia were in Jerusalem, probably to celebrate the Festival. Perhaps they had met Paul in Ephesus (19.28), and had regarded him as an enemy since that time. Then they heard a rumour that he had taken some Gentiles across the 'dividing wall' of the Temple into the Court of Israel (see Eph. 2.14). This wall or '*soreg*' separated the Court of the Gentiles from the inner courts, and on it was a notice: 'No foreigner may pass this barrier around the Temple and if anyone is caught doing so he must blame himself for his own death' (see diagram p. 197). The rumour about Paul was untrue, but they believed it, and they felt that they had a right to attack him. They dragged him out of the Court of Israel and tried to kill him (v. 31).

We can understand why these Jews (who were not Christians) were so angry. They thought that Paul was destroying the things that made Jews different from the rest of mankind, e.g. the custom of circumcision. We know how angry Muslims going to Friday prayers feel if they hear a rumour that a Christian has criticized the teachings of the Qur'an.

21.31–33: Word came to the tribune of the cohort . . . the tribune arrested him. Outside the north portico of the Temple area the Romans had built a large high tower called the Fortress of Antonia. They did this so that they could prevent anti-Roman demonstrations taking place in the courts of the Temple. During Festival times they kept 1,000 soldiers (a

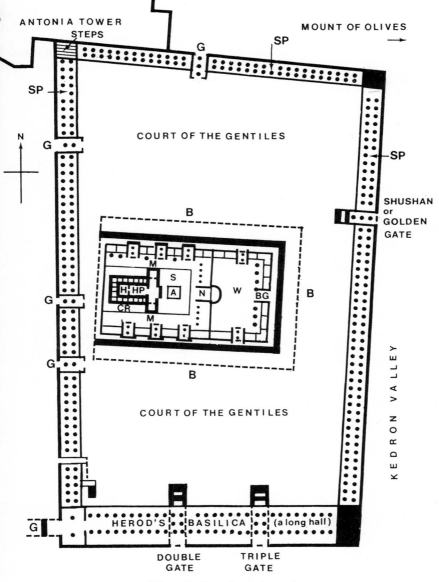

Plan of Herod's Temple at Jerusalem

A	Altar of sacrifice	HP	Holy Place
B	The Barrier	M	Men's Court (Court of Israel)
BG	Beautiful Gate	N	Nicanor Gate
CR	Council Room, for Sanhedrin	S	Sanctuary (Court for priests only)
G	Gates	SP	Solomon's Portico
H	Holy of Holies	W	Women's Court

'cohort'), with horses, in the tower.The commanding officer of these soldiers was their 'tribune' (major), in this case a Greek called Claudius Lysias. He took a body of soldiers down the steps that led from the Fortress to the Temple portico, and arrested Paul. Having arrested him, the soldiers had to carry him on their shoulders up the steps into the Fortress because the crowds were trying to kill him (v. 36).

STUDY SUGGESTIONS

REVIEW OF CONTENT

1. Give one reason why Paul travelled to Jerusalem.
2. At what three places in the journey did he meet groups of Christians?
3. Who was Philip, whom Paul met in Caesarea?
4. Why did James tell Paul to take part in a Jewish ritual?
5. What was the 'dividing wall' in the temple area?

BIBLE STUDY

6. 'Paul in making this journey was following Jesus who "went up to Jerusalem"' (p. 192). Match each of Jesus's experiences described in passages (a)–(f) in Luke's Gospel, with the corresponding experience of Paul described in one of the passages (g)–(l) in Acts.

Luke	Acts
(a) 18.31–34	(g) 21.13–14
(b) 22.54	(h) 21.33
(c) 22.66	(i) 21.36
(d) 23.1–2	(j) 22.30
(e) 23.14–15	(k) 24.1–2
(f) 23.18	(l) 26.31

7. 'Agabus acted his message, just as some Old Testament prophet acted theirs' (p. 194).
   According to each of the following passages, what did the prophet do, and what was the message which he acted?
   (a) 1 Kings 11.29–31   (b) Isa. 20.2–5   (c) Jer. 13.1–9
   (d) Ezek. 4.1–3
8. 'The Greek word here translated "ministry" is *diakonia* . . . Writers use it in five ways' (see note on 21.19). How is the word translated in each of the following verses, and in which of those five ways is it used?
   (a) Mark 10.45   (b) Acts 12.25   (c) Acts 19.22
   (d) Rom. 16.1   (e) 2 Cor. 3.6   (f) Phil. 1.1

DISCUSSION AND RESEARCH

9. 'God does offer guidance' (p. 193).
   (a) Give two examples of this truth from other chapters of Acts.
   (b) Is this true in your experience? Give examples.
   (c) 'We can never be completely certain that we have interpreted God's guidance rightly' (p. 193). What is your opinion? Illustrate your answer with an example.
10. 'Agabus acted his message' (p. 194).
    (a) Describe the actions of a speaker or preacher who acted his message in your presence, and say how effective the actions were in conveying the message.
    (b) What advantages can there be of 'speaking' in this way, and what are the dangers?
11. 'Many Christians mistakenly believed that they were not being real Christians unless they were being made to suffer' (p. 194).
    (a) Why do some Christians behave in that way?
    (b) Why did Paul endure suffering?
12. 'James told Paul to take part in a Jewish ritual publicly ... Paul decided to obey him?' (p. 195).
    (a) What would you have done if you had been Paul? Give your reasons.
    (b) Give examples of some present-day situations in which Christians face a similar dilemma. Say in each case whether or not you think they should compromise, and why.

21.37—23.11

Paul's Two Speeches to the Jews

OUTLINE

21.37–40: The Roman tribune allows Paul to make a speech.

22.1–21: Paul's speech to the Jewish crowd.

22.22–29: The tribune rescues Paul from the angry crowd.

22.30–23.5: The anger of the High Priest.

23.6–11: Paul's speech to the Sanhedrin.

INTERPRETATION

THE TWO AUTHORITIES

Paul, like every other Jew who lived in the Roman Empire, had two 'authorities' who expected him to obey them. One was the Jewish authority, of whom the High Priest was head, the other was the Roman Empire whose head was the Emperor. In the next five chapters of Acts (21.37—26.30) Luke records how Paul met both these authorities.

PAUL WITH THE JEWS

In this section, 21.37—23.11, we read of Paul's speeches to Jews, first to the crowd, later to the Sanhedrin. Although in some passages it is difficult to discover what happened, Luke has enabled us to see what the chief events were (see note on 22.30).

NOTES

21.37: Paul ... said to the tribune, 'May I say something to you?' Paul probably had to shout in order to be heard above the noise of the crowd, and he did so in Greek. The tribune had previously thought that Paul was the Egyptian guerilla-leader who unsuccessfully led a revolt against the Romans in AD 54 (v. 38). This man led an army of 4,000 Assassins ('dagger men') and was the only person to escape. When the tribune heard Paul using Greek, he asked him who he was, and Paul told him, 'I am a Jew, from Tarsus' (v. 39). Tarsus was one of the three chief university cities in the Roman Empire (the other two were Athens and Alexandria).

21.40: Paul, standing on the steps ... spoke to them in the Hebrew language.

On the steps. Paul stood on the high stairway that led to the Fortress of Antonia. Luke says that as he stood there, there was a 'great hush'. Perhaps this was because they were astonished at his appearance, his face running with blood and his clothes torn to shreds (the crowd had dragged him out of the Temple and tried to kill him, vv. 30–31).

He spoke to them. We especially notice in this speech: (a) That Paul spoke out of his own experience, chiefly about his conversion, not repeating what others had believed or done (see note on 15.8). (b) The contrast between the beginning and the end of the speech. At first Paul made himself one with his listeners, 'I am a Jew ... (22.3). But later he had to go further and tell them of the commission which he had received from God to minister to the Gentiles: 'I will send you far away to the Gentiles' (22.21). Then they rejected him.

In the Hebrew language. 'Hebrew' in this verse means 'Aramaic', the everyday language which Jews spoke throughout the eastern part of the Roman Empire. The Hebrew language was only spoken by highly educated Jews. It was because Paul used Aramaic that the crowd listened (22.2). He was a fully trained theologian, but was able to use the language of the people. Many inexperienced preachers of today lose the attention of their listeners because they use special theological language. They learnt it at college but have not learnt how to translate it so that ordinary people can understand.

22.3: Brought up in this city at the feet of Gamaliel. Paul had been taken to Jerusalem when he was young and later became a student under Gamaliel (see 5.34). Gamaliel was a famous Jewish theologian who was far less bound by tradition than most Rabbis. Paul, before he became a Christian, was stricter than Gamaliel (see Phil. 3.5–6).

22.4: I persecuted this Way. Paul shows his listeners that he was a strict Jew by telling them that he had persecuted the Christian Church. He calls it 'the Way'.

In the Bible the word 'way' often means a path or a road, but it also has special meanings, e.g.:

(a) The plan on which God has created the world, the way in which He intends that people should live. 'The Lord teaches the humble his way' (Ps. 25.9). Jesus commented that it was difficult to keep to that way: 'The way is hard that leads to life' (Matt. 7.14).

(b) Jesus called Himself 'the way' because He, alone of all mankind, was fully living according to God's plan (John 14.6).

(c) The first followers of Jesus were called the 'people of the Way' and in some verses 'the Way' seems to mean 'the Church', as in this verse and in 24.14. Other people could tell who the Christians were by the 'way' in which they behaved towards each other and towards others, rather than by their knowledge or their skill in preaching. During a long dispute between a Christian congregation and the local Muslims, their Bishop said, 'The way in which you conduct this affair is as important as the result.'

Note. Taoists in China use the phrase 'The Way'. They teach that human beings must follow the way in which the whole universe behaves. For Jews, '*halacha*' is 'the Way'. There is surely a link between such teaching and what Jesus taught about the 'Way'.

22.6: As I made my journey and drew near to Damascus. Here Luke gives us a second account of Paul's conversion (see notes on 9.3–25). This account is very like those in chapter 9 and in Gal. 1.15–16. But there are some differences: compare 22.9 with 9.7; 22.15 with 9.17; 22.17 with 9.27–30. 'About noon' occurs only in this account.

22.14: The God of our fathers appointed you to know his will, to see the Just One, and to hear a voice from his mouth. Ananias told Paul that the work which God had appointed him to do was: (1) to discover God's will, (2) to do this by treating Jesus (the Just One) as God's voice, and (3) to do so by listening to that voice rather than the voice of the world around.

22.15: You will be a witness for him to all men. According to this verse

Paul said it was Ananias who told him that he must be a 'witness for Jesus'. According to the account of Paul's speech to Agrippa in 26.16 he said that it was Jesus who gave him this message. The Greek word translated 'witness' is *martus*, from which we get the word 'martyr'; it is translated 'martyr' in Rev. 17.6. Very often when Christians 'witness' to what Jesus has done and what He wants His followers to do, they do suffer and even give their lives for it, as Stephen did (v. 20 and see note on 7.58a).

22.17: I fell into a trance. See note on 'visions' (p. 151), and see 23.11. Here Paul says that it was in a vision that he was told to leave Jerusalem, but according to 9.27–30 it was the Christians who persuaded him.

22.24: The tribune ... ordered him to be examined by scourging. When the crowd had refused to listen to Paul and had again demanded that he should be killed (vv. 22–23), the tribune decided to interrogate him by torture to see if he was a political agitator. Paul had been flogged with rods at Philippi (16.22–23) and probably at Ephesus, but the torture which the tribune now ordered was much worse. They stretched prisoners out on to a frame of wooden planks and kept on beating them with strips of leather to which they had tied bits of iron and bone.

22.25: Is it lawful for you to scourge a man who is a Roman citizen? Paul said this when he was about to be tortured. He told them that he was born a Roman citizen, that is, a privileged person (see note on 16.37). The tribune was astonished, and told Paul that he himself had had to buy his citizenship. He released him the next day.

Some commentators point out that Jesus never escaped suffering by claiming that He was a special person. They add that Paul, in saying this, was failing to place himself alongside those many unprivileged people in the world who have no rights. But others think that Paul believed that God wanted him to reach Rome alive and that he spoke about his 'rights' for the sake of the gospel rather than for his own sake.

It may not be wrong for Christians to 'claim their rights' when they do so for the sake of others. A priest who brought a very seriously ill woman to hospital was probably right to explain who he was and to ask for special attention for her. But too often those who hold important positions or who are rich demand special attention for themselves, e.g. the best seat in church or the first place in a queue.

22.30: He ... commanded the chief priests and all the council to meet. Luke's account in 22.30—23.10 of Paul being taken to the Jewish Sanhedrin ('the council') is not clear, and readers ask many questions e.g.: Did a Roman tribune really have the authority to 'command' the Sanhedrin to meet? Why did the Sanhedrin discuss resurrection instead of dealing with the charge against Paul (21.28)? How was it that Paul, a prisoner, was able to be in charge of events?

'Very often when Christians witness to what Jesus wants us to do they suffer for it, and even give up their lives' (p. 202).

In recent years many Christians in Korea have suffered arrest and detention without trial. The Korean poet Kim Chi Ha was sentenced to life imprisonment for courageously speaking out in defence of Christian principles.

But we can see what the main events were: (1) the tribune handed Paul over to the Sanhedrin; (2) the High Priest and Paul had a violent dispute; (3) the Sanhedrin failed to reach a decision; and (4) the tribune had to take Paul back into the Antonia fortress.

23.2: The high priest Ananias commanded those who stood by him to strike him. We should not confuse this Ananias with two others who had the same name (5.1 and 9.10), or with Annas, a previous High Priest (4.6). This Ananias was dismissed soon after this incident, and was later killed by Jewish guerillas for being pro-Roman.

His task on this occasion was to find out whether Paul was guilty of breaking the Jewish Law, but in giving the order to strike Paul, he himself was breaking it.

23.3: Paul said to him, 'God shall strike you'. It is not surprising that Paul was very angry. But how should we interpret his anger? Did he feel personally insulted and lose his temper? Or was he boldly following the example of the Hebrew prophets, and of Jesus Himself, in angrily denouncing evil (see John 2.15)?

23.5: I did not know, brethren, that he was the high priest. Paul said this when they accused him of 'reviling the High Priest'. Was he telling a lie in order to escape trouble? It is more likely that, because this was an informal meeting, the High Priest was not sitting in his usual seat, so that Paul did not know who had given the order to strike him.

23.6a: Paul perceived that one part were Sadducees and the other Pharisees. The Sadducees and Pharisees were two 'sects' or societies within the Jewish religion. Each group sent representatives to the Sanhedrin. They had been united in opposing Jesus, e.g. Matt. 16.1–6, but on many matters they disagreed. The Sadducees belonged to the wealthy families and the high priest was a Sadducee; they also depended on the Roman Empire to help them keep their power, whereas the Pharisees hated the Romans. There was another difference between them to which Paul refers here. The Sadducees kept strictly to the Law as it is in the first five books of the Old Testament, but the Pharisees were ready to interpret the Law and to apply it to changing circumstances. The Sadducees refused to believe in 'resurrection', i.e. that after death a person could be alive as a spirit or an angel (v. 8), because they did not find that belief in the Law. But the Pharisees believed in 'resurrection'. So when Paul spoke about Jesus's resurrection the two groups disagreed violently (v. 10).

23.6b: Brethren, I am a Pharisee. In Phil. 3.5–7 Paul wrote that before he was a Christian he had been a Pharisee, but he was one no longer. But according to this verse he says he is still a Pharisee. Some think Paul was being dishonest in order to gain the support of the Pharisees. But it is more likely that he was saying, 'I am a Pharisee by upbringing, but I believe that following Jesus is the fulfilment of being a Pharisee.'

23.11: The following night the Lord stood by him and said, 'Take courage'. This is another of Paul's visions. Because of it he knew that God was beside him whatever happened. He would save him *in* danger, though not *from* danger. He knew also that he must reach Rome (see note on 16.9).

STUDY SUGGESTIONS

REVIEW OF CONTENT

1. What were the two 'authorities' whom all Jews were expected to obey?
2. (a) Where was Paul born? (b) Where was he educated?
3. What did Paul say that made the Jewish crowd reject him?
4. What happened which prevented Paul from being tortured?
5. In what two ways did the Sadducees differ from the Pharisees?

BIBLE STUDY

6. 'I persecuted this Way' (22.4). As we saw, the word 'Way' has four different meanings. What is its meaning in each of the following passages?
   (a) Exod. 13.21   (b) Isa. 55.8–9   (c) Matt. 22.16
   (d) John 14.6   (e) Acts 19.9
7. 'Stephen thy witness' (22.20). Read the following verses and say in each case: (i) Who gave witness or were told to witness? (ii) To what did they witness? (iii) To whom did they give their witness?
   (a) John 1.15   (b) Acts 1.8   (c) Acts 3.15
   (d) Acts 22.15

DISCUSSION AND RESEARCH

8. Paul spoke to them 'in the everyday language which Jews spoke' (p. 200).
   (a) Why is it necessary for preachers to use the ordinary language of their listeners?
   (b) How would you translate the following New Testament words into the ordinary language of the people around you?
   (i) redeem   (ii) revelation   (iii) grace
9. (a) Note down three differences between Paul's account of his conversion in 22.3–21 and the account in 9.1–19.
   (b) What reply can you give to those who say that they cannot rely on Luke as a historian because of differences like these?

10. 'Paul told them that he was born a Roman citizen, i.e. a privileged person' (p. 202).
    (a) Was he right to do this? Give reasons for your answer.
    (b) When, if ever, is it right for Christians to claim their privileges'?
11. (a) 'Paul was very angry' (p. 204). When is it right for a Christian to be angry, and when is it wrong? Give examples.
    (b) 'Did Paul lose his temper?' (p. 204) What are the most harmful results when someone loses their temper? What sins are more serious than losing one's temper?

23.12—25.12

Roman Governors Examine Paul

OUTLINE

23.12–24: Some Jews make a plot to kill Paul.

23.25–30: The tribune asks Governor Felix to see Paul.

23.31–35: Soldiers take Paul to Felix in Caesarea.

24.1–9: The Jews' lawyer accuses Paul.

24.10–21: Paul makes his defence.

24.22–27: Felix postpones his decision, and leaves Paul in prison for two years.

25.1–12: Festus, successor to Felix, also refuses to pronounce a verdict, and Paul appeals to Caesar.

INTERPRETATION

From 21.17—23.11 Luke told how Paul defended himself to Jews. In 23.12—25.12 he describes Paul's defence before Roman governors.

Luke continued to emphasize the good treatment which the Romans gave to Paul and, on the other hand, the hostility of the Jews. He did not do this in order to stir up hatred against the Jews (see note on 2.23b), but for a different reason. He wanted to show his first-century readers, especially the Romans, that Paul was grateful to them for their protection, and also that he and other Christians were loyal members of the Empire.

NOTES

23.12: The Jews made a plot and bound themselves by an oath. These Jews ('more than forty') made a religious vow to kill Paul: 'May God curse us if we do not keep it.' They planned to murder him as he was being taken from the Fortress to the Sanhedrin. They were a group of fanatics, like the 'suicide-squads' among some present-day guerrillas. They were certain to be killed if they attacked Paul while he was with the Roman soldiers.

23.16: The son of Paul's sister heard of their ambush. This is the only verse in the New Testament which mentions Paul's family.

His nephew had overheard the Jews plotting and managed to get into the Fortress and see Paul. Perhaps he was able to do this because he was a child, one of those who took food to prisoners (see v. 19: 'the tribune took him by the hand'). When Paul heard of the plot, he persuaded a centurion to take the boy to the tribune.

23.23: Get ready two hundred soldiers. The tribune had to act quickly to prevent Paul being killed. So he ordered a body of 470 soldiers to leave at 9 p.m. that night ('the third hour') to take Paul to Caesarea, and Paul was given horses to ride.

23.24: Bring him safely to Felix the governor. Tiberius Claudius Felix became governor of Judea in AD 52. Roman historians describe him as an evil man and a cruel governor, who maintained so-called peace by killing huge numbers of rebels. Like Pilate he was dismissed from his position by the Emperor a few years after this event (24.47).

23.26: Claudius Lysias to his Excellency. In vv. 26–30 Luke gives us a summary of the letter which the tribune wrote. See v. 25: 'he wrote to this effect', i.e. 'he wrote this sort of letter'. Luke could not have seen the letter itself.

We note that: (a) Lysias hid the fact that he had tied up a Roman citizen without a trial (22.24); (b) he did not condemn Paul, because Paul had broken no Roman law (v. 29).

23.31: So the soldiers ... took Paul and brought him by night to Antipatris. It was 60 kms from Jerusalem to Antipatris, a long journey for foot-soldiers to make in one night.

Between Jerusalem and Antipatris it is hilly country and there were many Jewish rebels in the area, so a very large body of soldiers was needed. But between Antipatris and Caesarea it is open country and the inhabitants were mostly Gentiles, so the foot-soldiers were no longer needed and returned to Jerusalem.

23.33: They came to Caesarea. Caesarea, not Jerusalem, was the headquarters of the Roman Government in Judea, and the place where the governor lived. Although it was a great city with magnificent buildings and a large port, it was at this time the centre of trouble. Jews and Syrians fought each other and the district round the city was full of rebels. Many people expected that a national revolt against Rome would come soon, and so it did, in AD 66.

The soldiers gave the letter to the governor and handed over Paul, who was put in the 'praetorium'. This was one of the many palaces which Herod the Great had built, and was not the government headquarters. Paul speaks of the 'praetorium' in Phil. 1.13, which leads some scholars to think that he wrote that letter from Caesarea.

Felix was able to conduct Paul's trial because Paul had been born in a Roman province (Cilicia, v. 34).

24.2: Tertullus began to accuse him. Tertullus was the lawyer whom the High Priest had hired. He began with the sort of flattery which lawyers sometimes use in order to gain the approval of a judge. It was not true that they 'enjoyed much peace' (v. 2). And Felix had introduced no 'reforms'. Tertullus accused Paul of: (1) being a pest; (2) being guilty of 'sedition', i.e. stirring up people against the authorities; (3) belonging to the 'Nazarene' sect; (4) having 'profaned' the Temple.

Three of these accusations were of no interest to the governor. But the accusation of 'sedition' was very serious, as it would be today in any country, e.g. when the leader of a Christian congregation, living as a small minority in a country whose population is mainly Buddhist, Muslim or Hindu, is accused of sedition, i.e. plotting against the constitution.

Note: Tertullus called Paul a 'Nazarene' and Peter referred to Jesus as a 'Nazarene' (e.g. in 2.22), but except in this verse no New Testament writer used this name for Christians. It has, however, been used as a name for Christians in present-day Arabic and also in some other languages.

24.10: When the governor had motioned to him to speak, Paul replied. He said that:

(a) He had only been in Jerusalem twelve days and had not had time to do the things of which he was accused (v. 11);

(b) He had not disputed with anyone in public (vv. 12,18);

(c) He was a faithful worshipper of the God of the Jews and followed the Law and the Prophets (v. 14b);

(d) He admitted that he followed the 'Way'. He belonged to the group who believed that Jesus had fulfilled the old Jewish beliefs (v. 14a) and who believed in a resurrection (vv. 15, 21).

(e) He had not come to Jerusalem to cause trouble but to bring aid for the very poor (v. 17).

(f) He also pointed out that his accusers from the province of Asia were absent (vv. 18–19).

24.15: There will be a resurrection of both the just and the unjust. In this verse the word 'resurrection' means God raising human beings to new life after they have died. It does not refer to God's raising Jesus to life at Easter.

But there were (and are) two ways of thinking about this 'resurrection':

1. In this verse it means life after death for everyone, for 'the just and for the unjust'. Most Jews who were not Sadducees believed in that sort of resurrection at the time when Paul was speaking (see Dan. 12.2–3). Thus it means 'resurrection for all, but resurrection for judgement' as in John 5.28–29: 'All who are in the tombs will hear his voice and come forth, those who have done good, to the resurrection of life, and those who have done evil, to the resurrection of judgement.' But this is the only verse in the New Testament where Paul says that resurrection is for everyone.

2. In Paul's letters he says that it is only those who are 'in Christ' who experience resurrection: 'In Christ shall all be made alive' (1 Cor. 15.22).

So the Bible seems to contain two different views about resurrection. When a group of students studied those differences they expressed various opinions, e.g.: (a) 'Paul changed his mind during his life.' (b) 'Nobody knows what happens after death so these differences do not matter.' (c) 'Whichever view we hold, we know that there is life after death and that we are judged according to the way we have lived.'

24.16: I always take pains to have a clear conscience toward God and toward men. Greeks and Romans regarded 'conscience' as a natural power which everyone has, like seeing or tasting. Paul refers to this 'Gentile' idea in Rom. 2.4. But in the New Testament the word 'conscience' usually means being responsible to God and treating Him as the One who judges what is right and what is wrong (2 Tim. 1.3).

As Christians we need to keep our consciences fresh, as Paul says here, 'taking pains' to keep them 'clear'. Otherwise they become weak (1 Cor. 8.7–10) or sickly, e.g. making us feel that God is always condemning us.

24.17: I came to bring to my nation alms and offerings. This collecting of alms for the poor Christians of Judea was very important to Paul (see 1 Cor. 16.1–4 and note on 19.21–22). It was his way of trying to unite the Gentiles (who gave the money) and the Jewish Christians of Judea (who received it). In Rom. 15.25–27 Paul explains that when the Gentiles made a collection for the Jews, both were givers and both were receivers. The Gentiles had received the gospel from the Jews and the Jews were receiving aid from the Gentiles. The Gentiles gave the aid and the Jews had given them the gospel.

A large and well-established town congregation in West Africa sent a teacher and money to a small and very poor congregation who were being seriously troubled by the local chief. Both congregations discovered that they were receivers (the large congregation received inspiration from the courage of the others), and that both were givers. Real partnership and affection among the two groups resulted. Each had the pleasure of knowing that they had helped their fellow Christians.

24.22: Felix put them off, saying, 'When Lysias the tribune comes down, I will decide your case. Felix had probably realized that Paul had broken no Roman law. But in order to avoid trouble with the Jews he refused to pronounce a verdict. So he 'put them off'. As a result Paul was kept in prison.

24.25: He argued about justice and self-control and future judgement. Felix and his Jewish wife discussed 'faith in Jesus Christ' with Paul, but they sent him away when he spoke about matters which affected Felix closely. Felix was neither 'just' nor 'self-controlled' (see note on 23.24), and did not want to think about these three matters.

24.26: He hoped that money would be given him by Paul. He hoped that Paul would bribe him in order to gain his freedom. It seems that Paul had enough money to do so. We have already seen that he paid the expenses of the four men who were under a vow (21.24). He had also to pay for his own food while he was in prison, and later rented a house in Rome for two years (28.30). He may have earned the money from his trade, or perhaps local Christians made contributions.

24.27: Two years had elapsed. Paul was left in prison for at least two years, because he refused to bribe Felix. During this time he was not alone. According to v. 23 he was allowed to have visitors and had 'some liberty' (e.g. he could wash every day). Luke himself was probably in Caesarea for these two years, together with Philip the Evangelist and his family (21.8). John Bunyan and other Christians used their time in prison for writing, and Paul probably did the same, and wrote many letters to the congregations which he had founded. But it is not likely that these letters have survived. Most scholars think that Paul wrote to Philemon from Rome, and that, if he was the author of Ephesians and Colossians, he wrote them from Rome. It must have been a very difficult time for Paul, because he was an active person. He had to learn two lessons especially, which all Christians have to learn: (a) How to serve God while being forced to be inactive, whether through imprisonment, like Paul, or illness. (b) How to receive the ministry of others instead of ministering to others. Many people who have retired find this difficult.

It seems from Phil. 4.11–13 that Paul did learn these lessons.

25.1: When Festus had come. After the Emperor had dismissed Felix, Festus became Governor of Judea. Immediately the Jews made another plan to kill Paul by asking that he should be sent to Jerusalem (v. 3). At first Festus refused this request (v. 4). But he was determined not to offend the Jewish leaders. He therefore changed his mind, and suggested that Paul go to Jerusalem to defend himself there (v. 9).

25.8: Paul said, 'Neither against the law of the Jews ... nor against Caesar have I offended at all'. In three verses (8,10 and 11) Luke gives a brief summary of Paul's defence.

In v. 8 Paul shows how he, like other Jews, was expected to obey two authorities, the Jewish and the Roman. He had done no wrong to the Jews, so it was the Roman authorities who had to decide his case. But Festus refused to pronounce any verdict (see v. 12).

Caesar. People used the name of the Emperor, Caesar, when they were referring to the central government in Rome. In the same way Jesus had the central government tax in mind when He said 'Render to Caesar the things that are Caesar's' (Luke 20.25).

25.11: I appeal to Caesar. Roman citizens had the right to appeal to the central government if they could pay the cost. The Emperor himself may sometimes have taken part in hearing the appeal. When Paul appealed, the Emperor was Nero.

STUDY SUGGESTIONS

REVIEW OF CONTENT

1. 'Luke shows that Paul was grateful to the Romans' (p. 206). On which two occasions described in these chapters was Paul *not* grateful to the Romans in your opinion?
2. Why did the tribune send Paul to Caesarea?
3. Which one of the accusations which Tertullus made against Paul was the serious accusation in the opinion of the Governor?
4. For what two reasons did Felix refuse to give a verdict in Paul's case?

BIBLE STUDY

5. 'In 24.15 the word "resurrection" means God raising human beings to new life after they have died' (pp. 208, 209).
   (i) Which human beings will have this existence?
   (ii) What sort of existence will they have?
   What answers if any) to these two questions do we find in each of the following passages?
   (a) Luke 20.35   (b) John 5.28–29   (c) Acts 24.15.
6. 'I came to bring to my nation alms and offerings' (24.17). Paul had written to the Church in Corinth about these 'alms'. Read 2 Cor. 8 and say:

(a) Why did Paul tell the Corinthians about the Christians in Macedonia?

(b) What did he mean by the 'saints'?

(c) Why did these 'saints' need relief?

(d) Who helped Paul to collect the money?

(e) Why did Paul refer to Jesus when writing about the collection?

DISCUSSION AND RESEARCH

7. 'We need to keep our consciences fresh' (p. 209).

   (a) How can we do this?

   (b) How can we avoid having 'guilty consciences'?

8. 'In Romans 15.25–27 Paul explains that when the Gentiles made a collection for the Jews, both were givers and both were receivers' (note on 24.17).

   (a) In what ways were both Gentiles and Jews giving and both receiving?

   (b) Have you personally (or has your congregation) had the same experience, i.e. that when you gave generously to others you were also receiving something? If so, give examples.

9. 'Being in prison must have been a difficult time for Paul' (p. 210).

   (a) In what two ways would you have found that a painful and difficult experience if you had been Paul?

   (b) Have you ever been forced to stop active life (perhaps through illness), and discovered that you could use the experience usefully? If so, give examples.

   (c) What difference does being a Christian make to an experience of that sort?

25.13—26.32

Paul Meets Herod Agrippa II

OUTLINE

25.13–27: Governor Festus reports Paul's case to Agrippa.

26.1–11: Paul makes a statement to them about his life before he was converted.

26.12–18: He describes his conversion.

26.19–23: He tells them what happened afterwards.

26.24–32: Festus and Agrippa agree that Paul is innocent.

INTERPRETATION

The hearing described in this passage was not an official trial. It was a formal interview at which Festus and Agrippa examined Paul in the presence of many local officials and prominent people. During the interview they invited Paul to state his own case.

Here Luke is again showing that Paul was loyal to the Roman State (25.25; 26.31).

NOTES

25.13: Agrippa the king and Bernice arrived at Caesarea to welcome Festus. This Agrippa was the son of Herod Agrippa I. He was not a Jew, but like his father and all the Herods, he belonged to the Edomite people. The Edomites had been forced to adopt the Jewish religion and so Agrippa was regarded as a Jew. When he became 'king' of a small territory in Lebanon he had the difficult task of being a 'go-between', i.e. he used to speak to the Romans on behalf of the Jews and to the Jews on behalf of the Romans. Although he was called a 'king' he had far less power than the Roman Governor Festus, so from time to time he came to pay his respects to Festus.

Festus took this opportunity to consult Agrippa about Paul's case. He reported on two successive days what action he had taken (vv. 14.–21 and vv. 24–27), the action which Luke described in 25.1–12.

Bernice was Agrippa's sister, whom he treated as his wife. She was later the mistress of the Emperor Titus.

25.19: They had certain points of dispute with him about their own superstition. Festus made it clear that it was the Jews, not the Romans, who had a dispute with Paul, and that the dispute was about their religion. ('Religion' is a better translation of the Greek word than 'superstition', see note on 17.22.) Festus correctly understood that the Jews had prosecuted Paul because he spoke about the resurrection of Jesus.

25.23: On the morrow Agrippa and Bernice came with great pomp. Agrippa's examination of Paul was not a private affair. No doubt Agrippa and Bernice wore their purple robes and gold crowns, Festus was in his official red robes, a crowd of 'military tribunes and prominent men' stood round them, and Paul was alone in the middle, his hands chained together (26.29).

25.26: I have nothing definite to write to my lord about him. Because Festus had not released Paul, Paul had appealed to the Emperor. It was, therefore, Festus's duty to tell the Emperor of what crime against the state Paul was accused. But he knew that Paul had committed no crime. This was the problem on which he consulted Agrippa.

Festus called the Emperor 'my lord'. The Emperor Caligula told people to call him 'lord', and other Emperors followed his example. (Later, rightly or wrongly, Christian bishops used this title.)

26.1: Then Paul ... made his defence. In vv. 1–23 Luke records the statement which Paul made in the presence of Festus, Agrippa and the onlookers. Luke himself may have been present. In this speech Paul was not really defending himself, but witnessing to the resurrection of Jesus. In the first part (vv. 1–11), when he spoke of events before his conversion, he drew special attention to (a) his Jewishness (vv. 4–11), (b) his persecution of Christians (see note on v. 10), (c) the resurrection of Jesus (v. 8).

26.6: I stand here on trial for hope in the promise made by God to our fathers. The Jews had always hoped for a resurrection of some sort. Paul now repeated what he had said to the Jewish Council in Jerusalem: 'I am being tried for one reason only, namely that I say that this hope has been fulfilled' (see also 23.6).

26.7: To which our twelve tribes hope to attain. There is a popular saying that ten of the tribes were 'lost' after the exile in Babylon. In Burma people sometimes call the Karens (the large hill tribe) 'one of the ten lost tribes'. But there is no clear evidence on the matter. Paul here (and New Testament writers) speaks of '*twelve* tribes' (not thinking that any tribes had been lost).

26.10: I ... shut up many of the saints. Here Paul calls the Christians whom he imprisoned 'saints'.

The word 'saint' is a translation of the Greek word *hagios*, which is often translated 'holy'.

1. Today we often use these words to mean people whose lives were or are more Christlike than others. When a good person dies we may say, 'She was a "saintly" person'.

2. But in the Bible 'saint' and 'holy' do not have that meaning. In the Old Testament things or people were called 'holy' when they were set apart to be used by God for a special purpose (see e.g. Exodus 28.2).

In the New Testament 'saints' or 'holy people' are those who are set apart by God to represent Jesus Christ in the world, i.e. they are the members of the Church. That is its meaning here and in 9.13, 32, 41. Church members are called 'saints', not because they are superior to other people or live apart from them, but because they serve a different Lord, have different aims and have been given special responsibilities. This is the reason why Paul could call Christians in Corinth 'saints' (e.g. in 1 Cor. 6.1) although the congregation was doing wrong at that time. Saints do sin, but they belong to a body in which they can receive forgiveness.

3. Many outstanding Christians (like Paul) have been given the title of 'Saint' in the past. In the Roman Catholic Church this is still done, in order that modern Christians should thank God for the example which those outstanding Christians set and should follow it. Perhaps it is even more important that modern Christians should see *themselves* as 'saints' as the first Christians did, i.e. that as members of the Church they accept the special gifts which God offers and accept the special responsibilities which He gives.

26.13: At midday, O king, I saw on the way a light. In vv. 12–18 Paul again tells of his conversion. This account is very like the accounts in 9.3–18 and 22.6–16, but it is different in some ways, e.g.: (a) Here Paul says that he received his message from God Himself (rather than through Ananias, see v. 15); (b) He draws special attention to God's command to evangelize Gentiles (vv. 16–17).

26.14: I heard a voice saying to me in the Hebrew language, Saul, Saul, ... it hurts you to kick against the goads.

In the Hebrew language: Here Paul tells us something new, i.e. that the message which he had was not in Greek, but in the everyday language of his childhood, Aramaic.

It hurts you to kick: An untrained ox, pulling a plough, often kicks back at the driver. So the driver has a stick with spikes ('goads') on it. If the ox kicks, he hurts himself on the spikes. Paul discovered that it is painful to disobey God. God does not *send* the pain to those who disobey Him. They, like the oxen, bring pain on themselves. Peace comes through obedience.

26.16: Rise and stand upon your feet; for I have appeared to you for this purpose.

Rise. See 9.6 and 22.10. Paul's life had been changed, but he was told not to look back at the past, but to get up and follow God's instructions (see Ezek. 1.28b; 2.1–3). When we have faced our own sinfulness, and have fully accepted God's forgiveness, it is no longer a time for kneeling in penitence but for standing up in readiness to serve.

I have appeared to you. See also 'the things in which you have seen me and those in which I will appear to you'. Paul had visions throughout his life as a Christian. We do not understand his actions if we forget this, or if we think that all visions are the result of a sick mind (see note on 16.9).

For this purpose. Christians do not have visions in order to enjoy them, but in order to discover God's purpose for their lives. God's purpose for Paul was that he should 'open the eyes of the Gentiles' (see vv. 17–19).

26.17: Delivering you from the people and from the Gentiles. Paul said (v. 22) that this was true. God had indeed delivered him. But from what did God deliver him? He did not deliver him from imprisonment or physical pain or persecution or danger. Did Paul mean that God had saved him from despair or overpowering fear? From what does God promise to deliver present-day Christians?

26.18: That they may turn . . . from the power of Satan to God, that they may receive forgiveness of sins.

Satan. The Jews had several names for Satan: 'the adversary' (1 Pet. 5.8), 'devil' (Luke 4.2), 'the evil one' (John 17.15). Is Satan a person? Some Christians, like the Jews, regard Satan as a person, others as a powerful force of evil. But it is more important to realize Satan's power and to overcome it than to discuss whether Satan is personal or not.

Forgiveness. There were teachers before Jesus who said that God can forgive sinners (see e.g. Micah 7.18).

But it was Jesus who showed that anyone who 'repents' can receive God's forgiveness and be in the right relationship with Him (Luke 15.21–24). Jesus also taught that those who have received the gift of forgiveness show that they value this gift by forgiving others (Matt. 18.35).

According to Acts, the apostles constantly taught that forgiveness was 'through Jesus Christ' (see 2.38; 5.31; 10.43 and note on 13.38).

26.19: Wherefore, O King Agrippa, I was not disobedient to the heavenly vision. In vv. 19–23 Paul was explaining what happened after his vision, and how he was 'obedient' to it. As we saw in v. 16, Christians are not given visions to enjoy them but to obey them. Indeed it seems that everything Paul did as a Christian he did as the result of that vision (see 1 Cor. 15.8).

26.22–23: Saying nothing but what the prophets and Moses said would come to pass: that the Christ must suffer. Paul was telling Agrippa that he had not invented the teaching which he gave. What he said had been predicted by the Jews of long ago.

We do not know what sayings of Moses or what prophets Paul had in mind. Certainly there are verses in the Old Testament where we read that God will send a 'saviour' or a 'prophet' (e.g. Deut. 18.15). But as far as we know the Jews did not believe that the 'suffering servant' (Isaiah 53) was the same as the Messiah or 'Christ'. It was Jesus who explained to His astonished disciples that the Christ must suffer (Luke 9.20–22).

26.24: Festus said with a loud voice, 'Paul, you are mad'. While Paul was still speaking Festus shouted out, 'You are mad. You have been studying too much.' Why did he call Paul mad? Perhaps because Paul had spoken about his visions, or because he kept saying that Jesus had been seen alive after His death. But people like St Francis, Galileo, Martin Luther King were all called 'mad' because they brought new and different teaching to the world. Jesus announced a new way of living and His friends and His family and some of the most highly educated men in Jerusalem all called Him 'mad' (Mark 3.20–22; John 10.20–21). Paul explains this in 1 Cor. 1.18–25.

26.28: In a short time you think to make me a Christian! In vv. 22–23 Paul had said that the events which he preached had been predicted by Jewish prophets. In v. 27 he asked Agrippa, a religious Jew, why he did not believe those prophets. Agrippa avoided this question altogether and laughed at Paul: 'Do you really think that you can turn me into a Christian with a single remark?' People attack the Christian way of life in different ways. They persecute it and they argue against it, and by doing so are difficult to resist. But they may be even harder to resist when they laugh at it and treat it as too absurd to take seriously, as Agrippa did.

26.32: Agrippa said to Festus, 'This man could have been set free if he had not appealed to Caesar.' The interview was now concluded. Festus and Agrippa went away to decide what to do. Festus had to inform the Emperor what the charge was against Paul, but he knew that there was no charge. Luke does not tell us what Festus finally decided to say to the Emperor. But Luke in this chapter has clearly shown to any readers who might accuse Christians of disloyalty, that their leader Paul was a loyal member of the Empire.

ADDITIONAL NOTE: CHRISTIANS AND THE STATE

IN PAUL'S TIME

Paul received much help from the State (the Roman Empire) and was a loyal member. Like all Jews in the Empire he made use of its roads and the law and order it maintained. He was also a Roman citizen and could, therefore, ask for special treatment (Acts. 22.25). Luke reports a few occasions when the Roman authorities treated him unjustly (16.22; 21.33; 24.27). But he shows that the officers of the State were usually helpful and fair, e.g. Gallio protected Paul (18.12–17), the tribune rescued him from the crowd three times (21.33; 22.29–30; 23.31), and Festus allowed him to appeal to Caesar (25.12).

During the time when much of the New Testament was being written, the Roman State authorities continued to treat Christians well. They called them a Jewish sect and, therefore, they allowed them, as they allowed Jews, not to sacrifice to the Emperor. It was during this time that Paul wrote 'Let every person be subject to the governing authorities' (Rom. 13.1).

'Christians have a double duty to the state: to support it and to be its conscience' (p. 219).

Like this group of protest marchers, many Christians in Latin America today are demonstrating against the dictatorial and oppressive actions of their own government and the governments of other nations.

LATER

As Christians grew in number they were no longer regarded as a Jewish sect, and the Emperor demanded that they worshipped him. Christians regarded this as 'blasphemy' and could no longer obey him. Their duty now was to endure suffering. This is what is referred to in Rev. 13. vv. 1, 7, 10. The words which Peter used to the High Priest also describe what these later Christians believed, 'We must obey God rather than men' (Acts 5.29, see also 4.19).

TODAY

We cannot discover what the attitude of Christians to the State should be by reading single verses from the Bible. We need to rely on the guidance of God, and have also to take into account the way in which the government of our country is treating religious people. At the present time there are at least six different ways in which states are treating religions:

(a) They give special support to the Christian Church, e.g. in Greece, Scandinavia, Britain, and give freedom to other religions also.

(b) They are partners with a non-Christian religion, e.g. in Pakistan.

(c) They are 'neutral', i.e. they permit religions but have no link with them, e.g. in India, USA and many African countries.

(d) They officially disapprove of religions but permit them, though in some cases restricting religious activities severely, e.g. in China.

(e) They do not allow religion, e.g. as was the case in Albania.

(f) The state authorities and the religious authorities are the same, e.g. in Iran.

Christians have a double duty to the State:

1. To *support* the State loyally as far as possible, e.g. by keeping the laws, praying for its leaders, paying taxes, helping to create a better nation.

2. To *challenge* the State and to be its conscience; to make protests when it is necessary to remind its leaders that they are answerable to God, that they should treat minorities with justice, and that they have a duty to treat other nations with fairness. Many Christians have believed that it is their duty at times to disobey the State, as they did in the later Roman Empire, and as they are doing in many countries today.

STUDY SUGGESTIONS

REVIEW OF CONTENT

1. Why did Festus consult Agrippa?
2. Which two facts did Paul mention to Festus and Agrippa concerning his conversion which he had not mentioned in the other accounts of his conversion?
3. In what ways did Paul accept help from the State?
4. What was the difference between the way the State treated Christians during Paul's lifetime and the way the State treated them later?

BIBLE STUDY

5. 'I shut up many of the saints' (26.10).
   (i) What is a 'saint' according to the New Testament?
   (ii) In your experience who or what do people refer to when they use the word in ordinary conversation?
   (iii) In each of the following passages, who were the writers referring to when they used the word 'saint'?
   (a) Rom. 1.7   (b) Rom. 15.26   (c) 2 Cor. 1.1   (d) Col. 1.2
6. 'Forgiveness of sins' (26.18).
   Paul in his letters usually used the word 'justify' instead of the word 'forgive' (p. 216). In each of the following passages which word is used, 'forgive' or 'justify' or neither, and who is being promised forgiveness or receiving it?
   (a) Luke 5.17–20   (b) Luke 15.20   (c) Acts 2.38
   (d) Rom. 5.1   (e) Gal. 2.15–17   (f) Eph. 4.32

DISCUSSION AND RESEARCH

7. Festus called the Emperor 'my Lord' (25.26). Bishops are often called 'my Lord' (and, like Roman Emperors, wear purple). What is your opinion of these customs in the Church?
8. 'Delivering you from the people and from the Gentiles' (26.17).
   (a) From what, in your opinion, did God deliver Paul?
   (b) From what does He promise to deliver present-day Christians?
9. 'Some Christians regard "Satan" as a person, others as a powerful force of evil' (p. 216).
   In which of these ways do you think of 'Satan'? Give your reasons.
10. 'Agrippa laughed at Paul' (note on 26.28).
    (a) How far is it true to say that it is more difficult to resist those who laugh at us because we are Christians than those who persecute or ignore us?

(b) What do you do when people laugh at your religion?
11. 'Paul received much help from the State' (p. 217).
    (a) For what reasons should Christians accept help from the State?
    (b) What are the dangers of doing so?
12. To what extent is the Church in your country free:
    (a) to join with the State in forming national policies?
    (b) to challenge the State and to protest to it when that seems necessary?

27.1—28.31

The Journey to Rome

OUTLINE

27.1–8: The voyage from Caesarea to Myra, and from there to Crete.
27.9–20: The storm at sea.
27.21–38: Paul encourages the other passengers.
27.39—28.10: The arrival at Malta.
28.11–16: They sail to Italy and finally reach Rome.
28.17–29: Paul meets Jewish leaders.
28.30–31: Paul's two years in Rome.

INTERPRETATION

LUKE'S PURPOSE

In these last two chapters of Acts Luke gives a description of a long and dangerous journey. It is probably the most complete account in all Greek literature of a storm at sea, and Luke provides many details. But we shall be more concerned with Luke's purpose in writing than with the details.

First, Luke wanted to show that nothing could prevent God's plan to bring Paul to Rome, the city from which Christians could reach Gentiles in all parts of the Empire. Not even the worst storm could stop that.

Secondly, Luke wanted to show Paul's great trust in God. In spite of the dangers at sea and his fears concerning the future, Paul continued to have confidence in God (see 27.24–25, 33–38).

THE JOURNEY

The voyage from Caesarea to Rome took about four months and was in five parts (see map p. 120):

1. In one ship from Caesarea and Sidon to Myra, on the south coast of the country we now call Turkey;
2. In a second ship from Myra to Crete, and then
3. From Crete to Malta;
4. In a third ship from Malta to Puteoli on the west coast of Italy;
5. By land from Puteoli to Rome.

NOTES

27.1: They delivered Paul and some other prisoners to a centurion. When Paul began the journey he had Luke and Aristarchus as his companions. In addition there were the 'other prisoners', probably convicts being taken to Rome to provide entertainment by fighting with wild beasts, guarded by the centurion Julius and his soldiers.

27.2: A ship of Adramyttium. Adramyttium was a sea-port in the north of the province of Asia, and this ship was on its way back there, where it belonged. The centurion and his prisoners went aboard the ship at Caesarea, stopped at Sidon, and travelled with it as far as Myra, where they transferred to a 'ship of Alexandria sailing for Italy' (v. 6).

27.3: Julius gave him leave to go to his friends. The Greek phrase which is translated 'his friends' is '*the* friends', and this was probably another name for Christians. Compare the Quakers of the USA and Britain who in 1800 became 'The Society of Friends' (see 11.26; 26.10; 28.14 for other titles given to Christians).

Throughout the journey Julius showed Paul great kindness (see note on 28.2).

27.4: Putting to sea. The ship in which they put to sea from Myra was large, perhaps 500 tons in weight and 30m long. It had one mainmast with the mainsail, and a small foremast and foresail as well. The owner of the ship was on board, with the captain and the crew, taking their usual cargo of corn to Rome. Altogether this ship had 276 people on board (vv. 11, 37–38). See p. 226.

27.7: We sailed under the lee of Crete. After changing ships at Myra they sailed west hoping to get as far as Italy. As the wind came from the north, they sailed south of Crete ('under the lee' means 'in the sheltered part of') and reached Fair Havens (v. 8).

27.9: The fast had already gone by. This fast was the Jewish Day of Atonement, which took place early in October, i.e. it was already too late in the year to sail with safety in the open sea. At that time sailors had no compasses, and so when clouds and rain hid the sun and the stars in the winter months they could not tell in which direction they were going. No sailing at all took place between November 11 and March 11. This is the reason why Paul advised them to stay in Fair Havens. But they did not take his advice (vv. 10–12).

27.14: A tempestuous wind ... struck down from the land. Suddenly the wind changed and was so strong that the captain was unable to steer into the wind, but had to turn round and let the ship run with the wind ('we were driven', v. 15). So he did everything he could to save the ship from going down: he took the little boat on board (vv. 16,17), he 'undergirded' the ship (i.e. the sailors put a huge rope round it to prevent it from breaking into pieces, v. 17), he lowered the 'gear' (i.e. the mainsail, v. 17), he threw the corn overboard as it had become wet and heavy (vv. 18, 38), together with the heavy rigging ('tackle', v. 19).

27.21: Paul said ... 'Men, you should have listened to me'. He shouted above the noise of the wind to the centurion and the captain, 'I told you that this would happen'. Some people think that Paul should not have said this, and that Luke is here showing us a weakness of Paul. But he did not only blame them, he immediately encouraged them and perhaps saved the lives of everyone by doing so.

27.23: There stood by me an angel of God. Once again Paul reported a vision which he had had: 'Do not be afraid, Paul' (v. 24, see notes on 5.19 and 16.9).

As a result of his vision, as well as his previous experience of God's help, Paul was confident that God would save them: 'I have faith in God' (v. 25, see note on 20.21). He believed that God would save him, chiefly because he believed that God planned to take him to Rome (v. 24).

But God does not save from shipwreck everyone who has faith in Him. How can we explain this? (a) Some say, 'God has allowed chance to exist in His world and it is sometimes by chance that one person is saved while another is drowned.' (b) Others say that when believers are drowned God has for them a special purpose in the life after death and that their work on earth is completed. (c) Others say, 'We are human and not divine, and should not expect to understand everything.'

27.27: We were drifting: For fourteen days they drifted the 900 kms from Crete to Malta, passing the island of Cauda on the way. (The 'Sea of Adria' does not, of course, refer to the sea between Italy and Yugoslavia which we now call the Adriatic Sea.)

When they had drifted into shallow water near Malta some sailors tried to launch the ship's little boat, but soldiers prevented them (vv. 30–32).

27.33: Paul urged them all to take some food. No one had eaten for fourteen days, being too sea-sick to digest food, and everyone was becoming weak. So Paul persuaded them to eat. He was not only a highly-qualified theologian who could preach words of encouragement (vv. 22–26), he was also a leader who could take command in an emergency, and a person of great common sense who could take practical action (see also 28.3). Compare the practical action taken by Jesus after healing the girl (Mark 5.43).

The words of v. 35 are similar to the words which Paul used in 1 Cor. 11.23–24 when he was referring to the 'Lord's Supper' or 'Eucharist'. But Paul was not leading a religious service on this ship. He took a loaf of bread, mouldy and damp, broke it, and thanked God for it, as was the Jewish custom. Then he began to eat it, and others followed his example.

27.39: They noticed a bay with a beach. They arrived at last at the north-east corner of Malta, but the ship ran on to a sandbank between the mainland and the tiny island of Salmonetta, and began to break in pieces (v. 41). But they all reached the land. The centurion took a risk in allowing the prisoners to make their way ashore. If they escaped, he himself would probably be executed by the authorities.

28.2: The natives showed us unusual kindness. The Greek word here translated 'natives' means 'barbarians', a word which Greeks used in an insulting way for people who could not speak Greek. The inhabitants of Malta were Phoenicians and spoke Punic.

Luke emphasizes their kindness in making a fire for the cold and wet travellers. Some Christians are surprised and a little troubled when non-Christians show love and courage. A Christian student read about non-Christians in Vietnam treating escaped prisoners of war with great kindness and was very puzzled. He asked, 'What is the point of being a Christian if other people also show such kindness to strangers and foreigners?' Other people also have found that the question 'Why is there good in the world?' is just as important as 'Why is there evil?'

Paul partly answered these questions in his sermon in Lystra, 'God did not leave himself without witness' (14.17), i.e. God's Spirit and some awareness of God are·in each human being. Christians do not honour the gospel by denying the goodness in non-Christians. They honour it by thanking God for goodness wherever it is seen, and by working and praying so that that goodness may reach its completion in Jesus Christ.

28.3: Paul had gathered a bunch of sticks. Again Paul took practical action, and collected firewood (see note on 27.34). While he was doing this a viper clung to his hand (it is not certain whether it bit Paul or not).

28.4–6: No doubt this man is a murderer ... they changed their minds and said that he was a god. The inhabitants showed two mistakes in their ideas which are still common today: (1) They seem to have thought that bodily pain is always punishment for sin; but see Luke

224

13.4. (2) They thought that an unusual happening is a proof that some god has done a miracle, so they called Paul a 'god'; but we see God's actions in ordinary events as well as in unusual events (see Additional Note, Miracles, pp. 189, 190).

28.7: The chief man of the island, named Publius. The Greek word here translated 'chief man' is '*Protos*' or 'No. 1', which according to first-century writings was the title of the Governor of Malta at that time (see Special Note, Luke as Historian, pp. 56, 57).

Publius's father was ill and Paul healed him and others. Although Paul himself was never cured of his own trouble (2 Cor. 12.7), he was able to heal others, e.g. 14.8–10.

28.11: After three months we set sail. As soon as it was safe to be on the open sea, they sailed in another ship to Italy, to Puteoli which is in the Bay of Naples. This was the chief port where corn was unloaded on its way to Rome, a port as important at that time as Singapore and Rotterdam are today.

28.14: There we found brethren, and were invited to stay with them for seven days. Julius, who had been kind to Paul throughout the journey, allowed him to spend a week with the Christians of Puteoli.

Brethren. See note on 9.26, 'disciples', 3. As was his custom, Paul had fellowship with whatever group of Christians he met on his journeys, and received support from them (see note on 2.42).

We know that Christian traders or other travellers had brought the gospel with them to Italy before Paul got there, because Paul had written his letter to the Church in Rome some years earlier. Now we learn that there was a Church in Puteoli. Luke says nothing in Acts about these other travellers. He was not writing a complete history of the early Church, but selecting from it the events that seemed most important.

At the end of that week Paul set off for Rome, meeting Christians from Rome at the Forum of Appius, 70 kms from Rome, and at Three Taverns 50 kms from Rome. He greatly needed their fellowship because he was uncertain what would happen to him when he reached Rome. See v. 15 'He thanked God and took courage.' (Every Church leader needs the fellowship of the members.)

28.16: We came into Rome. Luke had already referred to this great event in v. 14, but v. 16 is the verse to which he was leading up in the earlier part of Acts. For him, and also for Paul, Rome was a sign of the truth that the gospel is for all nations and not for Jews only. When Paul entered Rome, they felt that Acts 1.8 had come true: 'You shall be my witnesses . . . to the end of the earth.'

28.17: He called together the local leaders of the Jews. Paul had two meetings with these leaders. In the first (vv. 17–22) he made a brief defence. He explained that he was not against Jewish traditions but that

'And so we came to Rome' (28.14). 'For Luke, and also for Paul, Rome was a sign of the truth that the gospel is for all nations' (p. 225).

From this 3rd-century stone-carving of a trading ship arriving in port we know what the ship which took Paul to Rome must have looked like. It shows the captain on the rear deck offering a sacrifice of thanksgiving to the Roman 'sea-god' Neptune (on the right with his trident), while a sailor in the ship's boat (27.32) attends to the steering oar.

Today the ship 'trademark' of the World Council of Churches reminds us of Paul's voyage, and stands as a sign that nothing can stop the spread of the gospel 'to the end of the earth' (1.8).

the traditions had been fulfilled by Jesus. All the Old Testament writers, he said, had hoped that Jesus would come one day (see v. 20, also 23.6; 26.6).

In the second meeting Paul spoke more severely, accusing them of disobeying God (see note on v. 26).

28.23: Testifying to the kingdom of God and trying to convince them about Jesus. Paul gave the Jews of Rome a double message: (1) By speaking of 'the kingdom of God' he referred to the *gospel which Jesus taught*; (2) By 'trying to convince them about Jesus' he was referring to the *gospel about Jesus*, i.e. that He was Messiah, which he and others preached.

The kingdom of God. (The phrase 'kingdom of heaven' in Matthew's Gospel has the same meaning.) We should note that:

1. When Jesus used these words He was teaching that God reigns and rules over the world and its people. To accept Him as King is to live fully by obeying Him. To reject Him as King is to lose the life He made us to enjoy.

2. When Jesus said 'the kingdom is at hand' or 'has begun to arrive' (Mark 1.15) He did not mean that God had not been ruling before that time, but that God was now ruling on earth in a new way because He, the Messiah, had come.

3. The 'kingdom' is 'in' those who accept God as King (Luke 17.21).

4. The 'kingdom' is not yet completed, and, therefore, we pray, 'Thy kingdom come' (Luke 11.2).

5. We cannot cause its completion but we can prepare ourselves and others for its coming (Matt. 25.1–13).

6. Thus the 'kingdom' is what God does. It is not a place or a 'state' such as the kingdom of Saudi Arabia. Nor is it the same as the Church. There are people outside the Church who accept God's rule and there are people inside the Church who reject it.

28.26: You shall indeed hear but never understand. Paul was quoting from Isa. 6.9–10 (we also find the verses in full in Matt. 13.13–15, and in part in Luke 8.10; Mark 4.12; John 12.39–40; Rom. 11.8). The meaning is this: those who hear the gospel and believe that it is true are at a cross-roads. They *can* become either better or worse. They are *either* more able to hear the truth *or* less able to hear it (they are 'hardened').

At first sight Paul seems to be saying in vv. 26 and 27 that God actually intended the Jews to reject Jesus. Perhaps some Christians at this time did think that. But Paul was not saying that. God never causes people to sin. By quoting Isaiah Paul was explaining that the prophets had always predicted that the Jews would reject the Messiah, not that God made them do so.

28.28: This salvation of God has been sent to the Gentiles; they will listen. Here Paul was repeating what he had said to the Jews in

Antioch-near-Pisidia (13.46) and in Corinth (18.6). Although he himself was a Jew he saw that in the future the Church would be a mainly Gentile Church. It is one of the saddest facts concerning the Church today that it contains so few Jews. The Church is weakened without them. It needs their gifts, e.g. their insistence on firm family life, their skill in music and writing, their conviction that God is equally concerned for religious and 'everyday' events.

But Paul did not give up hope that one day Jews would accept Jesus as Messiah: 'All Israel will be saved' (Rom. 11.26, and see vv. 25–32). **28.30: He lived there two whole years at his own expense.** Luke says very little about what Paul did during that time. We know from vv. 30, 31 that he was not held in prison at government expense, and that he paid for his own food and lodging, that all sorts of people came to visit him, and that he was free to teach and preach the gospel. But there are many questions to which we do not know the answers:

1. Which, if any, of the four letters, Ephesians, Philippians, Colossians, and Philemon did Paul write during this time?

2. Who was with him? If Paul wrote those four letters then at least eight of his friends were with him in Rome from time to time. (They are mentioned by name in the letters.)

3. Did Paul lead others to accept the gospel while he was in Rome?

4. What happened to Paul after two years? Was he acquitted and travelled to Spain, but finally condemned to death (as Clement, Bishop of Rome, wrote in AD 96)? Or was he tried twice and finally acquitted (as Eusebius wrote in AD 320)?

5. Why did Luke not record what happened? Did he die before he finished Acts? Or did he write another chapter which has been lost? Or if Paul was executed by the Romans, did Luke omit the fact in order not to offend the Roman official Theophilus to whom Acts was being sent (see note on 1.1a).

28.31: Teaching about the Lord Jesus Christ quite openly and unhindered. In this verse, the last in Acts, Luke points again to two facts which he had emphasized throughout the book:

1. That the Romans assisted rather than hindered the work of the Church;

2. That nothing can stop the spread of the gospel, even though its followers are imprisoned or persecuted in some places and at some times.

STUDY SUGGESTIONS

REVIEW OF CONTENT

1. What were Luke's two chief aims in writing these two chapters?
2. Why did they not sail ships on the Mediterranean Sea in the winter months?
3. Give (a) *two* examples from these chapters of Paul taking practical action, and (b) two examples of non-Christians showing kindness.
4. On what *two* occasions during this journey did Paul have fellowship with Christians and receive support from them?
5. 'Testifying to the kingdom of God' (28.23):
   (a) If it is true that the kingdom of God is 'within you' (Luke 17.21), why did Jesus teach us to pray 'Thy kingdom come' (Luke 11.2)?
   (b) What is the difference between the kingdom of God and the Church?

BIBLE STUDY

6. 'Friends' was probably another name for Christians (p. 222). What three other names were used for Christians according to Acts 9.32; 9.41; 17.10; 26.28; 28.15 and 1 Peter 4.16?
7. 'Paul did not give up hope that one day Jews would accept Jesus as Messiah' (p. 228). Read Rom. 11.25–32 and put briefly and in your own words the reasons why Paul was hopeful.
9. 'If Paul wrote those letters, then at least eight of his friends were with him in Rome' (p. 228). Who were they, according to the following verses?
   (a) Eph. 6.21   (b) Phil. 4.18   (c) Col. 4.10–14
   (d) Philem. v. 23?

DISCUSSION AND RESEARCH

9. 'As a result of his vision . . . Paul was confident that God would save them' (p. 223). But many people ask, 'Why does God save some believers from such disasters as drowning, but not others?'
   (a) How would you answer them?
   (b) What is your opinion of each of the three answers given in the note on 27.23?
10. 'The natives showed us unusual kindness' (28.2). Some Christians are surprised and a little troubled when non-Christians show love and courage (p. 224). What would your answers be:
    (a) To the student's question?
    (b) To the question 'Why is there good in the world'?

11. 'Paul had fellowship with Christians' (p. 225).
    (a) What is the difference, if any, between fellowship and 'friend-ship'?
    (b) In what practical ways can members of a congregation express 'fellowship' with their leader?
12. Imagine that you are Paul and that you keep a diary. What would you write on the day when you arrive in Rome?

Time Line

The following table provides the approximate order of events referred to in Acts. Many of the dates are uncertain, but an asterisk indicates that the date suggested is confirmed by evidence outside the New Testament.

AD	Events	Bible Reference
29 or 30	The Resurrection of Jesus	
	The Feast of Pentecost	Acts 1 and 2
32, 33, 34	Persecution of Greek-speaking Jews	
	Death of Stephen	Acts 8.1
	Paul's Conversion	Acts 9
	Paul to Arabia and Damascas	Gal. 1.17
34, 35, 36	Paul's first visit to Jerusalem after	Acts 9.26 and
	his conversion	Gal. 1.18
	Paul in Syria and Cilicia	Gal. 1.21
	Paul in Arabia until AD 45	
34–38	Christian mission to Gentiles in	
	Syrian Antioch	Acts 11.19
41	James, brother of John, killed by	
	Herod Agrippa I	Acts 12.2
44*	Death of Herod Agrippa I	Acts 12.23
45	Paul returns from Arabia to Cilicia	Acts 11.25
46	Famine in Jerusalem	
	Barnabas and Paul in Syrian	
	Antioch, then to Jerusalem	Acts 11.27–20
47	Paul's mission to Gentiles in Asia:	
	Pisidian Antioch, Iconium, Lys-	
	tra, Derbe (the 'First' Journey)	Acts 13.4—14.28
	Disagreement between Paul and	
	Peter in Syrian Antioch	Gal. 2.11
	Letter to the Galatians? (or in AD	
	56)	
48	Jerusalem meetings	Acts 15.6–29
49	Paul leaves Syrian Antioch and	
	begins his mission in Europe (the	
	'Second' Journey)	Acts 15.36
49*	Jews expelled from Rome	Acts 18.2

AD	Events	Bible Reference
50	Paul in Corinth	Acts 18.1
	Paul's first letter to Thessalonica	
51	Paul still in Corinth	Acts 18.12
51*	Gallio proconsul of Achaia	
52*	Felix procurator of Judea (till AD 58)	
53	Paul's mission in 'Asia' begins (the 'Third' Journey)	Acts 18.23
	Paul in Ephesus	
54	Paul still in Ephesus	
	First letter to Corinth	
	Paul's second visit to Corinth	
54*	Nero Emperor till AD 68	
55	Paul still in Ephesus	
	Second letter to Corinth	
	Letter to Philippi?	
56	Paul leaves Ephesus	Acts 20.1
	Letter to Galatians?	
	Paul's third visit to Corinth	2 Cor. 13.2
	Letter to the Romans?	
57	Paul in Greece	Acts 20.2
	Paul's journey to Jerusalem	Acts 21.15
	Paul arrested	Acts 21.27
	Paul in prison in Caesarea	Acts 23.33
58	Paul still in prison	
	Letters to Colossae and Ephesus?	
58*	Festus procurator of Judea till AD 62	Acts 24.27
59	Paul's journey to Rome	Acts 27.1—28.16
60, 61	Paul under arrest in Rome	Acts 28.17–30
62	Possible date of Paul's death	
	Death of James, brother of Jesus	
70*	Destruction of Jerusalem	
80–90?	'Acts of Apostles' written	

Some scholars think that the events from Paul's arrival in Ephesus until his arrival in Rome took place about two years later than is suggested above.

Key to Study Suggestions

Introduction

1. See p. 1, para. 2.
2. (a) See p. 1, para. 2.
   (b) It shows that the gospel spread from Jerusalem to Rome.
3. (a) To show that by sending Elisha to Naaman, who was not a Jew, God cares for all nations.
   (b) They did not understand that God cares for all races.
   (c) Both show that God loves all races equally.

1.1–11

1. See p. 4, numbered para. 1.
2. See p. 4, numbered paras 2 and 3.
3. See p. 7, note on 1.6.
4. Because the disciples did receive the Spirit and they did witness in Jerusalem and even in Rome.
5. See p. 7, note on 1.9–10.
6. Mary Magdalene and the other Mary; the Eleven; Cleopas and his friend; the disciples; Cephas; the Twelve; 500 brethren; James; Paul.
7. In Luke 24: It took place at Bethany, Jesus blessed them, and then 'parted'.
   In Acts 1: Jesus was 'lifted up', hidden by a cloud, and two men in white spoke to the disciples.
8. (a) and (b) Exalted at the right hand of God.
   (c) At the right hand of God.
   (d) At His right hand in the heavenly places.
   (e) Passed through the heavens.
   (f) Seated at the right hand of the throne.
   (g) Has gone into heaven and is at the right hand of God.

1.12–26

1. See p. 11, note on 1.12.
2. See p. 11, numbered para. 2 of note on 1.14b.
3. See p. 12, note on 1.16a.
4. See p. 11, lines 1–6.
5. See p. 13, lines 1–4.

6. Acts: (a) The disciples – because they had been released from prison.
(b) The Twelve – because they had commissioned 'the Seven'.
(c) Paul and Silas.
(d) Paul and Luke and the Christians of Tyre – because Paul was leaving Tyre and going to Jerusalem.
Luke's Gospel: (a) We need to pray when we begin on a new stage in life.
(b) We sometimes need to be alone in order to pray.
(c) We need to persevere in our prayers.
(d) Our prayers should be for other people and not for ourselves only.
7. That what the Psalmist had written was being fulfilled.
8. (a) God raised.
(b) Acts 10: It was something which God had done. 1 Cor. 15: God had done it and thus fulfilled what was written in the Old Testament.

2.1–13

1. See p. 15, Interpretation line 3.
2. See p. 15, note on 2.1a.
3. See p. 17, line 11.
4. See p. 17, numbered para. 3 of note on 2.4b.
5. See p. 18, note on 2.10.
6. (a) Bezalel – became a skilled craftsman.
(b) Seventy elders – prophesied.
(c) Gideon – became a leader.
(d) Ezekiel – stood up.
7. (a) The disciples – power. (b) Philip – guidance. (c) Those who heard Peter – guidance. (d) Agabus – guidance. (e) Prophets and teachers – guidance. (f) John's disciples – power.

2.14–41

1. See p. 25, note on 2.23b.
2. See p. 21, Interpretation, lines 1–2.
3. See p. 21, last 3 lines.
4. See p. 22, second half of page.
5. (a) and (b) See p. 26, note on 2.36.
6. See p. 27, notes on 2.37 and 2.41.
7. (a) Plainly. (b) Plainly. (c) Boldly. (d) Openly. (e) Boldly. (f) With confidence.
8. (a) 1. (b) 1. (c) 2 or 4. (d) 1, 2, 3 or 4. (e) 3. (f) 1 or 2. (g) 1. (h) 2 and 3.

2.42–47

1. See p. 30, note on 2.42a, last line.
2. See p. 30, last 5 lines.
3. See p. 31, note on 2.42c, last 2 lines.
4. See p. 32, note on 2.44, 3 lines from end.
5. (a) and (b) See p. 31, note on 2.42d.
6. See p. 33, note on 2.46b.
7. (a) A contribution. (b) Fellowship with God and fellow Christians. (c) Holy Communion Service. (d) and (e) Fellowship with other Christians. (f) Fellowship with Jesus Christ.
8. (a) A lonely place – a crowd of people were hungry.
   (b) The upper room – Jesus wanted to celebrate the Passover with the Twelve.
   (c) A village house – Jesus wanted to have fellowship with Cleopas and his friend.
   (d) An upper room in Troas – they were having a Holy Communion Service.
9. (a) Chloe's. (b) Stephanas's. (c) Aquila and Prisca's. (d) Narcissus's. (e) Gaius's. (f) Nympha's.

3.1–26

1. See p. 35, last 8 lines.
2. See p. 37, note on 3.12, numbered para. 3.
3. (a) See p. 37, note on 3.13.
4. That God raised up Jesus and that they must repent of the sin of killing Him.
5. See p. 41, last 4 lines and p. 42, lines 1–10.
6. (a) The man's friends. (b) The patient. (c) The patient. (d) The disciples. (e) The patient.
7. (a) Put His hands on them. (b) Put his hands on him and spoke. (c) Spoke to him. (d) Looked at him and spoke. (e) Prayed and put his hands on him.

4.1–31

1. See p. 44, note on 4.1, lines 1–5.
2. See p. 44, note on 4.1, lines 10–12.
3. See p. 44, lines 6–11.
4. See p. 46, note on 4.13a.
5. See p. 49, lines 8–12.
6. (a) From the evil of captivity. (b), (c) and (d) In order to have fullness of life. (e) As a gift that cannot be earned. (f) As a gift to be fully received at the last day.

7. See p. 47, note on 4.20, numbered para. (b).

8. In all these prayers, praise is given to God during a time of suffering and opposition.

9. (a) Peter and John. (b) Peter. (c) Paul and Silas. (d) Gaius and Aristarchus. (e) The High Priest and the Sadducees. (f) Herod. (g) Magistrates. (h) The High Priest and Tertullus.

4.32—5.42

1. See p. 52, Interpretation, lines 3–7.

2. See p. 53, lines 6–11.

3. See p. 53, note on 5.1, lines 1–7.

4. See p. 55, line 3.

5. (a) One invited Jesus to a meal.

(b) They spent too much time on details and forgot the purpose of life.

(c) One of them wanted to learn from Jesus.

(d) Some insisted that Christians must be circumcised and keep all the Jewish rules.

(e) Some became Christians.

(f) Paul was one who became a Christian.

6. (a) All passages describe Christians being joyful in times of suffering.

(b) In the references in Luke and Philippians there is no mention of joy.

Special Note A

1. (a) See p. 56, Special Note lines 3–12.

(b) See p. 57, lines 1–9.

6.1–15

1. See p. 58, Interpretation, lines 7–13.

2. See p. 59, lines 1–4.

3. See p. 60, note on 6.2b, line 5.

4. See p. 60, last 3 lines and p. 61, lines 1–5.

5. See p. 61, note on 6.9.

6. (a) They chose 7 men to share in the work of ministry.

(b) He appointed trustworthy men to be leaders and judges.

(c) He asked the disciples to help Him to feed the crowds.

(d) He sent Timothy to Philippi to look after the congregation till Paul could come.

7. (a) They accused Jesus of disregarding the traditions, and the Jews accused Stephen of the same thing.

(b) The Pharisees accused Jesus's disciples of disregarding their traditions.
8. See p. 63, lines 2–5.

7.1—8.1a

1. See p. 65, lines 4–7.
2. (a) See p. 66, notes on 7.2, 7.9 and 7.15; see p. 67, note on 7.20; see p. 68, note on 7.47.
(b) See p. 66, line 4.
(c) See p. 66, note on 7.9; see p. 67, note on 7.20, line 3.
3. (a) and (b) See p. 67, last 3 lines.
4. See p. 70, note on 7.56.
5. See p. 71, notes on 7.59 and 7.60.
6. (a) Physical. (b) Spiritual. (c) Physical. (d) Spiritual. (e) Spiritual. (f) Physical.
See also p. 66, note on 7.8, last 3 lines.
7. (a) Elijah, persecuted by 'the people of Israel'.
(b) Zechariah, persecuted by 'the people'.
(c) Uriah, persecuted by King Jehoiakim.
(d) Jeremiah, persecuted by King Zedekiah.
8. See Additional Note, p. 72.
(a) Para. 2, line 1. (b) Para 1, line 1. (c) Para. 2, line 1. (d) Para. 4, lines 3–5. (e) Para. 3, lines 3–5. (4) Para. 4, lines 3–5.

8.1b–25

1. See p. 74 , line 8 from foot of page, and p. 75, line 3 from foot.
2. See p. 74, line 11 from foot.
3. See p. 76, note on 8.9, lines 4–6.
4. See p. 77, lines 3–5.
5. See p. 77, note on 8.17, numbered para. 1.
6. See p. 77, note on 8.18–19.
7. See p. 79, lines 6–10.
8. See p. 79, lines 15–21.
9. (a) He did not want to quarrel with them.
(b) He believed that the spirit of God's compassion was in them.
(c) He was glad when one of them was grateful to God.
(d) He was willing to accept a drink from one, and to talk with her, although Jews did not talk to Samaritans.
10. (a) Repentance. (b) Instructions. (c) Belief. (d) Laying on of hands. (e) Receiving the Spirit. (f) Instruction. (g) Laying on of hands and receiving the Spirit. (h) Hospitality and rejoicing. (i) Laying on of hands, receiving the Spirit, speaking in tongues.

8.26–40

1. See p. 81, last para., lines 1–5.
2. See p. 81, para. 1, lines 4–7.
3. See p. 82, para. 'Our Evangelism', lines 6–11.
4. See p. 81, last 2 lines.
5. See p. 85, lines 4–5.
6. (a) and (b) See p. 86, lines 1–3.
7. (a) Angel. (b) The Spirit. (c) The Spirit. (d) Angel. (e) The Spirit. (f) Angel.
8. (a) A dream – Daniel was interpreter.
   (b) The Old Testament – Jesus was interpreter.
   (c) Isaiah 53 – Philip was interpreter.
   (d) Speaking in tongues – someone must interpret it.
9. (a) b. (b) a. (c) a. (d) a. (e) b. (f) b.

9.1–19a

1. See p. 88, lines 3–8.
2. See p. 90, note on 9.4.
3. See p. 90, note on 9.10, lines 3–9.
4. See p. 91, notes on 9.17b–18 and 9.19.
5. (a) The shepherds. (b) Peter, John and James. (c) Peter.
6. (a) Moses – to take off his shoes.
   (b) Isaiah – to go and speak to the people.
   (c) Jesus – that He was God's beloved Son.
   (d) Peter, James and John – to listen to Jesus.
   (e) Peter – to kill the animals and eat them.
7. (a) He saw Jesus.
   (b) Jesus appeared to him, although he had been a sinner.
   (c) God revealed Himself to him so that he should be a missionary to Gentiles.
   (d) As a result of the conversion he had to make a great change in his life.
   (e) It happened to him in spite of his sinfulness and because of God's grace.

Special Note B

1. See p. 93, para. 1.
2. See p. 93, para 2.
3. See p. 93, last 5 lines.

9.19b–31

1. See p. 96, numbered para. 2.

2. See p. 96, note on 9.20.
3. See p. 98, note on 9.29.
4. See p. 98, note on 9.31, lines 1–7.
5. See p. 98, note on 9.29, lines 6–7.
6. See p. 98, note on 9.31, numbered para. 3.
7. (a) Joseph of Arimathea. (b) James and John. (c) One of the disciples. (d) Andrew. (e) Ananias. (f) Tabitha (Dorcas).
8. (a) i. (b) ii. (c) ii. (d) i. (e) ii. (f) i.

9.32—11.18

1. See p. 102, note on 9.36 and p. 103, note on 10.1. For part 2 of the question see p. 101, line 3.
2. See p. 101, note on 10.3, lines 4–6.
3. See 10.19 and 10.22.
4. See p. 100, last 3 lines.
5. See p. 106, note on 10.48.
6. (a) See p. 106, note on 11.2, lines 4–6.
(b) See 11.2–3.
7. (a) They would be blessed because of Abraham's obedience.
(b) The Israelites would become a 'light' to them.
(c) God's salvation would be a 'light' to them.
(d) They would receive the gospel from Paul.
(e) Some of them tried to stone Paul.
(f) Some of them opposed Paul, but he would call on them to repent.
(g) When a large number of Gentiles had become Christian, then the Jews would be converted.
8. (a) Two or three people acting as witnesses to a disagreement.
(b) Two disciples fetching a colt for Jesus.
(c) Pairs of disciples sent out visiting by Jesus.
(d) Two servants of Cornelius sent to find Peter.
(e) Barnabas and Saul taking relief to the poor Christians in Judea.
(f) Timothy and Erastus sent to Macedonia by Paul.

11.19–30

1. See p. 108, Interpretation, lines 7–10.
2. See p. 108, last 2 lines
3. See p. 109, note on 11.19, lines 11–16.
4. See p. 110, note on 11.22.
5. See p. 53, note on 4.36–37 and p. 110, note on 11.22.
6. See p. 110, note on 11.25, line 8.
7. (i) (a) Disciples. (b) Saints. (c) Disciples. (d) Brethren. (e) Brethren.
(f) Saints. (g) Christians.

8. (i) (a) To put money aside every week for the poor Christians in Judea.

(b) and (c) To give as generously as the Macedonians had given.

12.1–25

1. See p. 115, lines 3–10.

2. See p. 115, note on 12.1, lines 5–7.

3. See p. 116, line 5.

4. See p. 118, note on 12.25.

5. (a) When Jesus went to Simon Peter's house.

(b) When Jesus went to Jairus's house.

(c) When Jesus went up a mountain to pray.

(d) When Jesus was sitting on the Mount of Olives.

(e) When Jesus was praying in Gethsemane.

6. In Rom. 14.8. Paul said: 'We are in God's hands whether we live or die.' Peter was able to sleep because he believed this.

7. (i) (a) (1). (b) (2). (c) (3). (d) (4). (e) (4).

13.1–12

1. See p. 121, Interpretation.

2. See p. 121, Interpretation, line 4.

3. See p. 122, note on 13.4.

4. See p. 122, note on 13.5a.

5. See p. 125, 'Those officially appointed'.

6. See p. 126, numbered para. 3, lines 6–10.

7. (i) (a) Because his child was very ill.

(b) Because He was about to begin his ministry *or* because He was being tempted.

(c) Because it helped them to pray *or* because they were waiting for God's guidance.

(d) In order to get a reputation for being holy.

8. (a) He assisted Barnabas and Paul.

(b) He left them, at Perga.

(c) He was not chosen to go with Paul on the next journey.

(d) Later Paul asked to see him because he regarded him as 'very useful'.

(e) Paul later called Mark his 'son'.

9. (a) Some of them predicted the future.

(b) They encouraged and strengthened the local congregation.

(c) They needed faith to carry out their work.

(d) Their work was only one way of exercising ministry.

(e) They spoke in a way which people could understand.

(f) They equipped and trained other Christians to be ministers.

13.13–52

1. See p. 128, Interpretation, lines 7–8.
2. See p. 128, Interpretation, last 3 lines.
3. See p. 131, note on 13.43, lines 3–7.
4. See p. 131, note on 13.44, lines 7–10.
5. See p. 132, note on 13.52.
6. (i) (a) Justified. (b) Justified. (c) Freed. (d) Acquitted. (e) Justified.
7. (a) All human beings will be judged, but the Jews will be judged first.
   (b) The Jews are his brothers and sisters, and he was willing to make any sacrifice in order to save them.
   (c) Paul prays that the Jews may be saved.
   (d) It is because of the failure of the Jews to accept the gospel that the Gentiles have received it: this may cause the Jews to receive it, through jealousy.
   (e) In order that everyone may accept the gospel, Paul makes himself one with the Jews and also one with Gentiles.

14.1–28

1. See p. 135, last 5 lines.
2. See p. 138, note on 14.23.
3. See p. 137, last 5 lines.
4. See p. 138, last 5 lines.
5. (a) In 14.15–17 his main message was that there is only one God, the Creator God whom they should worship; but in 13.16–41 he was speaking to Jews and God-fearers, and said that the coming of Jesus and His death and resurrection were the fulfilment of Jewish history.
   (b) Rom. 1.19–25 is very like Acts 14.15–17, but in it Paul judged his readers severely for not worshipping the one God.
6. (i) See 9.23; 9.26; 9.29; 14.2; 14.5; 14.19.
   (ii) (a) When we suffer for Christ's sake we are sharing His sufferings.
   (b) Christians cannot avoid sufferings and should not let sufferings overwhelm them.
   (c) Those who are living close to Jesus Christ are bound to experience suffering.

15.1–35

1. See p. 141, para. 1.
2. See p. 144, note on 15.7, lines 4–6.
3. See p. 144, note on 15.2b, para. 1.

4. See p. 145, note on 15.20, lines 11–14.

5. See p. 143, para. 2.

6. For example: vv. 4, 7, 8, 12, 14.

7. In Rom. 14.15–21 Paul wrote 'You may think that wine is a gift from God and should be enjoyed, but don't drink it if it will lead someone else into temptation.'

In 1 Cor. 9.19–21 he wrote that he made himself like a Jew in order to win Jews for Christ, and makes himself like a Gentile in order to win Gentiles.

15.36—16.10

1. See p. 148, Interpretation, para. 1.

2. See p. 148, Interpretation, para. 2 (b) and (c).

3. See p. 149, note on 15.39, lines 3–7.

4. See p. 150, note on 16.3, lines 6–14.

5. See p. 149, lines 5–3 from foot, p. 150, note on 16.3 and p. 151, note on 16.10.

6. See p. 151, note on 16.10.

7. Some of the Christians in Lystra had forgotten the gospel and returned to keeping traditional Jewish rules, so Paul wanted to bring them back to the real gospel.

8. Some helpful words about Timothy are: 'brother', 'God's servant', 'establish you', 'exhort you', 'genuinely anxious for your welfare', 'as a son with his father', 'served in the gospel', 'true child of the faith', 'sincere faith'.

9. (a) Ananias – heard the Lord – went and found Paul.

(b) Paul – saw Ananias in a vision.

(c) Cornelius – saw an angel and heard the Lord speaking – sent messengers to Peter.

(d) Peter – saw a great sheet – went down and met the messengers.

(e) Paul – heard a voice – allowed people to lead him by the hand.

(f) Paul – declared to people in Damascus that they must repent.

16.11—17.15

1. See p. 153, Interpretation, lines 1–6.

2. See p. 154, note on 16.12, lines 8–10.

3. See p. 155, note on 16.15.

4. See p. 155, lines 9 and 8 from foot.

5. See p. 157, note on 16.25.

6. See p. 155, last line and p. 157, lines 1–4.

7. See map p. 120 and a modern atlas showing the same area.

8. (a) He enjoyed fellowship with the Christians.

(b) He and they met opposition.

(c) The Christians gave much to Paul and received much from him; no other Church had such close partnership with Paul.

9. (a) Mary, Jesus's mother – she visited Elizabeth and praised God.
(b) Women of Jerusalem – they wept for Jesus as he walked to his death.
(c) Mary Magdalene, Joanna, Mary, mother of James, and other women – they told the Apostles that Jesus had risen.
(d) Mary, Jesus's mother, and other women – they prayed.
(e) Mary, John Mark's mother, and others – they were praying for Peter who was in prison.
(f) Priscilla – she gave hospitality to Paul.

10. (a) The Christians were persecuted, but in spite of it they rejoiced.
(b) They welcomed Paul and put away their idols.
(c) Paul worked to earn his living, and also did the work of preaching.
(d) Paul and the congregation members loved each other and enjoyed each other.
(e) The congregation was persecuted.

17.16–34

1. See p. 159, line 14 and p. 161, para 2, line 1.
2. See p. 161, note on 17.16.
3. See p. 160, Outline, lines 2 and 3 and p. 162, note on 17.18a.
4. **and 5.** See p. 164, note on 17.31, lines 8–11.
6. See p. 166, line 13.
7. (a) Discuss. (b) Argue. (c) Talked. (d) Talked. (e) Dispute. (f) Dispute.
8. (a) v. 24. (b) v. 26. (c) v. 27. (d) v. 29. (e) v. 31. (f) v. 30.

18.1–28

1. See p. 168, para. 1.
2. See p. 168, numbered para. 4 and following para.
3. See p. 170, note on 18.2 and p. 171, note on 18.9–10.
4. See p. 170, lines 1–5.
5. See p. 172, note on 18.18, last 3 lines.
6. (a) They were tent-makers and were willing for Paul to work with them.
(b) See p. 172, last 5 lines.
(c) They took great risks in order to rescue Paul. They had a house-church in their house.
(d) They had a house-church.
7. (a) and (b) He earned money by working at his trade.

(c) The Christians in Philippi sent him gifts.

(d) He worked at his trade day and night.

8. He led one group of Christians in Corinth, and followed up what Paul had begun. But he needed further instruction when he came to Ephesus. The Ephesian Christians gave him a good testimonial when he went to Achaia, where he greatly helped the Christians and was able to debate with the Jews.

9. (ii) (a) Being saved. (b) The work which Paul did. (c) The call which Paul received. (d) Comfort and hope.

19.1–41

1. See p. 175, Interpretation, line 2.
2. See p. 175, Interpretation, numbered paras 1, 2 and 3.
3. See p. 177, note on 19.9b.
4. See p. 179, note on 19.22.
5. See p. 179, note on 19.24, lines 10–12.
6. See p. 180, note on 19.29, (c) and (d).
7. (a) Almost killed. (b) Puzzled. (c) Flogged, almost killed. (d) Beatings, imprisonment, hunger. (e) Unhappy, deprived of his possessions ('poor'). (f) Imprisonments, beatings, almost killed.
8. (a) Speaking in tongues. (b) Speaking in tongues and praising God. (c) Faith, healing, working miracles, prophecy, distinguishing between spirits, various kinds of tongues, interpretation of tongues. (d) Love, joy, peace, patience, kindness, goodness, faithfulness.

Special Note C

1. See p. 182, Special Note C, lines 1–3.
2. See p. 183, lines 9–15.
3. See p. 183, lines 16–19.
4. (a) See p. 182, last 3 lines and p. 183, lines 1–2.

20.1–38

1. See p. 185, numbered paras 2 and 3.
2. See p. 185, note on 20.7, line 3.
3. See p. 185, note on 20.6.
4. See p. 186, note on 20.17.
5. See p. 189, note on 20.34.
6. (a) See p. 185, note on 20.4.

(b) Sopater was a member of Paul's family; Aristarchus was with Paul in Ephesus and on the ship going to Italy, and was in prison with Paul; Trophimus was with Paul at Miletus but became ill.

7. (a) The faith of friends can lead to the healing of a sick person.
(b) Faith is trusting in Jesus and trusting that what He says is true.
(c) Faith is trusting in God's generosity rather than in religious rules.
(d) Faith is trusting in God for the future, i.e. 'hope'.
(e) Faith in God is real if it is accompanied by action.

21.1–36

1. See p. 192, Interpretation, lines 4–6.
2. See p. 193, note on 21.4, and see 21.7 and p. 194, note on 21.8.
3. See p. 194, note on 21.8.
4. See p. 195, note on 21.23–24, para. 2.
5. See p. 196, note on 21.27, lines 4–10.
6. (a) with (g). (b) with (h). (c) with (j). (d) with (k). (e) with (l). (f) with (i).
7. (a) He tore his garment into 12 pieces – message: the tribes of Israel will be divided.
(b) He walked naked and barefoot – message: the Egyptians and Ethiopians will be led away naked and barefoot.
(c) He took his waistcloth and hid it in a rocky place where it got spoiled – message: the Lord will punish Judah by spoiling it.
(d) He made a drawing of Jerusalem on a brick, and made a little wall around it – message: Israel will be besieged.
8. (a) 'Serve' – Christ's giving of himself.
(b) 'Mission' – the service which Church leaders give.
(c) 'Helpers' – either being useful or service given by Church leaders.
(d) 'Deaconess' – the work of deacons.
(e) 'Ministers' – the service given by Church leaders.
(f) 'Deacons' – see (d) above.

21.37—23.11

1. See p. 200, lines 1–4.
2. (a) See p. 200, note on 21.37, line 8.
(b) See p. 201, note on 22.3.
3. See p. 200, note on 21.40, lines 12–15.
4. See p. 202, note on 22.25, lines 1–5.
5. See p. 204, note on 23.6a.
6. (a) See p. 201, note on 22.4, lines 4 and 5.
(b) and (c) See note on 22.4, para. (a).
(d) See note on 22.4, para. (b).
(e) See note on 22.4, para. (c), last 5 lines.

7. (a) John the Baptist – he witnessed to Jesus.

(b) The Apostles: they were told to witness to Jesus – to the people of Jerusalem and of all Judea and Samaria.

(c) Peter and John: they witnessed to the resurrection of Jesus – to the people in Solomon's Porch.

(d) Paul: he was told to witness to Jesus – to all people.

23.12—25.12

1. See p. 210, notes on 24.22 and 24.26.

2. See p. 207, notes on 23.12 and 23.23.

3. See p. 208, note on 24.2, lines 5–9.

4. See p. 210, notes on 24.22 and 24.26.

5. (a) i. Those who are accounted worthy. ii. They do not get married.

(b) i. Both the just and the unjust. ii. The just have life, the unjust are judged.

(c) i. Both the just and the unjust. ii. No answer.

6. (a) He wanted the Corinthians to be as generous as the Macedonians had been.

(b) and (c) See p. 209, note on 24.17.

(d) See 2. Cor. 8.6 and 16. (e) See 2 Cor. 8.9.

25.13—26.32

1. See p. 213, note on 25.26.

2. See p. 215, note on 26.13.

3. See p. 217, Additional Note, para. 1.

4. See p. 219, para. 1.

5. (i) See p. 214, last 10 lines.

(iii) (a) Christians in Rome. (b) Christians in Jerusalem.

(b) Christians in the Province of Achaia. (d) Christians in Colossae.

6. (a) 'Forgive' – the paralysed man.

(b) 'Compassion' – the son who had wasted the family money.

(c) 'Forgive' – the people who had killed Jews.

(d) and (e) 'Justified' – Christians. (f) 'Forgive'.

27.1—28.31

1. See p. 221, last 7 lines.

2. See p. 222, last 4 lines and p. 223, lines 1–4.

3. (a) See p. 223, note on 27.33 and p. 224, note on 28.3.

(b) See p. 222, note on 27.3 and p. 224, note on 28.2.

4. See p. 222, note on 27.3 and p. 225, note on 28.14.

5. (a) See p. 227, note on 28.23, numbered para. 4.

(b) See p. 227, note on 28.23, numbered para. 6.

6. Saints, brethren, Christians.
8. Tychicus, Epaphroditus, Aristarchus, Mark, Jesus Justus, Epaphras, Luke, Demas.

Index

This index contains only the more important names of people and places and the main subjects which occur in Acts or which are discussed in the Guide. The names of God and Jesus are not included because they appear on almost every page. Bold type indicates those pages or sections where a subject is discussed in detail.

249